Warmest wishes
from
Bedford Springs,
where history comes alive!

Jon Baughman

2011

The Bedford Springs Resort:
Its History and Rebirth

by Jon Baughman

2 - *The Bedford Springs Resort*

Table of Contents

A look at the Restoration	5
In the Beginning	15
Who discovered the Springs?	23
The Caledonia Iron Works	29
Early Days at Bedford Springs	33
A Pleasant Peregrination	49
In the Days of Buchanan	51
The Civil War years	67
The Rich and Famous	81
The Bancroft years	99
Other Area Resorts	127
The role in World War II	133
The Gardner Moore era	143
William L. Defibaugh	165
The Springs reborn	167

The author has made every reasonable effort to identify the photographers and/or owners of photographs used in this book. Any omission is strictly unintended.

Copyright 2009 by
Jon D. Baughman
20236 Blacks Drive
Dudley, PA 16634
All Rights Reserved
ISBN No. 978-0-615-32071-7

Printed by
Jostens Printing and
Publishing Co.
State College, PA

Photo on page 2, courtesy of Bedford Gazette, 2007
Photo above, courtesy of Gene Miller, 2005
Front cover photo, Jon Baughman

Introduction

On July 12, 2007 the historic preservation project of a lifetime came to fruition in Bedford, Pennsylvania. An historic old Hotel, suffering from decay and neglect, came back to life. New owners with a vision for the future invested $120 million dollars in the project, along with the federal and state contributions. The Bedford Springs Hotel, which seemed to have no future, would reopen after all.

The story of the Bedford Springs Hotel does not begin with the two-year restoration project, nor does it end there. The story began in prehistoric times when native Americans visited the fabled waters. It continued with the arrival of the pioneers, with the vision of founder Dr. John Anderson, and for another two hundred years until the hotel closed. And it will continue to evolve under the ownership of Bedford Resort Partners, Ltd. and the current management, Omni Hotels and Resorts.

Having worked as a newspaper editor and an author of local history books during most of my adult life, I had been keenly aware of the history and significance of the Bedford Springs Hotel. I followed the controversy surrounding the earlier efforts to save the hotel, and I also followed the efforts that led to the reopening. I knew that the restored and updated Bedford Springs Hotel would reopen in July, 2007. I was interested, but strictly from a newspaper editor's point of view.

Then came the wake-up call, provided by my biggest supporter and most trusted advisor, my wife Judy, who said, "This is the biggest story of the year. You really should get involved."

A week later, after I had begun to write news stories about the "new" Bedford Springs, she shared another insight with me. "The story of the Bedford Springs should be told in a book. I mean the entire history from beginning to the present. You need to see what information is available, and you should talk to people who worked there."

A few weeks later I met with William L. Defibaugh of Bedford, and with Bill's valuable and expert assistance and insight, work on this book was under way. It took two years of research and writing to get to this point, and you are now holding the finished product in your hands.

I was truly blessed by all of the people who helped with this project. I am very grateful to all who contributed to this book. First of all, to my wife, Judy, and to Bill Defibaugh, who have been very generous in their support; the *Bedford Gazette;* Gillian Leach and Ray Jackson and staff at the Bedford County Historical Society: the Bedford Springs Historical Society; Gene Miller for use of his photos; the Fix family and other former employees who shared their personal recollections; to Bedford Resort Partners Ltd. and Omni Bedford Springs Resort; and to all others who contributed in any way -- thanks very much!

Jon Baughman

A look at the Restoration

Between 2005 and the grand opening on July 12, 2007, hundreds of trades persons and dozens of contractors worked on the massive $120 million Bedford Springs construction and restoration project. Although the scope of the project is described in the final chapter of this book, please compare these construction photos of the historic restoration with the photos of the completed project to get a "before and after" feel for the scope of the work.

Photos in this chapter courtesy of Gene Miller, Bellefonte, PA

Top: contractor's note. Below, Evitt, Stone Inn, Swiss Cottage, Anderson House.

The Indoor Pool is shown undergoing restoration

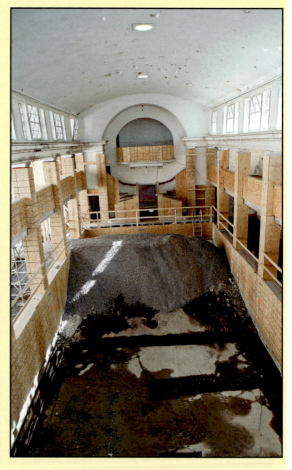

6 - *The Bedford Springs Resort*

Above, steel beams are being set for the new spa; behind the spa is the historic kitchen building and at right, the indoor pool. Below, right, a view of construction from the Colonial Building. Below, left, entrance to Colonial Building.

A look at the Restoration - 7

Inside the Colonial Building
(Colonnade)

The Evitt Building takes shape, inside and out

A look at the Restoration - 9

These photos were taken by Gene Miller of Bellefonte, PA during the restoration project in 2005.

BEDFORD SPRINGS

Medicinal values of these springs discovered about 1796. It soon became a leading resort visited by numerous notables. James Buchanan used the Springs as his summer White House while President.

PENNSYLVANIA HISTORICAL AND MUSEUM COMMISSION

A look at the Restoration - 11

12 - The Bedford Springs Resort

Do you remember?

Facing page: murals in the Reynolds Room.

Above: Promotional color photo for the indoor pool.

Left: Hand painted signs used for the entrance to the Reynolds Room.

Right: Bellhop uniform from the 1960s.

Courtesy of William L. Defibaugh and Bedford Springs Historical Society.

A look at the Restoration

Above: Landscaping is being completed for the Grand Opening in 2007.
Below: The new spa building nearing completion in 2007. Photos by Jon Baughman.

In the Beginning ...

Bedford Mineral Springs Resort was founded by Dr. John Anderson of Bedford, as early as 1796 and definitely by 1798, when he purchased the property. The often cited 1804 date appears to be too late than the actual beginnings of the Springs.

Before the Bedford Springs was founded by the good Doctor, there was a lot of activity going on in the narrow valley in which the Springs are located, going back to prehistoric times.

Dr. Anderson had a very colorful background, as did his parents. In fact, the story of how his parents Thomas and Alice Anderson ended up in America, and then in Bedford, rivals any modern day love story.

Dr. Hickok, in his *Bedford In Ye Olden Time*, tells it this way: "The early life of Anderson was a somewhat romantic one. In his native home in North Ireland he was known for his convivial and fox hunting proclivities as "Rollicking Tom Anderson," but he was warm hearted and generous to the last degree. He had won the heart and was promised the hand of the daughter of one of his father's neighbors, Alice Lyon, the aunt of the late Mrs. James Russell, and great-aunt of the late William Lyon, Esq. The alliance was objected to by the lady's father, a man of rigid views, on account of Tom's recklessness, and she was forbidden to see him. Finding, as all such fathers do, parental authority an ineffectual barrier against the cunning of the "subtle god," Mr. Lyon surreptitiously sent his daughter across the "deep, deep sea" to the care of her brother, who had emigrated to Carlisle a few years before.

"Tom sought her in vain amongst her kindred, and finally, disgusted and disconsolate, he sold his heritage and, gathering together his worldly gear, sought to forget his disappointments in the wilds of the new world. He made investments in Virginia. Some special providence drew him to Carlisle. As he was walking along the street the word "Tom!" reached his ear in tones "that made the heart of him lape intil his mouth" and looking in the direction of the voice he saw his Alice reaching her eager hands to him from an upper window."

In a short time, he took Alice to Virginia with him, where they were married. In 1765 following the end of hostilities in the French and Indian War, they came to Bedford, where they resided until their deaths.

Tom Anderson constructed a home in Bedford in 1766, which is described as a "long, low, two-storied log weather-boarded house" that stood on the corner of Pitt and Richard Streets.

John Anderson, second son of Tom and Alice Anderson, was born in 1770. When John was a child, his father had obtained title to numerous tracts of land around Bedford. His parents were also listed as tavern keepers in Bedford from 1780 to 1794.

At the outbreak of the American Revolution, Indian hostilities became more common in Bedford County. Bounties were being paid to the Indians for the scalps of white settlers, by the British at Fort Niagara and Detroit. Not much is recorded about John Anderson's youth, but one such incident involved a close call at the hands of hostile Indians.

Dr. Hickok writes, "In 1778 the mother of the late James Rea ... took him when two years old on horseback to her former home in Shippensburg to escape the Indians. The late Dr. John Anderson, when a boy of eleven years went one evening in company with a companion of about the same age into a pasture near town for his father's cows. They were pursued by Indians. Young Anderson succeeded in getting home but the other lad was captured by the savages and never heard from afterwards."

But not all of young John's encounters with the Indians were unfriendly. There are indications that he became friends with a few of the peaceful Indians who remained in the valleys of Bedford County after the American Revolution, and learned from them.

Bill Defibaugh states that Dr. Anderson knew many of the Native Americans who remained in the Cumberland Valley after the Revolutionary War ended. "He was chased by them as a ten-year-old and escaped with his life," he said. "It was the Native American who eventually taught Dr. Anderson about the springs and their medicinal values."

Let's digress for a few moments and journey back into the distant past, the prehistoric period before any white men came to Bedford County.

The region around Bedford was inhabited by native Americans for many millennia. The oldest evidence of these prehistoric people, from an archaeological standpoint, is at the Sheep Rock shelter in Huntingdon County, which is now covered by the waters of Raystown Lake.

This site was the setting for extensive archaeological excavations in the 1960s, coordinated by Penn State University and Juniata College. The earliest evidence of ancient man dated back 10,000 years to the paleo-Indian culture.

At Sheep Rock, the impressive finds included a bark bucket, remnants of a canoe, and a human skull believed to be 6,000 years old -- the oldest human remains found in the state.

In western Pennsylvania, the Meadowcroft rock shelter is even older. It is located near Avella in Washington County. The site was excavated from 1973 until 1978 by a University of Pittsburgh team led by James M. Adovasio. Radiocarbon dates from the site indicated occupancy as early as 16,000 years ago and possibly as far back as 19,000 years ago. If the 19,000 years ago dating is correct, Meadowcroft Rockshelter is the oldest known Native American cultural site in North America.

Given the established dates of these two sites, and that Bedford lies between them, it is apparent that early bands of Native Americans were in the region as early as 10,000 years ago, and perhaps earlier.

During that period the natives consisted mainly of small bands of hunter - gatherers, possibly living in extended family groups, who migrated to and from seasonal camps. There are a number of these "Archaic" camp sites in the county. One, near Saxton, dates back to 6,000 B.C. and was excavated by Penn State University and Juniata College between 1966 and 1973.

Agriculture gradually developed after 1500 B.C., and by 500 A.D. the natives were cultivating corn, beans, squash, pumpkins, etc. in fertile river bottoms, and were also making pottery. This is known as the Woodland culture.

It was during this Woodland phase that Bedford became the crossroads between two major Native American cultures. The Woodland culture, and subsequent Shenk's Ferry culture, is evident at village sites along the Raystown Branch of the Juniata River east and north of Bedford. Excavations at Saxton showed the existence of a substantial village containing circular bark huts.

Contrast this with the results of a joint Penn State - Juniata College "dig" at Old Bedford Village which began in 1977. To their surprise, the team members unearthed the remnants of a village from the Monongahela culture. The Monongahela People are known to have lived mainly in the region drained by the Monongahela, Allegheny and Ohio rivers. This was the first Monongahela village site found east of the Allegheny Mountains.

In Bedford, the Monongahela homes were dome shaped. Saplings were driven into the ground in a circle about 20 feet in diameter and bent inward until the ends met, were lashed together, and then covered with bark or mats made from rushes. These huts also had an anteroom added on the side, for storage.

Prof. Paul Heberling told this author that it is significant that Bedford may be the easternmost point of Monongahela culture, and Saxton the western-most point of Shenk's Ferry culture.

Farther west, the Monongahela People lived in large towns surrounded by palisades. There is no evidence that this was true at the Bedford site, which Prof. Heberling described as a number of small villages that occupied different parts of the Old Bedford Village property at different time periods, with never more than 150 residents.

Not much historical information is known about the Monongahela People, but they were closely related to the Mound Builders who lived along the Mississippi River and its tributaries. They vanished completely, for unknown reasons, before the arrival of the white settlers. Conquest, or the introduction of diseases such as smallpox for which they had no natural immunity, have been suggested as possible causes.

It is important to understand a little about these two Indian cultures because it may also help us understand what might have been taking place at the Bedford mineral springs.

The close proximity of two different Indian cultures gave ample opportunity for trade. It also offered an opportunity for people from both cultures to gather at, use and benefit from the healing powers of the mineral springs south of Bedford.

In the 1500s a new group began to move into the Juniata Valley and the West Branch of the Susquehanna -- the Susquehannocks. These were a highly organized people who possessed a superior political and military tradition. They lived mainly along the Susquehanna and the Potomac Rivers. The archaeological record shows that they were taking control of the Raystown Branch of the Juniata River either by migration or conquest. The Monongahela, just before their disappearance, suffered what archaeologists call an intrusion of Susquehannock influence -- whether this was through trade or conquest, it is not known. It is certain that the two cultures were interacting in the area around Bedford.

The Susquehannocks themselves, also called Mingoes or Conestogas, were almost completely wiped out during a long and protracted war with the Six Nations or Iroquois from upstate New York, which has been called the Beaver Wars. It was fought over control of the fur trade. In the interior of Pennsylvania the beavers were almost driven to extinction due to trade with the white men. The beaver trade was then extended west into the Ohio country, with the Susquehannocks acting as middlemen.

This brought them (and their Huron allies) into conflict with the Iroquois over control of the fur trade, which lasted for many years. By 1765 the Susquehannocks ceased to exist as a military power and were dispersed. Another theory is that their population was decimated by smallpox or another illness contracted through contact with the whites, for which the Indians had no natural immunity. This left vast regions of central Pennsylvania uninhabited by native Americans, and white settlers were able to move in and take possession of the land without any real resistance. As victors, the

Iroquois claimed the land as their own, including the area around Bedford.

But back to Bedford. In addition to being a contact point between two different native American cultures, it was also the crossroads for several major Indian trails, including both east - west and north - south trails. Specifically, the Raystown Path and the great Warriors Path intersected at Bedford.

Bedford Springs is less than a mile south of the Raystown Path, which followed the Raystown Branch of the Juniata River.

It has been suggested that the earliest Indian inhabitants of Pennsylvania followed trails left by deer and bison and other wild animals, adopting these trails and paths as their own. Paul A. W. Wallace pointed out in his *Historic Indian Paths of Pennsylvania* that "Early man did use animal tracks when he found them going in his direction," such as in finding the best mountain passes over the Alleghenies. "But wild animals do not harbor the same thoughts nor pursue the same objectives as men." He added, "Let us give honor where honor is due....It was the Indian, not the four-footed beast, who located our first thoroughfares, choosing where to follow and where not to follow the tracks of buffalo, bear and deer."

Thus Wallace reaffirms that the early Americans had their own objectives in mind when they blazed foot paths through the wilderness. Some of those objectives could have been reaching seasonal campsites, trading, or even war.

We do know that springs have been held as sacred by countless ancient cultures. They were especially sacred to the Celts of northern Europe. Perhaps the Indians also revered springs for their life sustaining properties. This could have been especially true of the Bedford Springs, which had medicinal value and could have attracted native Americans from far and wide.

The Raystown Path ran from Carlisle to Burnt Cabins, to Juniata Crossing, then followed the Raystown Branch of the Juniata River to Bedford. It continued west, ascending the Alleghenies and continued west to Shannopin's Town at present day Pittsburgh. It was a major thoroughfare.

There were two north - south paths that intersected the Raystown Path in Bedford County. The great Warriors Path went south from Standing Stone (Huntingdon) to Everett, where it intersected the Raystown Path, and then south to Opessah's Town in Maryland. People traveling the Warrior's Path sometimes went west to Bedford on the Raystown Path, and then south on a branch or variation of the Warriors Path to Maryland. Or, at Bedford, they could go north on the Frankstown Path to Hollidaysburg, or west on the Conemaugh Path to Conemaugh (Johnstown).

There is some evidence that this second branch of the Warriors Path at Bedford went past the Bedford Springs. Wallace's map of Indian trails of Pennsylvania shows the path going south from Bedford, either following Cumberland Valley Run or Shober's Run -- perhaps both; coming together in Cumberland Valley for the journey south. This would have provided the Indians with easy access to the healing waters of the Springs.

In prehistoric times, as in the early 20th Century, the Springs may have been a seasonal resort. The Indians preferred to travel during certain seasons. Wallace writes, "The best time to travel was in the spring and fall; in the spring after the ice had broken up and floated out of the streams, but before the flies and heat of the summer had set in; in the fall when the mosquitoes had disappeared and the nights were crisp, but before the snow came."

Does this mean that the natives didn't visit the Springs in the summer? Not necessarily. I'm sure they could bear the heat of the summer and the mosquitoes in search of a cure.

Indian medicine was not as primitive as we might imagine. Many of their cures were later incorporated into medical science. The sweat lodge (sauna, as we call it today) was used as a cure for various ailments. A patient remained inside a sweat lodge for half an hour or more, drinking a concoction specially prepared for him. When he came out, he plunged into a cold stream (spring?) or, in winter, rolled in the snow. This alternating of hot and cold was often repeated three times.

Indians also had their own physicians, and most Indians had a good knowledge of medicinal herbs.

But did the Indians believe that springs could hold medicinal power? An example of this is the so-called Medicine Spring, which was located on the Cornplanter Reservation in northern Pennsylvania. It was here that Chief Cornplanter's half brother Handsome Lake received the vision that helped revitalize the Iroquois Nation after their disastrous defeat during the Revolutionary War. The vision told Handsome Lake how to restore the Iroquois; it became the basis for a new Iroquois religion that placed emphasis on strict morality.

The Medicine Spring was also called a sacred spring, and it remained sacred to the natives until it disappeared beneath the lake formed by the Kinzua Dam.

The same can be said of Warm Springs, an early gathering place for invalids, west of Huntingdon. Historian Albert M. Rung writes, "The Indians are said to have regarded the waters of Warm Springs for unknown ages as possessing healing powers of such nature that they frequently came here from great distances. Early Virginia settlers are believed to have learned of the springs from the Indians and were possibly the first white people to make a pilgrimage to the locality."

Further evidence of the use of medicine springs by native Americans is found at Hot Springs, South Dakota, on the edge of the Black Hills. Dr. William E. Fitch, who later developed the "Bedford Cure" at Bedford Mineral Springs, said this about Hot Springs, S.D.: "They were (the springs) the resort of Indians long before the white man found his way into the jealously guarded realms of the Black Hills and were considered by the Red Man as a panacea for all ills. This water has been found useful in the treatment of chronic diseases of the gastrointestinal tract, diseases of the liver and biliary passages, and in rheumatism and arthritic joint disturbances, gout and others."

At Hot Springs the Minnekahta Spring near the center of town was used by the Indians who had hollowed out a rock basin into which in the spring water flowed and was used as a bath tub. Most likely, the town received its name from this spring which means "Hot Water" in the Lakota Sioux language. The mammoth spring at the north end of the interior of the plunge is known as the "Old Original Indian Springs." Here the Indians drank and bathed in its warm healing water.

With regard to the Indians congregating at the Bedford Springs, Bill Defibaugh writes, "The discovery of the celebrated Springs was shrouded in Indian legend. Long before the advent of the European the curative powers of the waters were known to the many Indian tribes of the East Coast. Their legends describe a "Medicine Spring" as shaded by majestic oak, giant pine and graceful maple. Tuscarora, Iroquois, and Shawnee tribes held powwow at this glen, a four-week journey from the ocean to the west. They smoked their peace pipe near the flickering fire of a Council meeting and consecrated that area around the medicine spring as neutral ground --- where wounded and sick could freely drink water to regain their health. Bedford Springs was known and revered by the Red Man centuries before the coming of the White man. The gathering of the Indians first caught the attention of early settlers and resulted in the discovery of the springs.

"For perhaps centuries the Indians knew of the curative values of these seven springs, and it may be that they could differentiate between them and could prescribe the use of one spring over another for a particular medicinal need."

He continues, "In the eighteenth century between 1750 - 1770 there was an awareness of these springs because of all the Indian activity one mile south of the town of Bedford. However, they did not know that there were seven different springs, nor did they know about the curative minerals of these springs."

As stated previously in this chapter, the Iroquois Confederacy or Six Nations claimed title to Central Pennsylvania as their reward for the defeat of the Susquehannocks. Following that defeat, the Iroquois governed this vast region from their regional capital called Shamokin, near Sunbury. Many of the eastern tribes were being displaced by white settlers, and those displaced were welcomed by the Iroquois, who invited them to live in the central part of the state. This was especially true of the Delaware tribes, whom the Iroquois believed would help hold the land against encroachment from the whites. Also, the Shawnee lived in this area for a short time, particularly at the "Shawnee cabins" near Schellsburg.

The Penn family, proprietors of Pennsylvania Colony, recognized the Iroquois claims, and went to great lengths to prevent settlers from encroaching on Indian lands -- even removing settlers by force and burning their cabins. The exception to this were the traders who ventured into the wilderness via the Indian paths to set up trading posts. One such trader was Robert Ray, who opened a trading post at the present-day site of Bedford. Ray came to trade with the natives, so there must have been an Indian population residing in the Bedford area. The only whites in the county consisted of about 12 families who came to Beans Cove from Virginia about 1728 with the Joseph Powell expedition. The numerous trails intersecting the Bedford area, plus the presence of a large number of friendly Indians nearby at the Bedford Springs and at Shawnee Cabins, would have made Bedford an ideal location for Ray's trading post.

As far as we know, Ray operated this post until his death which occurred in 1756.

Before Ray disappeared from the scene, war clouds were on the horizon. The French and British were already at war in Europe, and would also be fighting for control of North America. On July 9th, 1755 a British army led by General Edward Braddock, who had hoped to capture the French Fort Duquesne at the forks of the Ohio, was ambushed by the French and Indian allies. It was a disastrous defeat for the British, and Braddock was killed.

As the summer of 1755 wore on, the few whites in the wilderness fled east due to Indian hostilities perpetrated by France's Indian allies, including the Delaware and Shawnee. It was unlikely that a single white person remained in the area between Carlisle and Fort Duquesne.

General Edward Forbes arrived in America in 1758. The plan devised by Forbes was to amass an army of 5,850 men, cut a road through the wilderness, and capture the French fort. To this end, he planned to build a series of forts along the route to serve as strongholds and supply points, among them Fort Bedford and Fort Ligonier.

In fact, a scouting party led by a Capt. Hamilton, had reached Raystown (the site of Ray's trading post) in 1757. He reported finding no sizeable number of Indians in the area (Bedford Springs being a mile south of the trading post).

Forbes began his expedition westward from Carlisle in July, 1758. The army arrived at Raystown under the command of Col. Henry Bouquet. It was here that the army met and joined with the Virginia militia commanded by Col. George Washington. Fort Bedford was constructed as the supply base for the English advance over the Alleghenies. Gen. Forbes named the fort in honor of John Russell, fourth Duke of Bedford.

To briefly summarize, Fort Ligonier was erected in October, and the final assault began. Fort Duquesne fell on November 25, the crowning achievement of Gen. Forbes, who was ill, and who died the following March 11, 1759. As the army under General Forbes approached Turtle Creek, they heard a great explosion. The commandant of Fort Duquesne had blown up the fort and fled. Forbes' men found the wreckage of the fort "with the chimneys of the houses alone standing in their stark outlines."

Soon, French power in North America would come to an end. The British erected a new fort at the Forks of the Ohio, just east of Fort Duquesne, and named it Fort Pitt in honor of British Prime Minister William Pitt the Elder.

Fort Bedford remained an English stronghold for more than a decade and a garrison was stationed there. One of the terms of the 1763 peace treaty was to stop the advances of white settlers from the east. This was a condition requested by the Iroquois as their reward for being staunch allies of the British during the assault on Fort Duquesne. The garrison at the fort was maintained to prevent settlers from going any farther west.

After the conflict ended, the Iroquois and their allies were again free to visit Bedford Springs without interference from the garrison at the Fort.

Peace would not last.

At the outbreak of the American Revolution, some tribes of the Six Nations favored the 13 Colonies; others the British, so the Indian

Confederacy was divided. The British Indian allies, particularly the Senecas, conducted numerous raiding parties from upstate New York into Pennsylvania, especially against settlements located along the Great Warriors Path. This placed the pioneer families of Bedford County directly in harm's way.

During the American Revolution, many pioneer families took refuge in Fort Bedford, which was deteriorating but still standing. The fort provided protection from Indian raids and was one of the few safe strongholds in the wilderness. The raids were very bloody and included the massacre of men, women and children.

I will give one example, that being the massacre of the Tull family, near Bedford. "In the year 1777 a family named Tull resided about six miles west of Bedford, on a hill to which the name of the family was given. There were ten children, nine daughters and a son; but at the time referred to, the son was absent, leaving at home his aged parents and nine sisters. At that time the Indians were especially troublesome, and the inhabitants had to abandon their improvements and take refuge at the fort, but Tull's family disregarded the danger and remained. One William, who had made a settlement about three miles west of Tull's, and near where the town of Schellsburg now stands, had returned to his farm to sow some flax. He had a son with him and remained out about a week. The road to his improvement passed Tull's house. On their return as they approached Tull's they saw a smoke, and coming nearer, discovered that it arose from the burning ruins of Tull's house. Upon a nearer approach, the son saw an object in the garden which by a slight movement had attracted his attention, and looking more closely they found it was the old man expiring. At the same moment the son discovered on the ground near him an Indian paint bag. They at once understood the whole matter and, knowing that the Indians were still near, fled at once to the fort. Next day a force went out from the fort to examine, and after some search found the mother with an infant in her arms, both scalped. A short distance away a daughter was found, and finally all bodies were found within a short distance of the home."

At the conclusion of the Revolutionary War, the power of the Iroquois was broken and settlers flooded into the region. A few peaceful natives remained in Bedford County and lived among the white settlers.

It was these natives who provided Dr. Anderson with knowledge about the healing powers of the waters at Bedford Springs.

Archaeological excavations, like this one along the Raystown Branch of the Juniata River, have revealed a great deal about the Native American culture in the region around the Bedford Springs. Additional photos, next page.

Photo by Jon Baughman

Shaker screens, shown at left, were used to sift the soil to locate the tiniest artifacts.
Photos by Jon Baughman

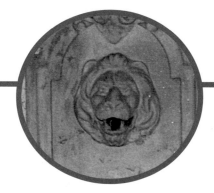

Who discovered the mineral springs?

One of Robert Ray's contemporaries at the present site of Bedford was another trader, Garret Pendergrass, who constructed a cabin at Bedford along the river. Pendergrass figures prominently in the early history of Bedford County. In 1752 he purchased a large tract of land from the Indians. The deed, one of the first to be recorded when Bedford County was formed in 1771, can still be seen at the Courthouse. It contains marks of the turtle and a circle within a circle, the signatures of Chief Anonguit and the "White Mingo."

Pendergrass, finding his land occupied, obtained another deed from the Indians for land where McKeesport now stands; this too, was occupied. He obtained a third deed at what is now Allegheny City.

Several published histories of Bedford County record that Pendergrass headed east for safety from marauding Indians just prior to the construction of Fort Bedford. A map of Fort Bedford from the French and Indian War period clearly shows the location of Pendergrass's cabin on the south bank of the river. Next to it is the log house of John Fraser and wife Jean, who were the first permanent white residents. The Frasers traded with the Indians and also operated what would become known as Fraser's Tavern in the log house. Mrs. Fraser cooked meals for the British officers at the fort.

Here their son, William, was born in 1759, and it is believed he was the first white child born in the county.

In 1761 the Manor of Bedford, including the site of Bedford Borough and additional lands, was surveyed by Col. John Armstrong on land owned by the Penn Family, Proprietors of the Colony.

Then in June, 1766, Surveyor-General John Lukens laid out the town of Bedford. The streets formed east and west lines parallel with the house of Capt. Lewis, commander of Fort Bedford. Lots were sold, and Bedford began to grow. This growth was accelerated when Bedford became the seat of government of the new County in 1771.

The community was certainly growing when Tom Anderson and his wife arrived here in 1766 from Virginia.

John Anderson, founder of the Bedford Springs, was born hin 1770. Today we might call him a "Renaissance Man," as he had a love of learning and pursued numerous interests and occupations during his productive lifetime.

Who discovered the mineral springs? - 23

He studied medicine in Carlisle, and returned to Bedford in 1796 to practice medicine, according to Waterman - Watkins History of Bedford County. There are some indications that he was practicing medicine in Bedford before that date.

Another source states that Anderson graduated from Dickinson College, Carlisle, in 1789. The college was founded September 29, 1783 by Dr. Benjamin Rush. The first president (1784), Charles Nisbet, established high standards of education and scholarship for Dickinson students. After graduating, Anderson studied medicine in Philadelphia and returned to Bedford to practice in 1791.

Anderson was living in Bedford in 1794 when President George Washington stopped in Bedford to review the Army of General Harry Lee, stationed in Bedford for a few days, during the Whisky Rebellion. Washington stayed in Bedford for two days, and was a guest in the Espy House, home of Capt. David Espy. Both Tom Anderson's tavern and that of Jean Fraser were still in operation at that date.

Espy was the second Prothonotary of Bedford County, succeeding General Arthur St. Clair.

John Anderson married Mary, daughter of Capt. Espy. The young doctor traveled far and wide on horseback to see his patients and to treat the sick during his years practicing medicine.

Dr. Hickok writes, "His field of practice reached some sixty miles either way, but chiefly to the west and north. He was obliged to make his professional visits on horseback; to go armed for fear of Indians and wild beasts; and oftentime he was obliged to carry a lighted fagot or a lantern as a protection against the wolves. He relinquished medicine at an early day and turned his attention to his large landed estates."

Dr. Anderson was not destined to practice medicine his entire life. He was, as his biographer writes in the Waterman - Watkins history, "a man of affairs and was possessed of all the essential qualities of a man *predestined to success in business.*"

During his lifetime he served as Prothonotary of Bedford County; he was president of the Allegheny Bank of Pennsylvania, at Bedford; was president of the Chambersburg and Bedford Turnpike; and he owned a large quantity of land in the county and elsewhere. He and Mary, were the parents of four children: George Woods, Espy Lyon, Elizabeth and Mary.

When Dr. Anderson returned from Carlisle, Bedford was still a small town. As an officer of Gen. Lee's army wrote in 1794, "The town of Bedford does not, indeed, contain many houses; but some of them are sufficiently large and very convenient. A number of the buildings are stone, a few of them are brick, and the work not illy executed."

Dr. Anderson first learned about the Bedford Springs through contact with friendly Indians who remained in the county after the Revolution. His second contact with the property came when he acquired the Naugel mill property.

The original land warrant for the site of the Bedford Springs was issued in 1767 to Josiah Shoenfelt; he conveyed title to the land to Frederick Naugel (also spelled Nawgel) in 1772. Naugel is listed as a tavern keeper in Bedford in 1771. The names recommended to the Governor for license as tavern-keepers in 1771, were

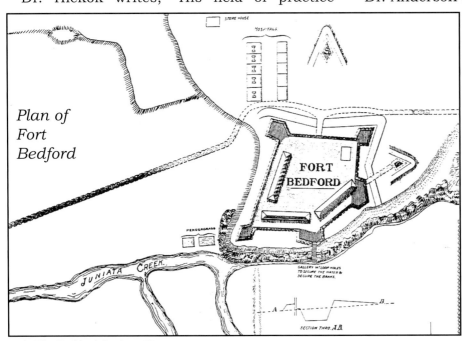

Plan of Fort Bedford

Margaret Fraser, Jean Woods, Frederic Naugel, George Funk, John Campbell, Joseph Irwin, John Miller, and Samuel Paxton. Naugel's Inn was located on West Pitt Street.

Please note that Margaret was John Fraser's daughter, and in 1771 she was still a minor.

William P. Schell, in his "Reminiscences" published in the Bedford Gazette, March 9, 1906, states that Naugel built the stone grist mill about 1797 along the banks of Shober's Run (other histories suggest that the mill was built in 1796). Over the years, the stone mill has been a landmark on the Springs property, as is the nearby log house, called the Miller's house, and another log house, called the "Chefs' House," as it was at one time used as a dwelling by chefs employed at the Resort.

Schell writes that in 1798 this mill property was sold by Sheriff Bonnett to Robert Spencer, presumably for debt incurred in erecting the mill. Spencer sold a portion of the property to Dr. John Anderson a short time later. He purchased the remainder of the 204 acres in 1808.

I feel certain that the mill was built before 1796, and that Dr. Anderson was already in possession of it, perhaps through a lease. Naugel's Last Will and Testament, dated September 17, 1775, leaves one-third of the money from the sale of his plantation and mill on Shover's Run to his wife. Apparently a mill existed before 1775. Was this the stone mill or an earlier structure? This earlier date for the stone mill is plausible because a number of stone buildings were erected in Bedford between 1767 and 1795 "from stone quarried on the summit of what is known as Boher's Hill, on the Anderson estate," according to Dr. Hickok.

In 1796 Dr. Anderson is listed as "a single man, 3 horses" on the Bedford Borough tax rolls. In the same year the list of single freemen included " --- Hunter, a storekeeper at Anderson's mill." The footnote to this name, in the Waterman-Watkins history, states "The old stone structure, yet standing near the Springs."

This confirms that Dr. Anderson was in possession of the Mill and store in 1796, possibly earlier. It also means that Dr. Anderson, by that date, was well acquainted with the Springs property of 204 acres on which the mill was located.

The Historic Sites Survey of Bedford County (1995) says that Naugel's son, Jacob, succeeded his father in the milling business and was involved in the milling business with Dr. John Anderson.

In July, 2003 Bill Defibaugh of Bedford was able to purchase a ledger from Anderson's mill and store (Naugel's mill), with entries dated between 1801 and 1805. Defibaugh had desired to purchase this ledger since first seeing it in 1964, but was unable to do so until the death of its owner, Armstrong Farber.

A close examination of the ledger revealed that this was more than a mill and store. The operation served as a bank, a trading post, and a warehouse to which goods were shipped into and out of Bedford for Dr. Anderson and others. In fact, Mr. Hunter, the storekeeper, arranged for wagoners to haul the goods to and from Baltimore, Philadelphia, Chambersburg, Conemaugh and other points.

As Defibaugh points out, "People borrowed money, paid back the same, exchanged British/Colonial pounds, shillings and pence for U.S. dollars and cents."

The Anderson operation also arranged for the shipment of bar iron to the nearby Caledonia Steel Works, and the shipment of blister steel and steel-edged tools from Caledonia.

Who discovered the mineral springs? - 25

Dr. Anderson's Mill

When Dr. Anderson purchased the land from Robert Spencer in 1798, did he buy it for the Mill or for the springs? It appears that the good doctor was already aware of the healing power of the springs before 1798. So, who discovered the Bedford mineral springs?

The actual origin of the resort is somewhat clouded in mystery. No less than three versions of the story of how the mineral springs were discovered have been written down by various historians and writers, over the decades.

Version one: This story is attributed to I. D. Rupp, who recorded it in his history, published in 1846. Rupp claimed that one Nicholas Stouffler discovered the mineral springs, and gave the date of discovery as 1796. He called Stouffler a "queer sort of a man," who was obsessed in a search for gold in the eastern spurs of the Allegheny Mountains and along the streams found therein. His quest led him to Shober's Run, where he thought he saw the specks of gold among the rocks.

Rupp writes, "He immediately built a rude furnace and commenced his work of melting the stones and evaporating the water. Enraptured with the idea of now having found the El Dorado of his wishes, he went to Thomas Vickroy and told him he had found something valuable." No, not gold. He told Vickroy it was better than iron, silver or gold. It was the Bedford mineral spring, with its healing powers.

Version two: The second of these stories was recorded by Bedford dentist Dr. C. N. Hickok, author of *Bedford In Ye Olden Time*. This booklet was based on two lectures that Dr. Hickok, a scholar and historian, delivered in Bedford in 1886.

He wrote an article which was published in Dr. Engle's "History of Pennsylvania," 1876. Here is his version of the discovery:

"In the year 1804 a mechanic of Bedford, James Fletcher, went fishing for trout in the stream near the principal fountain, was attracted by the beauty and singularity of the waters flowing from the bank and drank freely from them. They proved purgative and sudorific. He had suffered for many years from rheumatic pains and formidable ulcers on the legs. On the ensuing night he was more free from pain and slept more tranquil than usual, and this unexpected relief induced him to drink daily of the waters and to bathe his limbs in the

This log house once stood along the road to the Springs.
Both photos, Bedford County Historical Society collection

fountain. In a few weeks he was entirely cured. The happy effect which they had on this patient led others, laboring under various chronic diseases, to the Springs. In the summer of 1805 many valetudinarians came in carriages and camped in the valley to seek from the munificent hand of nature their lost health. Since that period the Springs have become widely famous."

Version three: This version was written by H. F. Foulke, son of George D. Foulke, M.D., and is found in Blackburn's "History of Bedford County," 1906. Dr. George Foulke began to practice medicine in Bedford shortly after 1800. He returned to his native Carlisle in April, 1803. He married Mary Steel on May 1, 1804 and they returned to Bedford. Here their son, H. M. Foulke was born, May 16, 1805.

H. M. Foulke writes that in addition to practicing medicine, his parents owned a small grocery and candy store, which his mother operated. He writes that his father contracted a severe illness of rheumatism, and at one time was near death, but recovered. He suffered from this until his death in 1849. The family returned to Carlisle in 1809.

During the family's years in Bedford, H. M. writes, "Father early made the acquaintance of George Anderson, M.D. (son of John Anderson, M.D.) and a strong, lasting friendship was the result. In the fall of 1803 they went for game, became thirsty, looked for a stream. They discovered one and drank. They found the water strongly impregnated medicinally. The place was marked by placing a gum in it -- the Bedford Springs of widespread reputation. A ball was given in honor of the discovery. Dr. Anderson and Mrs. Foulke and Dr. Foulke and Mrs. Anderson opened it as partners. Mother often told me about it, and no doubt father did also, but I remembered better from mother telling me."

The Waterman-Watkins history states that a mechanic from Bedford discovered the Springs; his name is not given (Fletcher?). Dr. Hickok felt that both Fletcher and Dr. Foulke played a role in the discovery of the Springs.

In "Bedford In Ye Olden Time" Dr. Hickok states that "The discovery of the Bedford Springs lay between him (Dr. Foulke) and Jacob Fletcher, who was a typical "Izaak Walton," and an eccentric character in his day." In other words, Fletcher was a a dedicated angler whose trout fishing trips would have taken him to the Springs property on a frequent basis.

Dr. Anderson must be given credit for establishing the Bedford Springs, regardless of who actually made the discovery. For he realized the economic potential of this location, and acted upon it.

I propose the following time line, and future researchers are welcome to modify it if new information becomes available.

1796: Dr. Anderson, who has already learned about the "magical powers" of the Springs, spends some time along Shober's Run, marking their locations. However, his medical practice and duties at the mill and store do not allow time for further investigation.

1797: Dr. Anderson continues to investigate the Springs but is unable to purchase the property.

1798: The Springs property is sold by the Sheriff. The buyer, Robert Spencer, agrees to sell a portion of the land (and mill) to Dr. Anderson. According to historian Schell, Dr. Anderson immediately made some improvements at (began digging out) the mineral springs. At this point, Fletcher makes his discovery -- not the springs -- but their medicinal powers. He tells others. The wagoners hauling goods to and from the mill and store carry the news to other communities, near and far. A few travelers arrive in Bedford in search of the mineral springs.

1799: Dr. Foulke arrives in Bedford, two years earlier than historians have suggested, and he learns about the Springs from Fletcher and from customers at the mill.

The arrival of Dr. Foulke allows Dr. Anderson to spend less time treating patients and more time at the mineral springs, as the number of visitors has gradually increased. Foulke and George Anderson visit the Springs together while on a hunting trip.

1800: Something amazing is taking place in the valley south of Bedford, which will change the community forever.

The people of Bedford embraced the Springs because they loved Dr. Anderson. "He was a fine physician for his day. I have newspaper stories dating back to 1806 that talk about Dr. Anderson walking down the streets. Children would come running and circle him because he was so kind, so loved. He was a generous man," Bill Defibaugh said.

The Magnesia Spring today.
Photos by Jon Baughman

MINERAL SPRING & MAGNESIA SPRING PAVILION

The Mineral Spring, initially called Anderson's Spring after Dr. John Anderson, the resort's founder, has also been referred to as Magnesia Spring because of its high concentration of magnesium salts. The spring water, which has been described as clear, lively, and sparkling, issues forth from a fissure in a limestone rock outcropping about thirty feet above the level of Shober's Run. The most popular of the spring waters, this highly mineralized water was once thought to have laxative and purgative qualities, and was once appealing to those with ailments related to the digestive track.

The temperature of the Mineral Spring was recorded at fifty-eight degrees Fahrenheit on May 28, 1825.

The Magnesia Spring Pavilion, constructed in tandem with the Colonnade Building, was completed by 1843. Originally, the temple-like pavilion was situated parallel to Shober's Run and located about a few hundred feet west of its present location. In 1905, the pavilion was moved eastward, and turned ninety degrees to correspond with the centerline of the Colonnade Building. The Magnesia Spring Pavilion evolved as a collegial gathering place where mineral water was available in the nineteenth century, and cocktails were served in the twentieth century. The current pavilion, a replication based on historic photographs, was constructed in 2007.

Caledonia Iron Works: the first steel in PA

In the decade leading up to the "discovery" of the Bedford mineral springs, there was a separate enterprise in operation on the present-day Bedford Springs property. It was called the Caledonia Iron Works.

The iron works was built by William McDermott (sometimes spelled McDermitt or McDermett) who was born near Glasgow, Scotland and who came to America about 1783, landing in Philadelphia. He learned the process of smelting iron in his native land. There are reports that his wife's family possessed considerable wealth, and that this capital enabled him to establish a forge in this area.

He journeyed westward from Philadelphia in search of a favorable location to erect his forge. Upon his arrival at Bedford, he found a good location south of town, which he named Caledonia.

McDermott purchased a farm and erected the forge at what is called the Black Spring, and here he built a dam to provide water to power the water wheel that operated the forge's trip hammer.

This location was originally the pioneer homestead of John Black and family, who received a land warrant in 1785 for 229 acres. They built a large log house and barn, plus outbuildings. McDermott, who secured the property from the Blacks, was drawn to the site because the flow from Black Spring, 600,000 gallons a day, was enough to power his operation.

The exact date of McDermott's arrival at Bedford is unclear. Many writers have assumed that he came to Bedford in 1783. The American Revolution had just ended. The surrender of General Cornwallis took place Oct. 19, 1781; peace was not officially declared until April 19, 1783. McDermott and his young wife probably landed in Philadelphia after 1781. But did he go to Bedford County right away?

The presence of iron ore deposits in the vast and unsettled Juniata Valley region must have been known as early as 1767, because in that year the Juniata Iron Company was chartered.

There were charcoal iron furnaces in operation in eastern PA prior to that date. The famed Cornwall iron mines and furnace were opened in Lebanon County in 1742.

Historians have incorrectly assumed that Bedford Furnace at Orbisonia was the first iron furnace west of the Susquehanna River. Bedford Furnace Company was organized in 1784, and began to acquire land grants in 1785. The furnace was placed in blast no later than 1787. Even if Bedford Furnace was not the first iron furnace west of the Susquehanna, McDermott's Caledonia Iron Works at Bedford certainly came after Bedford Furnace.

I believe McDermott learned about the construction of Bedford Furnace while in Philadelphia, and then came to Bedford County to see for himself the potential for iron manufacture, and that this took place no earlier than 1787. Orbisonia was then located in a part of Bedford County.

The name of Thomas T. Cromwell is connected with Bedford Furnace as the driving force behind this operation. His success was followed closely by Barree Forge in Spruce Creek in 1794, Freedom Forge in Lewistown in 1795, Huntingdon Furnace (Spruce Creek) in 1796, and Lemnos Furnace at Hopewell, 1801.

In the early days pig iron and bar iron were hauled great distances to market, either on horseback or in wagons. Pack horses and freight wagons were transporting the iron as far as Pittsburgh, to be made into other products like nails, stoves, guns, etc.

Today it is difficult to separate fact from fiction with regard to McDermott's enterprises. Much of what we know was written down by his grandson, Judge William A. Porter, who was the son of Gov. David Rittenhouse Porter and Josephine McDermott Porter. Judge Porter served on the state Supreme Court. His brother, General Horace Porter, was the personal secretary to President Grant; vice president of the Pullman Company from 1873 to 1897; and Ambassador to France, 1897 to 1905. It was Horace Porter who discovered the grave of Naval hero John Paul Jones buried under a trash dump in Paris, and had the body returned to the United States at his own expense.

It is believed that the Caledonia Iron Works was in operation at the Black Spring near Bedford Springs for about 15 years. Judge Porter claimed that his grandfather was successful in making steel at this location, with the exact process kept a secret by McDermott.

In 1876 the Centennial Exposition was held in Philadelphia, and on display were articles made at the old Bedford Furnace (Orbisonia), including a stove plate cast there in 1792. James Park, Jr., of Pittsburgh, saw the exhibit and thought his old friend Judge Porter would be interested. Judge Porter replied to the letter from Park by recalling that his grandfather, William McDermett held the distinction of being the first successful producer of steel in the Commonwealth.

Judge Porter recalled how the Caledonia Iron Works were in successful operation for over ten years until McDermett endorsed a note of one of his good friends who had met financial difficulties. He recalled that the note was called in, and the Sheriff foreclosed on the iron works, which was closed because no-one else knew the process for making steel.

The letter from Judge Porter continues, "McDermett moved with his family into the village of Bedford and lived for a few years in the stone house which stands on one of the corners of the public square. When General Washington passed through Pennsylvania he rested at Bedford (Whiskey Rebellion) and was the guest of Mr. McDermett. Several of the children often repeated the pleasant things the General had said to them during his visit."

In his recollections, Dr. Hickok stated, "There was in Bedford at an early day the firm of McDermot & Dunlop. They dealt in iron and also carried on general blacksmithing. Mr. McDermot afterward kept the Caledonia House (an Inn) at the Black Spring, one mile south of the Bedford Springs.... Here was born his daughter, who afterward became the wife of David R. Porter, Governor of Pennsylvania from 1838 to 1845.....Mrs. Porter was a lovely character, esteemed for her excellent sense, as well as for her gentle, unostentatious piety."

It is known that Josephine was born in 1803. At the time of her birth, her father was 49 years old.

A few years after Josephine was born the family relocated to Spruce Creek, near Colerain Forge, where McDermott's nephew, Thomas, had established a forge which was called Claybank or Claybunk, and later Millington Steel Works. The elder McDermott assisted in its operation, and was probably the driving force behind it. Again, the manufacture of steel was successful at this newer location along Spruce Creek. The plant remained busy until the close of the War of 1812, when a severe depression brought many industries to financial ruin. Claybank did not reopen.

An article in the *Huntingdon Gazette,* Feb. 18, 1826 provided this description of the operation: "Millington Forge, now tenanted by Messrs. Gloninger, Anshutz & Co. is situated 14 miles from Huntingdon, N.W. on Spruce Creek. This forge manufactures about 150 tons of bar iron annually. There was formerly at this place an extensive steel manufactory, established by Mr. W. M. McDermitt. Steel of a fine quality was made and commanded a ready market, but since the death of the late proprietor, this branch of the iron manufacture has been abandoned."

The elder McDermott passed away in 1816 at age 62. His death notice, published in the *Huntingdon Gazette,* December 5, 1816: "Died -- Suddenly, on the morning of the 27th ultimo, Mr. William A. McDermett, of Millington Steel Works, in this County, in the 62nd year of his age."

Huntingdon County Historian Albert M. Rung suggested that "Worry over financial difficulties undoubtedly shortened McDermett's life, as imprisonment for debt was the usual fate of such unfortunates in those days." The law allowing imprisonment of debtors was not abolished until 1842.

There is information on record that the Caledonia Iron Works was in operation in 1807, as stated in Blackburn's History of Bedford County (quoting William M. Hall, 1897). Hall had in his possession an 1807 article from the *Bedford Gazette* in which a visitor to the Bedford Springs, who drove from Hancock, recalled hearing the "rhythmical sound of the trip-hammer, which drew his attention as he paused in his journey at the top of the mountain to enjoy the view."

David R. Porter was born Oct. 31, 1788 near Norristown, a son of the Revolutionary War General Horace Porter, and later Surveyor General of Pennsylvania. Young Porter planned to attend Princeton, but a disastrous fire at the university in 1802 ended those plans. He then assisted his father as Surveyor-General from 1809 until his father's death in 1813. He then went to Huntingdon to study law under Edward Shippen, and here he became interested in the iron industry. He was a clerk at Dorsey's Forge for a short time, but ups and downs in the iron trade forced him to seek a new career by 1819 -- politics. He held several row offices in Huntingdon County, served in the General Assembly, was elected to the State Senate in 1836, and Governor in 1838.

He married Josephine McDermott in 1820; she was 17, he was 32.

The old log house of the Black family, and later McDermott, was torn down in 1896-97 on the Bedford Springs property. The *Bedford Gazette* in January 1897 stated "...it was here that the first steel edge tools are said to have been made in Pennsylvania." It continued, William McDermott "was a blacksmith and edge tool maker by vocation and operated a trip hammer forge; manufacturing axes, hatchets, augers, and the like."

"In the log house which has been torn away, a daughter was born to Mr. and Mrs. McDermott, who afterwards became the wife of Governor David R. Porter, and the mother of William A. Porter, who became a justice of the Supreme Court of Pennsylvania; Dr. George W. Porter of Harrisburg; and General Horace Porter.

So exactly what did McDermott make at Caledonia, and later at Millington? It is believed he made steel by the cementation process, which was perfected in England after 1619. The steel was made by increasing the carbon content. Wrought iron bars were placed inside a stone pot, which was heated inside a furnace. In the pot, iron bars and charcoal were placed in alternating layers. This was heated for about a week, then allowed to cool, which took about 14 days. The resultant product was called blister steel, because of the marks made by escap-

This log house is the last remnant of Bedford Furnace, Orbisonia, PA, where William McDermott obtained his bar iron. Photo by Adam L. Watson.

ing bubbles of gases.

Blister steel was then turned into shear steel by wrapping the bars together, heating them and then forging them. The action of the forge hammer welded the bundles together to the required size. The process required a lot of labor and was expensive.

McDermott could have learned this process in England or Scotland before leaving for America at age 29.

The Anderson store ledger, mentioned in the previous chapter, makes it clear that McDermott was obtaining his iron from other furnaces, which was transported in wagons by teamsters to Bedford. Numerous entries in the store ledger state that wagoner Abraham Ritchey hauled thousands of pounds of iron from Thomas Cromwell's furnace and from Judge John Gloninger's Huntingdon Furnace to the Caledonia Iron Works at the Black Spring. The distance from Gloninger's would have been more than 60 miles in one direction.

The ledger also reveals that teamster Jacob Kerns and wagoner and blacksmith Jacob Daviebaugh hauled blister steel from McDermott's to Baltimore, while wagoner and carpenter Hill Wilson transported blister steel for McDermott to Conemaugh (Johnstown). These shipments took place prior to 1805. Please keep in mind that these shipments were handled through Dr. John Anderson's mill and store. The entries make it clear that McDermott operated a forge on the Bedford Springs property, and not a charcoal iron furnace as is commonly believed, as he was obtaining his iron elsewhere.

After 1740, when the crucible process was invented by Benjamin Huntsman, crucible steel was made in England and the manufacture of blister steel was eventually discontinued. However, in America, crucible steel was not made in large quantities until 1832. It was expensive and harder to work. Most American manufacturers preferred wrought iron, which was softer and easier to work in a rolling mill.

Gov. David R. Porter, incidentally, was a frequent visitor to Bedford Springs during his political career, which is described in detail in another chapter of this history.

32 - The Bedford Springs Resort

Early days at the Bedford Mineral Springs

They came in carriages. They came on foot. They came on horseback, and they came by stage coach. And they never stopped coming.

News of the curative powers of the spring waters had traveled far and fast. Curiosity seekers, persons seeking a cure, and others made the trek to Bedford to check out the healing waters.

William P. Schell, in his book, *The Annals of Bedford County, Pennsylvania"* asserts that after he purchased the property from Robert Spencer in 1798, Dr. Anderson made some improvements to several of the springs. He cleaned out the magnesia spring to make it accessible to the public, and over the next five years would make additional improvements to the property.

No doubt some of the persons making use of the springs were Dr. Anderson's own patients. Others made the long trip to Bedford. In 1799, according to a time line established by Bill Defibaugh, Dr. Anderson made several improvements on the side of Shober's Run opposite the Resort. He constructed an underground reservoir and bathing pool and a small bath house. A small house for guests was added the following year, also on the opposite side of the "Run." A foot bridge crossed the stream.

In the very beginning, a few visitors stayed at Anderson's farm near the Springs, and at the Caledonia House owned by Ironmaster William McDermott at the Black Spring.

An article in the *Pittsburg Gazette,* Dec. 30, 1803, reported. "Very valuable mineral springs have lately been discovered in the vicinity of Bedford, Pennsylvania, which, from the extraordinary cures they have effected during the last summer, are beginning to excite very general attention."

In 1998 another article, this one from the *Pittsburgh Post-Gazette,* dated June 28, 1811, was discovered by James B. Whisker and was reprinted in the *Bedford Gazette* under the heading, "That magical Springs water." It provides an important glimpse into those early days at the Mineral Springs. "In the summer of 1805 a great number of valetudinarians came in carriages and encamped in the valley to seek from the munificent hand of Nature, their lost health. A dense copse of shrubs had enveloped the springs until about this time, and rendered it difficult to approach them. The inhabitants of Bedford now began to make improvements.

Upon digging away the bank, it was found that about twenty feet from the spot where the waters first issued, they poured themselves through the fissure of limestone rock.....About fifteen perches south of this, there is another mineral spring, which discharged on the 16th of last March, 6 gallons of water per minute; the sensible qualities of which differ but little from the other."

There was a problem. People making the journey needed a place to stay, and the good doctor had not anticipated the demand. Fortunately for Bedford and Dr. Anderson, the old Forbes Road became a well traveled road following major improvements and relocations that were made by the state beginning in 1785. Many of the steep grades along the mountains between Shippensburg and Ray's Hill (Breezewood) were moderated, making travel easier for wagoners hauling goods along the road between Philadelphia and Pittsburgh. Pioneers used the road to go west. After the improvements were made, this route was called the Great Road or Western Road.

Like the National Road farther south in Maryland, the Great Road was a major thoroughfare for the westward migration.

Travelers needed a place to lodge at the end of a long day on the road and a hot meal. At regular intervals along the route, taverns and inns sprung up. Many were located along Pitt Street in Bedford, which was the main route through town. On August 1, 1804 the first through line of stage coaches was established between Philadelphia and Pittsburgh, passing through Bedford on the Great Road.

Dr. Hickok lists the various taverns in the period shortly before, and after, 1800, along Pitt Street. Among them are, the Cross Keys, Thomas Rea's, Brice's, the Dean's, Naugle's and Funk's taverns, the Rising Sun (formerly the Fort House, owned by Henry Wertz), then Hafer's (or the Bedford House, kept by Robert Spencer as the Proctor House), Thomas Anderson's tavern, and others. In this time period, Dr. Hickok states that there were 16 taverns in Bedford, and several others outside the village, such as the Bonnett and Defibaugh taverns.

Dr. Anderson worked with many of these establishments to provide housing and meals to visitors to the Springs, as early as 1800. The Anderson mill and store ledger, owned by Bill Defibaugh and mentioned in previous chapters, shows Dr. Anderson paying for lodging for springs visitors to Jacob Bonnett, John Defibaugh (Daviebaugh), George Funk and others. Keep in mind that these establishments were already busy just from the traffic on the Great Road.

Dr. Anderson had an especially close working relationship with members of the Defibaugh family, who were wagoners and who also ran the Defibaugh Tavern east of Bedford in Snake Spring Township, later called The Willows.

States Bill Defibaugh, "The 1803 ledger shows John Daviebaugh buying restaurant items like many sets of dishes, teapots, tea and spices. At the same time John Daviebaugh bought large quantities of blue and white fabrics." This provided Dr. Anderson with suitable sleeping and eating quarters while the larger buildings at the Springs were under construction. In later years, a trip to the Defibaugh Tavern gave Springs patrons a fun-filled 20-minute ride on the stage coach (called the "Tally Ho") for the tavern's legendary chicken dinners.

Some Inns catered to drovers who were driving cattle or sheep to market. They also provided lodging to the drivers of large freight wagons. The drivers spread their bedrolls on the floor inside the bar room, with their feet towards the fire place.

Inns that catered to stage coach passengers provided sumptuous meals to the guests, who could sit down at the large dining room table with the proprietor. All types of food were available in generous quantities.

Although the idea of staying in a tavern or inn sounds very quaint today, that was not the case. In those days people were expected to share beds or sleep on the floor. The large bedrooms contained six to eight beds, with up to three persons allowed in a bed. Sharing a bed with strangers was common. It was difficult to find a bed that did not have bed bugs or fleas.

In 1800 a small boarding house was added at the Springs, on the Hotel side of the stream, to help meet the needs of visitors. It still wasn't enough. Having no place to stay, in the summer

This often - reprinted artist's sketch of the early Bedford Mineral Springs buildings shows the Stone Building, also called the Stone Inn, at right, Crockford in the center, and a bath house, at left.
Bedford County Historical Society collection.

of 1805 hundreds of persons set up camp in the valley with no shelter, so they could seek a cure at the Springs.

By this time, Dr. Anderson had a partner, Dr. George Foulke. As you may recall, Dr. Foulke played a role in the "discovery" of the Springs. Dr. Foulke returned to Carlisle in 1803; on May 1, 1804 he married Mary Steel and they immediately returned to Bedford.

In Blackburn's history, Dr. Foulke's son recalls, "Dr. Anderson and Mrs. Foulke and Dr. Foulke and Mrs. Anderson opened it as partners." He added that a Ball was given in honor of the discovery.

The partnership would not last because Dr. Foulke contracted a severe case of rheumatism, which afflicted him his entire life. In 1809 they moved back to the family home in Carlisle, despite his wife's objections.

Another Bedford physician was connected to the Springs, but not as a partner. He was Dr. William Watson, the eldest (there were three generations of doctors by that name).

Dr. Hickok wrote, "Dr. Watson came to Bedford in 1805, I think, and was celebrated far and near as a physician. It was a common occurrence for parties to come from the extreme southern states to Springs, to be under his treatment. He was almost a giant in physique, being six feet four inches in height and weighing three hundred and forty pounds. He was, not withstanding his weight, active, spending much of his time on horseback and was said to be one of the lightest dancers among the habitues at the Springs."

Dr. Watson, after commencing practice at Bedford, was responsible in part for the increase in visitors to the Springs. At Dickinson, Dr. Watson and Dr. Anderson had attended classes together. He practiced medicine in Carlisle but in 1805, his first wife having died, he moved to Bedford, no doubt at Dr. Anderson's urging.

Dr. Foulke was still a close associate of Dr. Anderson when they commenced the construction of the first of the larger buildings to be erected at the Springs, the Stone Building. This is the only one of the original early buildings at the Springs that is still standing. The Stone Building underwent extensive restoration during the 2006-07 reconstruction project.

Bill Defibaugh determined that construction

on the Stone Building, 2-1/2 stories and 130 feet long, began July 29, 1806 under contract with Joseph McCall and John Sterner. The Anderson store ledger shows Dr. Anderson paying the bills for the materials used in the construction of the Stone Building; also contracting with local blacksmiths and forges (particularly McDermott's forge) for steel lintels, beams and tie bars; nails, spikes, and sprigs (brads); and latches, screws, hinges, locks and many other items used in its construction.

The contract called for Dr. Anderson to pay McCall and Sterner one hundred and ten dollars and five gallons of whiskey. Bill Defibaugh explains that the stone used in the project was taken from the limestone outcrops on the western slope of Federal Hill, and chiseled to the proper form and dimensions "with William McDermott's hardened steel-edged tools."

The Stone Building had 24 guest rooms, each with a separate fireplace for heat and cooking; a kitchen with a large fireplace for preparing meals, dining room, living room, drawing room and lobby. It was four times the size of the largest Inn in Bedford proper. In 1848, another story would be added.

Today the Stone Building provides not only guest rooms, but the rustic setting of the Frontier Tavern. In one of the dining rooms in the Tavern can be seen the original stone fireplace that was used to cook the very first meals on site for patrons of the Bedford Springs.

Several published sources suggest that the Stone Building was the handiwork of Bedford builder and architect Solomon Filler, but this is not possible since Filler was born in 1798. Bill Defibaugh, who has in his collection a number of sketches by Espy L. Anderson, believes that E. L. may have drafted the plan for the Stone Building.

Though not formally educated, Filler designed his buildings in the classic Federal style. Filler's best known work is the Bedford County Courthouse, completed in 1829, which is the oldest building in Pennsylvania that is still in use as a working courthouse.

Present day visitors to Bedford Springs who take advantage of the walking tours of historic Bedford will also enjoy looking at several other buildings that show Filler's handiwork, including the Presbyterian Church (1829), the Russell House (1816) and the Lyon House (1834).

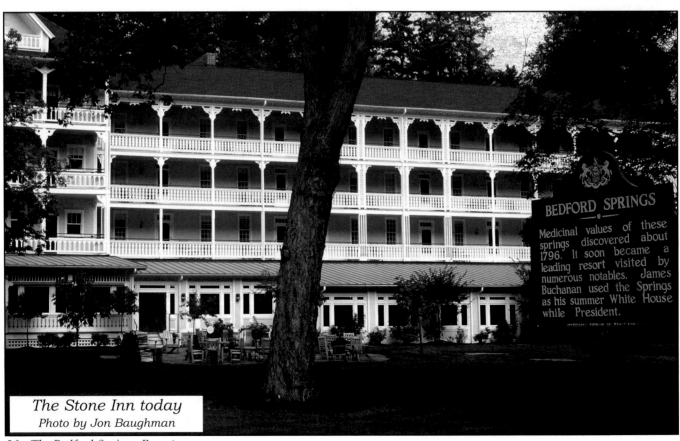

The Stone Inn today
Photo by Jon Baughman

Within a few years the Stone Building could not handle the growing patronage at the Springs. Even at that early date, the Springs was evolving from a therapeutic center to a fashionable resort. Guests were looking for other activities to help them pass the time, other than the therapeutic baths. Lawn croquet, badminton, and billiards were being added. Some of the guests now included political figures and business leaders.

Among the first notables who visited the Bedford Springs was Aaron Burr, who came there in 1806 to meet his daughter Theodosia Burr Alston and his grandson. Mrs. Alston arrived July 21, and soon her son seemed to be improving. Burr arrived in August, riding to Bedford from Philadelphia with two associates.

History records that Aaron Burr Alston was born in 1802, and after the birth of her son Theodosia was concerned with her own health, making trips to Saratoga Springs, New York and Ballston Spa, near Saratoga. But it was the child's health problems that led her to Bedford Springs. She later met her father in Ohio, taking her son along. There Aaron met Harman Blennerhassett, who had an island estate in the Ohio River in what is now West Virginia. Historians believe the two men made plans to form a western empire, and were later joined by General James Wilkinson. Burr and Wilkinson meant to separate Louisiana and parts of the west from the United States, with Burr ruling from Mexico, which would be invaded.

In 1807 Burr was tried for treason but acquitted. For the rest of his life he was discredited. As for Theodosia, her son died June 30, 1812. After that, she set sail on *The Patriot*. The ship was lost at sea and Theodosia was never heard from again.

In the 1920s brochures promoting the Bedford Springs Hotel began to list two other distinguished gentlemen as guests. The brochures state, "On its register appear the names of Benjamin Franklin, Henry Clay, Alexander Hamilton, Daniel Webster and many of their contemporaries."

Franklin passed away April 17, 1790, nearly a decade before the first "guests" came to Bedford Springs. There is an explanation for Franklin's name appearing on guest registers.

Helmut Leuck, Food Service Director in 2007, displays the original fireplace in the Stone Inn where the first meals were prepared for Bedford Mineral Springs guests. Photo by Jon Baughman.

Franklin did make trips to Bedford and his signature appears on documents in the Courthouse. While in Bedford he could have stayed at the National House on Pitt Street, also called the Golden Eagle Tavern, which was built and operated as an inn by Tom Anderson, Dr. Anderson's father. This was the first brick building in Bedford. It is possible that these registers were taken to the Springs. Some of the guest registers are missing today.

Alexander Hamilton's signature also appears on documents that are preserved at the Courthouse. Hamilton was shot and killed in a duel with Aaron Burr on July 12, 1804. It is

Early days at the Springs - 37

Crockford was named after a famous English gambling house.
Courtesy of Omni Bedford Springs Resort

possible that he visited Bedford before his death.

One of the earliest published accounts of the early Springs was in the form of a letter written to the *Lancaster Journal,* dated December 20, 1803, reprinted here in its entirety.

"Very valuable mineral springs have lately been discovered in the vicinity of this place (Bedford) which, from the extraordinary cures they have effected during the last summer, are beginning to excite very general attention. There are three in number, all issuing out of Dunning's Mountain, about one mile and a quarter south of this town; -- and they are now known by the names of the Yellow Spring, the Sulphur Spring and the Moss Spring.

"The first or Yellow Spring, (so called from the yellow tinge it gives to the substances it passes over), is considered the most valuable and salutary, and is the only one that has yet been used for medical purposes. It is a bold beautiful stream, bursting from the side of the mountain about three or four perches from Shover's Run beneath, and about fifteen feet above the level of the run. It is exceedingly limpid, of a mild temperature, (tho' not quite so warm as the Berkley waters in Virginia) and much lighter than common water. It has a peculiar taste, not unlike an infusion of tartar, -- to some not agreeable, but generally esteemed by those who have drank of it, by no means unpleasant. From the observation of some men of science, and from a few experiments lately made on the water, it is supposed to be more highly impregnated with foreign principles, and with a greater variety of them, than any spring yet discovered in this country. Of the four classes of mineral waters generally known, it unites the quality of at least three of them, viz. The Saline, the Sulphurous and the Martial -- but of the Sulphur it is only lightly tinctured.

"The water may be drank in great quantities with great ease and safety -- and its usual effects on people in health, are immediate and powerful Diuretic, a gentle Cathartic, and a considerable increase of Perspiration. Only a few diseased persons have yet made use of the water; but in every instance where used, they have been salutary, and in some, they have effected perfect and rapid cures. In one case particularly, a violent and alarming gravel, in a few weeks was totally removed; -- another person, affected with a severe and excruciating rheumatic affection, together with a general debility, was entirely relieved; -- and many others variously afflicted, have been much benefitted by only using the water occasionally at their own houses, some miles distant from the fountain.

"The Sulphur spring rises in the bottom of Shover's Run, about 150 yards below the Yellow spring, and is very strongly impregnated; -- but besides Sulphur, there is some other quality mixed with it, which at certain times, gives it a beautiful red colour; -- When in a glass, it appears as if currant juice had been plentifully poured into it. At other times, it is only blue, the natural colour of water highly charged with Sulphur.

"The Moss Spring discharges immediately into the Run about 100 yards above the Yellow Spring, and is a singular curiosity.

"A large rock about 8 feet in diameter, projects over the run; -- To the under parts of the rock is attached a beautiful thick green moss, from which, throughout the whole breadth of the rock, there falls a continual and rapid shower of pure limpid water, distilled from the rock.

"When this chrystal shower is viewed in the sunshine, nothing can be more brilliant. Whether the water has any medical properties is not yet known; but it is peculiarly sweet and pleasant, and may be made a very convenient shower bath.

"Besides these three, there is another spring remarkably cold, issuing out of the same bank, a few perches above the Sulphur Spring. It is a fine bold stream, rushing out of a cave, in the margin of Shover's Run, and may be appropriated to valuable purposes.

"The opposite bank affords convenient and pleasant situations for the building and accommodations contemplated. The romantic valley between is about 150 yards wide; it, and the adjoining ridges, abound with a great variety of Game, which, together with the great variety of fine trout that may at any time be caught in Shover's Run, will be a continual source of agreeable exercise and amusement to those who may frequent the waters."

There is one error in this description, that being a reference to Dunning's Mountain, which is north of Bedford, not south. The Springs are flanked by Evitts Mountain on the east and Wills on the west.

In 1811, the first section of the two-story building known as Crockford was constructed.

Dr. Anderson decided that Crockford would serve as a bachelor's quarters, and the Stone Building would be reserved for ladies and families. Crockford was a two-story, wood frame building.

Originally, this building did not bear a name. It was eventually given the name "Crockford" after a London gambling house constructed in 1827 by William Crockford, a fish monger and book-maker. After winning a large sum of money, he built his luxuriously decorated gambling house and organized it as a club with regular membership. Almost every English celebrity became a member.

At Bedford Springs the bachelors were fond of card playing, and named their building of choice after the better known London establishment.

In 1809 the facilities were described in *The Journal of Joshua Gilpin* (Pennsylvania Historical and Museum Commission, 1975): "...he has built a handsome and large frame lodging house and several smaller ones for families -- warm and cold baths, and a billiard room -- the accommodations are therefore very good and of all watering places I have seen in America, there seems to be none which for the beauty of the spot, and of the country around and their decided health appears more worthy to be visited."

A more detailed description appeared in the *Intelligencer and Weekly Advertiser,* Lancaster, PA, June 29, 1811: "The improvements shall now be concisely noticed. There are, at present, a large reservoir under ground: two commodious cold baths; two warm. A large boarding house, and two small detached buildings for lodging rooms. Besides which, the proprietor is now engaged in erecting large additions to the means of accommodation at the Springs. The inns and boarding houses of the town, will also be rendered more convenient and comfortable to those who may visit the springs during the ensuing season." This same description was also printed in the June 28, 1811 edition of the *Pittsburgh Post Gazette,* which added a number of testimonials, including this one, "Here amidst the mazy forest, or rugged landscape, they steal the roses of youth from the zephyrs of the mountains and valleys, and purify their feelings, whilst they lave their bodies in the translucid streams, sparkling with the richest gems of Hygeia." This was probably the first article that connected the Bedford Mineral Springs with Hygeia; it would not be the last.

In 1812 a room at the Springs cost about $1.00 per person. Breakfast cost 25 cents and dinner 50 cents. A bottle of whiskey was 75 cents.

From the very beginning, the Bedford Springs was always a seasonal resort, closing during the cold months. It was not until the 1950s that the Springs offered year-round lodging.

Another famous -- or infamous -- character who was known to have frequented the Springs property was David Lewis the Robber, also referred to in some circles as the "Robin Hood of Pennsylvania" for his custom of coming to the aid of poor widows.

Lewis became a wanted man after a trial by court martial for being AWOL from the Army, for which he received a life sentence. He managed to escape from the Jail at Carlisle. For many years he passed counterfeit money in a number of states. He returned to Pennsylvania in 1815, passing bogus notes in a number of communities before arriving at Bedford where he was arrested and jailed. Following a trial in which he was found guilty and sentenced to six years, in February 1816 he escaped from the Bedford lockup by cutting a hole through the plank floor and burrowing under the wall.

Lewis passed so many bogus notes and committed so many robberies that when he stopped at a public place, he was uneasy and always kept looking around the room. On the other hand, he was bold enough to join a posse that was looking for him.

His reputation as a "Robin Hood" is traced back to a widow he intended to rob in Mifflin County. He stopped at a farm house and intended to ask for change for a $5 bill so he could learn where their money was kept. But the widow who lived there said she had no money, adding that the constable was expected any moment to repossess the farm.

Lewis gave her the required money, told her to give it to the constable, and left. After the constable was paid she demanded a receipt, which was given. Far down the road, when the constable appeared, Lewis jumped out, pistols drawn, and robbed him of the money.

On October 3, 1819, a merchant named McClellan was traveling on the Great Road and was robbed of $1,500 by Lewis at Sideling Hill, accompanied by two sidekicks named Connelly and McGuire. Connelly wanted to kill the man, but Lewis intervened (during his life, he never killed a single man).

The trio were promptly apprehended and again taken to the Bedford Jail, but the following month all three escaped, along with other men confined there.

The robber's career came to an end July 13, 1820 when he died in the Bellefonte Jail. He had been shot in the arm by a posse. The arm was badly shattered but he refused to have it amputated. He was 30.

Lewis was no stranger to the Bedford Springs property. A cave located on the eastern base of Constitution Hill is called the "Davey Lewis Cave" and is pointed out as a secret hiding place of the outlaw. Bold as he was at times, it is not hard to imagine Lewis walking the grounds of the Mineral Springs, observing the people, and trying to pick out a sucker to which he could pass counterfeit bills.

Throughout Central Pennsylvania Lewis had a number of secret cabins in the dense forest and caves that were used as hideouts and pos-

The old Bedford Courthouse and Jail, from which David Lewis made his escape.

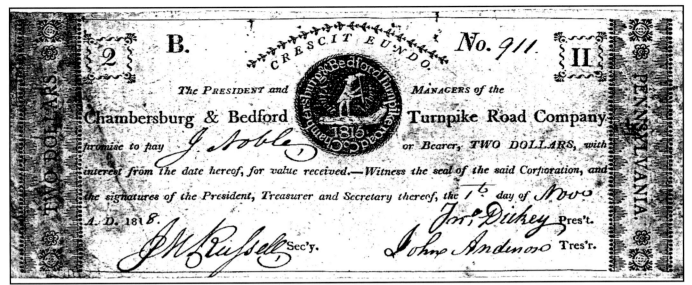

Chambersburg & Bedford Turnpike Company stock certificate
Collection of Adam L. Watson

sibly as places where he hid his loot. Even today, it is believed that Lewis hid more than $4,000 in glass bottles on the mountain near Three Springs, and also on the mountain above Colerain Forge near Spruce Creek.

William P. Schell wrote in 1906 that in 1816 Dr. Anderson sold the two mineral springs on the east bank of Shober's Run, the sulphur spring at the mill dam, the bath house, walks and certain adjacent lands to the Bedford Mineral Springs Company (reserving the boarding house (?) and all lands not granted). The new company consisted of Dr. John Anderson, Jonathan Walker, Dr. William Watson, Josiah M. Espy and Samuel Riddle. Dr. Anderson now had partners who were willing to invest money in the Springs.

The 1816 deed stated that the managers obtain a charter of incorporation, but this was never executed. The Bedford Mineral Springs Company was not incorporated until 1854.

The next significant expansion of the facilities at the Springs was made by the Bedford Mineral Springs Company in the 1820s, as business continued to increase. By 1825 the small boarding house on the "springs" side of the Run had been torn down. A similar structure on the opposite side of the Run was also removed so that "Crockford" could be doubled in size (1825). Also, about 1825 a new women's bath house was added along the road. Between this bath house and the Stone Building was placed a large fountain, in the shape of the Greek goddess of Health, Hygeia. There are few surviving photos of this fountain, but numerous descriptions exist. A pipe passed through the center of the statue, made of brass, and out the top of the head, which provided a thirty foot fountain spray that could be seen from many vantage points on the front lawn. The statue and fountain sat in the center of a large circular pool.

Next to Crockford, along the road, a new bath house was added in 1830, plus a stable and a barn. Also, in 1830, the Evitt frame building was constructed. It was two and a half stories, and 130 feet long, the same dimensions as the Stone Building.

The increase in visitors and the need for additional lodging was due, in part, to the construction of the Chambersburg and Bedford Turnpike, a project in which Dr. John Anderson was intimately involved as President of the company, but which eventually caused him financial loss. As noted earlier, Dr. Anderson was the founder and president of the Allegheny Bank of Pennsylvania, which at one time was the only bank west of Carlisle. Because of Dr. Anderson's involvement in the Turnpike, the bank eventually failed.

The Great Road, due to its route over the mountains, became unable to handle the great increase in traffic, especially larger and larger wheeled vehicles. Rather than raise taxes, the

Early days at the Springs - 41

Commonwealth felt the best way to fund transportation was by creating private turnpike companies which would construct roads by selling stock. An act authorizing that was passed by the legislature on February 24, 1806. The legislature envisioned a more direct route west, which would pass through Carlisle, then Chambersburg, McConnellsburg, Bedford, and end in Pittsburgh, essentially bypassing the Great Road west of Shippensburg. At first six companies were authorized; the number was reduced to five in 1814 and the route was divided into sections.

Tolls were to be collected at regular intervals along the route. These funds would be used to maintain the road and to pay debt service.

Construction of the various sections did not begin until 1816, after the companies acquired land, cut down trees and began to build culverts and bridges. Dr. John Anderson, fully aware of the impact a turnpike would have by making it easier for patrons to reach Bedford Springs, invested heavily in the Chambersburg and Bedford Turnpike, and also sold stock for the company.

Hayes Eschenmann of Shippensburg, an authority on early roads, stated that when he (Dr. Anderson) sold stock in 1818 to the Marine Insurance Company of Philadelphia he personally guaranteed 8% annual dividends. Later the stock failed to earn the promised 8% and caused Dr. Anderson financial embarrassment......The road deteriorated due to heavy use and neglect so lawsuits were filed for injuries due to accidents, tolls were high, and canals and railroads were being developed for transportation. People began to bypass the tollgates..."

The state tried to help the distressed Chambersburg and Bedford Company through the purchase of 2800 shares of stock. But the Allegheny Bank was forced to close on September 21, 1832. All of the assets were turned over to William Hartley of Mt. Dallas, a friend of Dr. Anderson (and also an investor in the Turnpike). Hartley paid all the bank's liabilities so that none of the depositors lost a single dollar.

Hartley was very successful in business, having invested in Conestoga freight wagons and stage coach lines. He may also have had an interest in Bedford Mineral Springs, as his sister, Eliza, was married to Dr. Watson.

The exact details of the Turnpike's struggles are not known because the office and early records of the company were destroyed on July 30, 1864 when the Confederate Army set ablaze a large section of Chambersburg.

For Dr. Anderson, the bank failure was an embarrassment but not a major setback. In time, the Turnpike proved its worth and continued to be a driving force in the success of the Bedford Springs. There is little question that "Bedford's convenient situation along the greatest traveled highways from the East across the Alleghenies" gave Bedford Springs a distinct advantage over other spas.

After the Turnpike opened to Bedford, a stage coach office was opened in the Exchange Hotel, located at the corner of Pitt and Richard Streets. It remained open until the railroad reached Bedford in 1874. It offered service to stage coaches, Conestoga wagoners, packhorse trains and drovers taking their animals to eastern markets -- sort of a modern day travel agency.

Starting in 1819 coaches with four horses would travel from Philadelphia to Pittsburgh, making the 303 mile trip in 60 hours, for a fare of $18 to $22. As the coach approached the town of Bedford, the driver would whip the horses into a full run, while sounding horns. As an additional excitement for passengers and spectators, if more than one coach was arriving, a race would ensue, noisily announcing the arrival of more visitors.

Guests arriving at the Exchange Hotel by stage coach were met by Hacks -- two or four seated carriages -- to transport them and their luggage to the Springs. The fee for the trip, a distance of 1.5 miles, was $3.00.

The daily stage line between Philadelphia and Pittsburgh was established in 1828 by James Reedside and Samuel B. Slaymaker with a fare of $18 to $22. Writes Ned Frear in *Bedford County: A Brief History,* "The Good Intent fast mail, for which John Piper was agent in Bedford, eventually made the run in three days, for a fare of $12.

The improvement in transportation also

made it feasible to ship the Bedford Springs mineral water throughout the United States and to Cuba. Water was shipped in mulberry barrels at $8 per barrel. Mulberry wood was used because it was thought to preserve the medicinal value of the water.

Dr. William Watson of Bedford is credited with launching the mineral water trade at the Springs, and he continued to supervise this operation until his death in July, 1835. By 1831, quart and pint glass bottles of the water were being advertised for sale in Philadelphia and other eastern cities.

The bottled water was advertised in the *National Gazette and Literary Register,* Philadelphia, Sept. 8, 1831, as "Carpenter's Bedford Springs Water" by Geo, W. Carpenter, 801 Market Street, Philadelphia. "The subscriber has made arrangements with the proprietors of the celebrated Bedford Springs in this State, and received the exclusive privilege of the water for bottling, and will have it carefully put up under the superintendence of Dr. Watson, an eminent Physician, who resides at the Springs, and is now pleased to offer it to the public in quart and pint bottles.

"These waters, as a gentle aperient and tonic, are equal, if not superior to any native spring in the United States. It is resorted to annually by numerous persons in various parts of the United States, who have received the most salutary and beneficial effects from the use of it. It is a safe and gentle purifier of the blood, and affords a great relief to those of plethoric habits residing in crowded cities without sufficient exercise, and those who participate freely in the luxuries of life..."

But wait. There's more. Carpenter was also marketing a unique product that he called "Carpenter's Bedford Spring Powders." If a person could not get Bedford Spring waters due to distance or costs of freight, "particularly those in the Southern States, all they needed to do was order the powders which were a "valuable substitute for the bottled water." He also warned the public about imitations -- "the emulator putting up different articles and calling them by the same name..." which should be boycotted.

Today many of the early glass bottles are on display in the hallway near the entrance to the Bedford Springs Resort Spa.

Dr. Watson was also responsible for the growing popularity of the Springs with Southern folk -- a lucrative patronage that would continue to grow until the Civil War. As Dr. Hickok wrote, "It was a common occurrence for parties to come from the extreme southern states to the Springs, to be under his treatment."

Several excellent descriptions of the facilities at the Springs in the 1820s survive. One, dated July 1, 1824, was published in the *National Gazette and Literary Register.* This item calls the Springs "The Montpelier of America" due to the medicinal properties of the waters, and calls it a "celebrated establishment and fashionable resort..."

"The buildings are large and the rooms spacious and airy; the arrangements of the bed chambers so much praised by the visitors last summer will, if possible, be rendered still better this season as an additional number of new mattresses has been obtained. The hot and cold baths are supplied from the mineral springs, and are in the best order. These inducements, with the salubrity of the mountain air, the delicious water, (independent of the mineral springs) make it to the valetudinarian one of the most desirable places in the United States. Whilst music and balls in the evening, billiard tables, quoits, bowling alleys, &c., a convenient distance from the house and the great abundance of game in the neighborhood, affords to the lovers of sport and exercise an opportunity of indulging in every innocent recreation and amusement.

"The table will be supplied with every thing in season, and the epicure gratified with the finest mountain mutton and venison, -- The wines and liquors have been selected with the most particular care, and the best servants and music procured."

The Evitt building had been completed and in use when this description of the Springs was published in the *Bedford Gazette,* May 9, 1833, by Samuel Blackwood. He describes the Stone building thus: "containing 35 neat and comfortable lodging rooms, well furnished. To this is attached a spacious building (Evitts), containing an elegant drawing room, tastefully fur-

Early days at the Springs - 43

nished; including a fine toned piano; and adjoining thereto a large dining room, 88 feet in length, and 30 feet in width. This building contains 22 lodging rooms, recently constructed -- airy sweet and comfortable." Crockford: "The frame building West of the Springs, and by many considered the most pleasant, presents many advantages to invalids, and contains 38 lodging rooms with a fine parlour. All of the above buildings have Piazzas round them, where exercise can, at all times, be taken free from exposure."

An article dated 1832 in the *Gazetteer of Pennsylvania* was not so impressed with Crockford: "At the distance of 15 or 20 rods South of the principal buildings, there has been erected, much to the injury of the prospect, a two story frame building, 140 feet in length. From its spacious balconies, however, the visitors have an agreeable prospect to the North."

This article does give a valuable description of the springs themselves: "The principal access from the principal houses of accommodation, to the springs, is by a raised way across the valley to a small bridge over Shover's creek. From the springs, zig-zag walks are cut upon the western slope of Constitution Hill, to its summit, which, but for the towering forest trees, would afford in all directions a most interesting and romantic view. The valley opposite Anderson's spring is about 150 yards wide and in its entire length, almost a perfect level, which is beautifully adorned by forest trees of native growth, dotted over its surface."

These articles describe the Mineral Springs that were first visited by the young James Buchanan, when he first came to Bedford in 1816, and on numerous occasions thereafter. These describe the Springs that were visited by John C. Calhoun, Secretary of War, in 1821, who came Pennsylvania to explore his prospects for the presidency. He toured the state until mid-September and returned to Washington "full of rosy hopes for the future," which did not materialize.

In June, 1824, Louisa Adams, wife of Secretary of State John Quincy Adams (who would become president the following year) came to Bedford Springs for her health. Her husband did not join her at Bedford, as he had intended. Instead, he visited his father, the former president, in Massachusetts

Numerous persons of wealth and fame were visiting the Springs. Of these, the name of the famed orator Daniel Webster certainly stands out. Webster came to Bedford Springs in the summer of 1834. His name

"A fountain featuring a statue of Hygeia, goddess of health, sat at the main entrance." Courtesy of Omni Bedford Springs Resort.

appears in the old Hotel registers. When he departed for Chambersburg he was accompanied by Attorney Alexander King. In 1854, King would become a part owner of the Springs.

As Dr. Anderson advanced in years, his children became actively involved in the day to day operation of the Bedford Springs, particularly his son Espy L. Anderson. Patronage at the Springs continued to increase each year. In the late 1830s it became obvious that the resort needed a much grander building and additional facilities to meet the needs of wealthy and influential clients who were now "regulars" at the Springs.

In 1838, a year before Dr. Anderson's death, Solomon Filler was called upon to design and build a structure at the Springs. This structure was modeled "after some of the Greek Revival style buildings in Washington, D.C. and Federal and State buildings in our State capital," according to Bill Defibaugh. "This architectural achievement, called the Colonial Building, brought much dignity and visual significance to a former cottage type inn," Defibaugh adds.

In 2008 a newspaper, *The Juniata Gazette,* dated August 10, 1819, surfaced in Fulton County, which was examined by Bill Defibaugh. Published in Lewistown, PA, the article stated "The author of the Declaration of Independence, Thomas Jefferson, is now at Bedford (Pa.) Springs where we understand he intends to remain two months."

Defibaugh contacted a librarian at Monticello, Jefferson's estate near Charlottesville, VA and asked if they had any evidence that Jefferson had visited Bedford Mineral Springs. The researcher told him that the same article had appeared in at least 12 newspapers published in 1819, but the Monticello staff had no record of the President visiting Bedford Springs.

She added that, since it is known that Jefferson visited his personal retreat, Poplar Forest, near Bedford, VA, in 1819 it could have been a case of mistaken identity. Jefferson's personal letters, which are preserved, allowed researchers to reconstruct evidence of his many trips, including those to Bedford, VA hot springs.

The *Thomas Jefferson Encyclopedia* states that Jefferson did not travel to Bedford Springs, PA in 1819, and that "A retraction of these reports was later printed by *The Carlisle Republican* in Carlisle, Pennsylvania."

Defibaugh then began to search for circumstantial evidence, and he soon found it, in the form of the architecture of several buildings in Bedford, PA. Thomas Jefferson is well known for his architectural design, and as a self-taught architect he left his mark on the design of the Rotunda at the University of Virginia, Charlottesville, and also in a number of Court Houses in Virginia.

The Bedford County Courthouse in Bedford, PA and the Courthouses in Virginia are very similar. Said Defibaugh, "We have two buildings in downtown Bedford that look like Jefferson's handiwork, the Courthouse and the Presbyterian Church."

The Bedford, PA buildings also resemble the designs of architect Benjamin Henry Boneval Latrobe, who was born in England but came to the United States in 1796. A close associate of Jefferson, Latrobe incorporated many of Jefferson's ideas into buildings he designed, particularly the Richmond Penitentiary. It was Latrobe who gave the U.S. Capitol Building and the White House their polished forms.

But the most striking of the Bedford buildings to show a possible Jefferson influence is the Colonial Building at Bedford Mineral Springs.

Defibaugh believes that Thomas Jefferson did stay at Bedford Mineral Springs in 1819, and in conferring with Dr. Anderson he suggested that a very grand hotel building be constructed that would be fitting of a famous resort such as Bedford. Taking this idea one more step, Jefferson may have even suggested or provided the architect's plans for the new building.

While many people believe that Bedford's Solomon Filler was both a builder and an architect, Filler was probably not an architect in the traditional sense, but followed the plans of others.

Defibaugh explains that if one looks head-on at the University of Virginia buildings and the Colonial Building at Bedford Springs, the buildings are very similar.

He added that the foyer at Monticello looks

Early days at the Springs - 45

Above, Colonial building and attached kitchen at left; Crockford at right.
Courtesy of Omni Bedford Springs Resort.

Below, the steps and bridge leading to the Magnesia Spring.
Bedford County Historical Society collection.

like a miniature Bedford Springs Colonial Building lobby.

Even if Jefferson did not visit Bedford Springs in 1819, circumstantial evidence suggests that he could have been here at some point in his life.

It took four years to complete the Colonial building, along with a new attached kitchen building (of brick, two stories, 70 feet long and 40 feet wide). Dr. Anderson passed away in 1839 (his wife Mary had passed away in 1818), and from that point on, the management of

46 - The Bedford Springs Resort

the Springs was generally referred to as the Anderson Heirs.

Following completion of this major expansion, Espy L. Anderson took up permanent residence at the Springs and was closely involved in its operations.

Defibaugh said the walls of the Colonial Building are five bricks thick, requiring 500,000 bricks for construction. The bricks were fired on the front lawn at a cost of $3.75 per thousand bricks. He adds, "The large 23 ft. long exterior columns that support the piazza and the overhanging pediment roof are 31 inches in diameter and are hewn out of white pine from the Springs property."

He continues, "The interior was planned with large and gracious common areas, such as the lobby with its high relieved ceiling. The grand staircase was designed much like the antebellum southern plantations with a large landing halfway up the stairway that overlooked the lobby. The stairway led directly into a very large dining room on the second floor. The dining room ceiling was supported by many beautiful Roman columns and pilasters."

In an excerpt from the National Register of Historic Places -- Bedford Springs, it is noted that the Colonial Building was the signature building of the Resort... "The large three-story hip-roofed building, brick facade and full two-story colonnade with projected pedimented portico announced to all visitors the resort's prestige."

The Colonial Building was erected at a cost of $25,000 and was first opened to the public in the Spring of 1842. In addition to the large dining room, the second floor also featured a drawing room, and 12 guest rooms, 12 by 18 feet each. The third floor had guest rooms of 15 by 20 feet.

The vastly improved Bedford Springs were described in 1842 in *The History and Topography of Dauphin, Cumberland, Franklin, Bedford, Adams and Perry Counties:* "The improvements made by the present enterprising proprietor, are in every respect commensurate with the place.

"The buildings are 1 large centre building, 162 feet long, 3 stories high and 70 deep; 2 other large 3 story buildings, 130 feet in front each; and 1 other building, 120 feet in front -- giving a front of 557 feet -- besides 4 or 5 other buildings.

"In front of the buildings there is a fine yard and on the mountain there are graded walks. There are cold and warm plunge and shower baths, and in short every comfort and convenience that could be wished. This is a palace in the wilderness -- here you have the 'urbs in rure' -- the city in the woods.

"Just below the yard is a mill dam with a beautiful artificial island. Dr. H. Heyden, in a letter written for Silliman's Journal in 1832, says -- in relation to the Springs, 'In find the beauteous and wonderful supply of water which flows from no less than seven highly medicinal springs, all within the radius of a stony cast; the beauty of the valley and its susceptibility of the highest state of improvement, the lofty adjoining hills; and the extensive and beautifully romantic view from their summits to the north and east, present a combination of attractions hardly surpassed in this or any other country on the globe. -- Add to this the facility of obtaining all the delicacies and comforts of life, including wild and tame animals, and vegetables of almost every kind and quality, and move over the high value of the perennial and other medicinal waters, which are not excelled in certain complaints by any in the world. All these circumstances combine to recommend the Bedford Springs as a place of unrivaled attraction.

"This is the general opinion of all who visit the Bedford Springs." -- R. Weiser.

Please do not get the impression that the Colonial Building and attached kitchen was the only improvement made in this time frame. It was not. By this time Espy L. Anderson had added the brick third floor of the Stone Building. According to the National Register of Historic Places, some $170,000 in improvements were made in 1840s... "Existing buildings were enlarged; others built, new bath houses were constructed and a fountain featuring a statue of Hygeia, goddess of health, sat at the main entrance."

Next to the Stone Inn, the three story Swiss Cottage, 120 feet in length, was constructed to provide additional and badly needed guest rooms. The verandas matched those of the Evitt and Stone buildings.

Notes Bill Defibaugh, "It was at this time when the tradition began for the 7:30 a.m. bugle call to summon guests to the magnesia spring, where each drank two tumblers of water, half an hour before breakfast. The water was always taken prior to meals."

The management of the Springs had also solved the problem of refrigeration. A lake was developed a half a mile south of the resort, at the Black Spring where a dam was constructed. The lake froze thick with ice in the winter. Teams of workmen would saw the ice into large blocks, which were taken to several ice houses on the property, covered in sawdust for insulation, and stored until summer. Ice was chopped into smaller blocks as needed and placed in "refrigerators" to keep the food from spoiling. The impoundment became known as Lake Caledonia, after the old iron works.

Ironically, one of the well-known hotel guests of this time period had close ties to the Caledonia Iron Works. He was David Rittenhouse Porter, who was born in 1788 in Montgomery County, Porter moved to Huntingdon in 1813 to study law, but soon became employed in the iron industry as a clerk at Barree Forge. Two years later he entered a partnership with Edward Patton on Spruce Creek. But a recession following the War of 1812 brought financial ruin over the next decade and changed his life. He was elected to the General Assembly in 1819 and served for two terms. He then filled several row offices in Huntingdon, but found that the financial returns were meager.

Through his involvement in the iron industry he met Josephine McDermott, daughter of the old ironmaster William McDermott. Josephine had spent her early years at Caledonia Iron Works, just south of Bedford Springs, and through his bride Porter became deeply familiar with the Bedford area. She had, as a small child, lived at both Caledonia and in Bedford. They were wed in 1820; she was 17, he was 32.

Porter ran for the State Senate in 1836 and won easily. He was immediately recognized for his leadership abilities, and only two years later was nominated for Governor in an effort to deny Gov. Ritner a second term. Porter won by a slim margin and was inaugurated Jan. 15, 1839.

He insisted that the state pay interest on its public debts, which restored the Commonwealth's credit rating at home and overseas. He supported the construction of railroads and canals to improve the state's economy.

He was running for a second term when he visited Bedford in June, 1841. He and Josephine combined a campaign stop with a sentimental visit to the site of the former Caledonia Iron Works at Bedford Springs.

Dr. Hickok wrote, "Mrs. Porter was a lovely character, esteemed for her excellent sense, as well as for her gentle, unostentatious piety."

Porter won that election also, and served until 1845, the longest term as Governor as allowed by the Constitution. He then returned to the iron industry.

One of his acts as Governor was to abolish the imprisonment of people for their debts. There is little doubt that the financial difficulties of his father-in-law, as well as his own difficulties in the iron industry, had influenced this decision.

He was a close friend of James Buchanan, and they corresponded regularly over a long period of time. He supported the candidacy of Buchanan for President, and may have joined Buchanan at Bedford Springs on several occasions.

Excerpts from *A Pleasant Peregrination through the Prettiest Parts of Pennsylvania, 1836,* performed by Peregrine Prolix

Bedford Springs, August 10, 1835.

The weather has been very fine, and the days pass so pleasantly that they seem too short for the time of year. If Aurora has not previously raised your eyelids, a bell breaks your slumbers at 7 a.m.; you rise and drink three glasses of the mineral water; (that is enough;) you dress and descend to the lower piazza, where half an hour's walk will conspire with the water to do you service. The bell for breakfast rings at eight, previous to which even the drawing-room has been gradually filled with the early and hungry fair, who are to eat, and the table has been filled with the boiled and baked and broiled fare, that is to be eaten. The etiquette of the table is similar to that observed at the Virginia Springs, and will be found described in our letters on those delightful watering-places in pages 19 and 20; to which we refer our curious and intelligent readers. There is abundance here, not only of edibles and potables, but also of room and time; circumstances which are extremely favourable to a full and fair discussion of the subjects that are laid before the company.

After breakfast, all who are able to walk, may be seem sauntering over the bridge, and wandering along the further bank of the stream; and some more ambitious than the rest actually carrying their breakfasts to the top of Constitution Hill; there to sit awhile and chew the cud of sweet and bitter fancy.

In an hour or two the ladies retire to read or sew, perchance to sleep or so; and when tired of their rooms, they tyre for dinner. There are some enterprising exceptions who take a drive in a barouche or a ride on horseback. The masculine amusements are billiards, shooting, fishing, and politics; the ladies also indulge a little in the two latter diversions; but then they are fishers of men, and use their angles with success and grace.

At two p.m. the bell again invites to the table well covered with flesh, fowl, fish and vegetables. Among the honoured viands are mountain mutton and wild venison; the former as good as that of Wales, and the latter better than that of Blenheim Park; as it is very tender and has a fine wild game flavour. It is plentiful here, and paradoxical, for though it is deer, yet it is cheap. Among the vegetable preparations, one of the most enticing and satisfactory is hominy; and it sometimes disappears with such amazing velocity and voracity, that on one occasion we were obligated to request our friend the President Judge of the district, who sat vis a vis, to issue a writ de homine repelgiando. Hominy is made of maize or Indian corn, the grains of which are cracked into several pieces and the skin rubbed off. One-fourth of its bulk of a small dried bean is mixed with it, and it is boiled or simmered for seven or eight hours. It is enriched with butter and seasoned with salt, and served up smoking hot and white as snow. It is in truth a lovely and a wholesome compound, and very worthy to accompany a piece of roast or boiled corn-fed turkey and a slice of Maryland ham, down the hungry throat. The dainty is but little known to the unhappy people who dwell east of the river Hudson, and but few transatlantics have ever heard its name. It is for the benefit of such that we have noticed it, and shall describe every thing we see in Pennsylvania.

"Planius ac melius Chrysippo et Crantore;"
in order that they may understand better
"Quid sit pulchrum, quid turpe, quid utile, quid non."

The afternoon is divided between occupation and idleness, much after the manner of the morning. An hour before tea the purlieus are again enlivened by the appearance of numbers of both sexes; many of whom visit the principal mineral spring to imbibe a little of its liquid treasure. At 7 p.m. the welcome summons the bell recalls the wanders to the festive board, now spread for supper. After this last meal of the day, the company collect in the drawing-room, which communicates with the dining-room by a folding door. Here they pass a chatty hour, whilst the familiars are arranging the latter for a dance, by withdrawing the tables to the further end. When the metamorphosis is complete the ballroom is not very grand;

'The ceiling boasts no polymyx,
No drapery the window;
The folks think more of politics
Than finery within doors.

Kentucky Ballad.

The musicians have no orchestra, but sit in chairs upon the floor, and are all members of one German family, consisting of a father and five or six sons, who play admirably upon different instruments, whose first harmony draws the dancers to the floor; and the more sedate are left to the pleasures of talk, or whist, or chess, in the drawing-room. By 11 p.m. another day is added to the past, and every sound is hushed in sleep.

On Sunday the occupations are different, for all that can find a place of worship agreeable to their religious views, go to church. If it should happen that a clergyman of the Protestant Episcopal church be sojourning at the springs, Sunday converts the dining room into a place of worship; and most of the company are satisfied to stay at home and attend the solemn and edifying service of the church.

(Continued on page 50)

Bedford Springs, August 13, 1835.

The weather has been very fine since our arrival, and the temperature delightful; the nights are cool and apt for snoozing, the mornings and evenings mild, and the days comfortable, warm and bright.

The bottom of this valley is about one thousand feet higher than the site of Philadelphia, which sufficiently accounts for the superiority of its summer climate.

There are several springs, the most important of which is Anderson's; which gushes abundantly from a lime stone rock on the western side of Constitution Hill, at an elevation of thirty feet above the rivulet and at a distance of sixty feet from its eastern bank. The water is transparent and sparkling, and exhibits a temperature of fifty-eight degrees according to the scale of Fahrenheit, when the same thermometer would stand at seventy in the surrounding air. It has a slight saline taste, but no smell. When exposed in a vessel to the air, it becomes flat, but retains its clearness, and deposits no sediment.

The stream from the spring deposits carbonate of iron, on those substances it continually flows over.

Doctor William Church of Pittsburg, gives the following analysis of a quart of the water from Anderson's spring.

A quart of water, evaporated to dryness, gave thirty-one grains of a residuum. The same quantity of water, treated agreeably to the rule laid down by Westrumb, contained eighteen and a half inches of carbonic acid gas. The residuum, treated according to the rules given by Dr. Henry, in his System of Chemistry, gave the following result: Sulphate of Magnesia or Epsom

Salts, -	20 grains.
Sulphate of Lime -	3 3/4
Muriate of Soda -	2 1/2
Do. of Lime -	3/4
Carbonate of Iron-	1 1/4
Do. of Lime -	2
Loss -	3/4
	31 grains.

To which must be added 18 1/2 cubic inches of carbonic gas.

At the distance of one hundred and fifty yards to the south of Anderson's spring, another abundant spring called Fletcher's, flows from a limestone rock on the western side of Constitution Hill.

Doctor Church's experiments on the water of this spring, produced nearly the same results as above described, with respect to Anderson's spring; except in detecting a little more iron and common salt; and a little less magnesia. With the surrounding air at seventy, the water in the spring exhibits fifty-five degrees of Fahrenheit.

These waters are antacid, mildly cathartic and tonic, and not being nauseous, may be taken with comfort by the most delicate stomach. Experience has proved that they are capable of putting to flight an army of diseases; and when the body personal is thoroughly soaked with them secundum artem, like Pandora's patent box, it parts with an Ilias malorum, and hope remains behind.

Any persons possessing any of the undermentioned diseases, may become the beneficiaries of these benignant waters: Diseases of the stomach and intestines; dyspepsia; hemorrhoids; worms; calculus; gravel; anasarca; suppression or excess of various secretions; diabetes; gout; debility remaining after acute diseases; and all those chronicobilious affections originating in southern climates.

The waters have acquired so great a reputation, that immense quantities are sent away daily in barrels to perform long and expensive journeys by land, to go and cure those, who cannot come to them. The price of a barrel filled, and ready booted and spurred for its journey is three dollars; and that is enough to last a regular and prudent toper four months.

Visitors at the Springs grow so fond of the water, that Brandy, Gin, Usquebaugh, Rum, Champagne, and the rest of their old and virtious loves, are soon routed from their affections, and whistled down the stream of oblivion. It is feared that this may excite the jealousy of the temperance societies, as trenching somewhat upon their ground; and that it may prevent poets from spending a few pleasant days at the Springs; because Horace says, -

Nulla placere diu nec vivere carmina possunt, Quae scribunter aquae potoribus - Epist. 19. Lib.1

It is however probable that he did not mean Bedford water; therefore let the Poets come, and resist the watery seduction if they can.

There is also a very copious spring of limestone water issuing from several crevices in a rock at the western foot of Constitution Hill, about two hundred yards north of Anderson's spring, and forty feet below its level. Its volume is sufficient to turn an overshot mill, and its temperature is fifty-one.

On the western side of the rivulet, and at a distance of two hundred yards from Anderson's spring, rises a spring whose water exhales a strong odour of sulphuretted hydrogen gas, and is covered by a thin whitish pellicle. Doctor Church's experiments proved it to contain carbonic acid and sulphuretted hydrogen gas; and small quantities of lime, magnesia, and common salt. Its temperature is fifty-six.

The place is also blessed with two pure springs, clear as light, and cool as the cave of Calypso. The element flowing from these sources is so pure that the chemical tests do not discolour it. The springs are situated on the eastern side of Federal Hill, and from their tasteless purity and delicious coolness, have obtained the name of Sweet. Their temperature is fifty-two.

In the days of President Buchanan

"My first visit to Bedford was in 1816, the year in which the Turnpike was commenced. What I am about to tell occurred in 1818, the year in which the road was finished. It was my fourth summer on the roads. I had come from Lancaster in my gig and stayed for the night at Christian Beamer's on the old road, at the foot of Sideling Hill. I was about starting in the morning for Bedford on the old road, as I had found the day before places along the turnpike which were yet unfinished and hardly passable. As I was starting Mr. Beamer suggested that the turnpike was nearly fit for use and that I could get through by going that way. You will recall that the old road ascended the mountain on the north side of the gorge and that the new pike went up the southern side of the valley. After a little thought I concluded to try the new way and I turned my horses onto the pike. I had driven without any obstructions, north three miles, when I was brought to a standstill by a short piece of road that was not fully opened, not being entirely cleared and graded. There was about an eighth of a mile of clogged road to hinder my passage but things necessitated my going back fully two and a half miles to get on the old road again, and then traveling the same distance to as far as I had already gone. There were several men at work at this point and I stopped a little while in conversation with them. They were nearly all Irishmen, one an intelligent kindly young Irishman seemed to be the head of the rest, as I judged from their talk.

"After some conversation, he promised that if I could walk over an eighth of a mile of unfinished road, one of their number would lead my horse and four would carry my gig, and a little further on they could put me back on the way again and save me the lost time of the trip back again.

"You may be sure I gratefully accepted their kind offer and was soon on my way again, with a warm heart towards them all. Now whom do you suppose that warmhearted Irishman was? You have heard of him often. He was afterwards educated and is now Archbishop Hughes of New York." -- James Buchanan, quoted by Hayes R. Eschenmann.

James Buchanan, the future President, visited Bedford Springs on a regular basis, beginning in 1816. During his four years as the nation's chief executive, the Springs was referred to as his "Summer White House."

When Buchanan first visited the Springs, the buildings consisted primarily of the Stone Inn and Crockford. He witnessed firsthand how the resort grew and prospered over a period of more than four decades.

A bachelor, he was sometimes accompanied to the Springs by his niece, Harriet Lane, whom he raised.

A lawyer, Buchanan lived in Lancaster, from where he was elected to the state legislature in 1814, serving two terms. It was during this time that Buchanan became engaged to Ann Coleman of Lancaster, who died suddenly. Rumors claimed that her death was a suicide. Ann's father was a wealthy ironmaster, perhaps Pennsylvania's first "millionaire."

Buchanan had made a trip to Philadelphia to represent a Mr. Jenkins of Lancaster. Upon his return he stopped at Jenkins' house to relay the outcome of the hearing. During the visit Jenkins' sister-in-law, Miss Grace Hubley, engaged Buchanan in conversation, which stretched late into the afternoon. Either Hubley or a friend of hers sent Ann Coleman a note that stated that Buchanan had stopped to see Hubley. Angry that Buchanan didn't call on her first, Ann promptly broke off the engagement and made a hurried trip to her sister's home in Philadelphia, where she died suddenly.

Buchanan sent a note of sympathy to Ann's father, but it was refused at the door and returned unopened.

Miss Coleman's death played heavily on Buchanan's spirit, and he chose to remain a bachelor. He also threw himself into politics. An inscription on Miss Coleman's grave at St. James Churchyard, Lancaster, states that she was the sweetheart of James Buchanan, 15th President of the United States. It was shortly before her death that he made his third visit to Bedford, stopping on the way to Bedford at Mercersburg to announce his engagement to his parents.

He was elected to the House of Representatives from Pennsylvania in 1820, serving for nearly ten years. In 1828 President Jackson appointed him Minister to Russia, during which time he negotiated the first commercial treaty between Russia and the United States. Diplomatic life did not agree with him, and he resigned after two years. He was then elected to the U.S. Senate in 1834.

A visit to the Bedford Springs by Senator Buchanan in 1837 is described in the biography of the President written by Philip S. Klein. "Buchanan went to Bedford Springs in July for several weeks of pleasant recreation, walking with his old fiend Judge Henry Shippen of Meadville along the wooded stream which rippled through the glades below the huge hotel. In the morning they would stop at the little white summer-house enclosing the beautiful mineral spring and "drink of the waters," according to their doctor's prescription. Until noon the guests ordinarily stayed within easy reach of the other little white houses until the volcanic effects of the "waters" had subsided. After midday all sought the rocking chairs which lined the huge porch or promenaded up and down, greeting newly arrived friends and gossiping. In the evening there was dancing in the great ballroom with schottisches, polkas, and a new step called the hop-trot dubbed by some rakes the rabbit hop. Buchanan loved to dance and spent more evenings in society than he should have, considering the amount of work he had planned to do. But the ladies insisted and he was always a willing respondent to a roguish eye."

During his trips to Bedford Buchanan always stopped to visit his sister, Jane Lane and family in Mercersburg. The entire family, especially the children, were very fond of him.

After a long illness, Jane died in 1840, and her husband, Elliott, died the following year. The two sons were of age, and could take care of themselves, but the two girls were given a choice on where they would like to stay. Harriet, age 11, wanted to stay with her favorite uncle, James Buchanan, and she took up residence with him at Lancaster.

Buchanan took charge of her education, sending her to private schools. Little did young Harriet realize that she was about to enter a world full of excitement and famous people.

Buchanan, meanwhile, was actively engaged in politics. In 1844 he was nominated for president of the United States as Pennsylvania's favorite son. James K. Polk of Tennessee also sought the nation's highest office, and in exchange for his support, made Buchanan his Secretary of State. It was off to Washington for Buchanan, Harriet in tow to be introduced to the fashionable circles in the capital "in the best manner" as Buchanan had promised her.

> **After Harriet's first visit to Bedford Springs, Buchanan expressed some regret he had given his permission for her to come, disapproving of her "keen relish for the enjoyments there."**

An August, 1845 entry in the Bedford Springs hotel has proven to be somewhat of a mystery, for the bill was for Buchanan, "Wife and Nurse's Board." In fact, the "wife" could have been Miss Lane, and the entry could have been made by a clerk who did not know that Miss Lane was his niece. It is known that she sometimes accompanied him to the Springs. In fact, after her first visit, Buchanan expressed some regret that he had given his permission for her to come, disapproving of her "keen relish for the enjoyments there."

After that first visit to Bedford Springs, Harriet got into trouble at school for having started a "clandestine correspondence" with a boy she met at Bedford. Her teacher had intercepted and destroyed his letters.

The August 5, 1845 entry in the Bedford Springs cash book reads, "Hon. James Buchanan, Ice cream, champagne, Bottle Madeira," etc. That year, a notice was published by the Bedford Mineral Springs, that "Espy L. Anderson, prop. Respectfully informs the public that he has fitted up and newly furnished the above celebrated watering place in a style of superior attraction and comfort. The establishment will be placed under the superintendence of A. S. Barnum, prop. of Barnum's Hotel in Cumberland."

Another notice published in 1845 stated, "The buildings are undergoing a thorough repair and will be furnished in a style that will bear comparison with every other watering place in the United States, Among the visitors expected are Hon. James Buchanan; Pa. Gov. Francis R. Shunk; Sec'y of State Jesse Miller; Atty. Gen'l John R. Kane and President James Knox Polk."

But before long, and while he was still at the State Department, Buchanan allowed her to go on summer vacations with some of his friends (among them the Walkers, Bancrofts, and Pleasantons) to Rockaway Beach, Saratoga Springs and Bedford Springs, while he stayed behind.

Buchanan, as Secretary of State, urged the annexation of Texas into the Union, which promptly led to confrontation with Mexico. Congress declared war and, despite much Northern opposition, he supported the military operations. American forces won repeated victories and occupied Mexico City. Finally, in 1848, Mexico ceded New Mexico and California in return for $15,000,000 and American assumption of the damage claims.

President Polk added a vast area to the United States, but its acquisition precipitated a bitter quarrel between the North and the South over expansion of slavery.

Utterly exhausted, Polk sought escape from Washington. His destination -- Bedford Springs. There is no doubt that Secretary of State Buchanan had suggested that the President seek some rest at the Springs. In addition, Robert J. Walker, Secretary of the Treasury, had studied law in Bedford under his father, Judge Jonathan Walker and was intimately familiar with Bedford Springs. Judge Walker is listed as one of the owners of the original Bedford Mineral Springs Company (beginning in 1816).

Polk made the trip to Cumberland, MD by stage coach, and on August 19, 1848 left that city by coach for Bedford.

Polk kept a diary, and the diary entries described his stay in Bedford in great detail. The diary was published in 1929 in London by Longmans, Green & Co., 420 pages. The book was edited by Allan Nevins.

To make this account as complete as possible the diary entries are being reprinted here in their entirety. Words added are in parentheses.

Saturday, 19th August, 1848. -- After breakfast this morning I left Cumberland, Md., for

Girls at the Magnesia Spring.   Courtesy of Omni Bedford Springs Resort.

the Bedford Springs, Penn., in a special coach furnished for my accommodation by Mr. Johnson, the very obliging stage contractor on the line. Mr. Johnson accompanied me to see that I was properly accommodated. My company in the coach consisted of my nephew, Samuel P. Walker, Dr. Foltz, Surgeon of the U.S. Navy, and Col. James Polk of Maryland. The latter gentleman fills the office of Naval officer at Baltimore. He descended from the same family as myself, and is distantly related. At the half-way house between Cumberland and the Bedford Springs (Anderson's) the teams in the coach were changed & we procured fresh horses. A number of farmers in the neighborhood were there. They had heard the day before that I was expected to pass the road to-day. I shook hands and conversed with them. I soon found that they were democrats. One of them, named Cisney, was a sensible man, and talked more than any of the rest. He told me that the valley between the mountains in which we were is called Cumberland Valley, and that in politics it is a little Berks of a place. Berks is the great Democratic county of Pennsylvania, using (usually) giving between four and five thousand of a Democratic majority. He pointed to (a) house in view, which he informed me was the place of voting in that District, and informed me that at the Presidential election of 1844 out of 208 votes polled 192 of them were given to Polk & Dallas, and that they intended to give as good a vote to Cass & Butler this fall. I took leave of these honest farmers & we proceeded on our journey. I was requested by Mr. Cisney to call at a house which he described a mile on the way and shake hands with his elder brother, who was now 88 years old, and as he said, always opened the election at their precinct by giving the first Democratic vote. I called at the House and found the old gentleman absent from home. I got out of the coach and shook hands with the old lady. She expressed her grief that the old gentleman was absent and said he would be almost beside himself when he heard I had been there. She said he had rode off down to Esquire ____'s. I do not remember the name of the "Squire," as she called it. I promised her to call and see him on my return, which seemed greatly to delight her. We proceeded on our way to the Springs, where we arrived about 1 O'Clock P.M. It was known at the Springs that I was expected to-day, but I was not looked for until about 4 O'Clock, the usual hour for the arrival of the stage. It was not known that I would come over in a special coach and, arriving two or three hours earlier than the usual hour for the arrival of the Stage, the proprietor and company at the Springs were taken by surprise. I was informed after I arrived that the Citizens of the Village of Bedford, situated about 2 miles from the Springs, and the company at the Springs, had made arrangements to give me a formal reception, and had provided a band of music for that purpose. I prefer to have arrived quietly as I did than to have had a public reception. I found about 50 visitors at the Springs, and among them was my old friend, the Hon. John Laporte (Tennessee), with whom I served in the Congress many years ago. Col. (Samuel) Black, lately commanding the U.S. Volunteers in Mexico, and his wife, Mr. Magraw of Pittsburg, Mr. McKinley, Editor of the leading Democratic paper at Harrisburg, were also of the number. In the course of the evening, Gen'l Bowman and a number of other citizens of the village of Bedford came out to see me. In the evening I was requested to walk into the Ballroom, where there was music and a number of young persons dancing. I remained but a short time and then retired for the night. I find the buildings large & the accommodations good. The Springs are situated in a valley between two mountains. The valley is not more than 200 yards wide. One of the head streams of the Juniata runs between the mountains, and the Springs flow out of the sides of the mountain. The Spring of greatest medicinal virtue and chiefly used is a bold, strong fountain. I have not been furnished with an analysis of its properties. The water, however, contains portions of magnesia & iron; & when used operates chiefly on the kidneys & bowels. There are also a white sulphur springs; a Slate Spring; a very large limestone Spring, and three or four other springs, all within a circumference of less than three hundred yards in diameter. The walks and grounds are neat & well shaded, and everything about the establishment has the appearance of comfort. I used but little of the water this evening. There is a great difference between the hot & sultry atmosphere of Washington & this place. I slept under a blanket to-night and would have been uncomfortable without it.

Sunday, 20th August, 1848. -- I rose early this morning and walked to the main spring and drank some of the water, and then ascended the mountain by a winding path to its Summit, where a summer-house or shed had been erected. The fog rose and prevented the view over the valley below, which is said to be very fine. I returned and drank more of the water before breakfast. This being the sabbath was a quiet day and I remained chiefly in my chamber. I wrote letters to Mrs. Polk & to J. Knox Walker. In the afternoon I ascended to the top of the mountain again & had a fine view of the valley below and of the surrounding country. At dinner & in the afternoon I shook hands with a number of people from the village & the neighbourhood, who from curiosity had come to see the President of the United States. The day became cloudy and the atmosphere cold, so much that about 2 O'Clock I had a fire made in my room. Towards sunset a cold rain commenced falling. At 8 O'Clock P.M. the company assembled in one of the large parlours and an excellent sermon was preached by the Rev. Mr. Purviance of the Presbyterian Church (G. D. Purviance of Baltimore). After the service was over I retired for the night. The rain continued to fall when I retired, and I slept very comfortably under two blankets.

Monday, 21st August, 1848, -- The weather was cloudy and cool this morning, and I fear will be unpleasant during the short stay I propose to make at the Springs. I walked to the

Springs and drank freely of the water before breakfast this morning. It begins to produce its effect on my system. Several of the visitors left this morning, and others speak of leaving soon in consequence of the unfavourable character of the weather. I find the company pleasant. Several persons from the village of Bedford & surrounding country visit me to-day. In the evening Mr. Meek, the Marshall of the Oregon Territory, arrived from Washington bearing dispatches to me from Mr. Buchanan, the Secretary of State, & a communication from Mr. Cave Johnson, the Postmaster Gen'l. By them I learned that Gen'l Shields of Illinois, whom I had appointed Governor of Oregon, had, by a Telegraphic dispatch, declined to accept. Before I left Washington I had made known my intention, in the event Gen'l Shields should not accept, to appoint Gen'l Joseph Lane of Indiana to be Governor of Oregon. This being known, Mr. Buchanan forwarded to me by Mr. Meek a commission for Gen'l Lane, all complete except my signature. I signed it and wrote a letter to Gen'l Lane. I delivered the commission and letter to Mr. Meek, with directions to proceed immediately to Gen'l Lane's residence on the Ohio River, near Evansville, Indiana, and deliver them to him. I prepared a Telegraphic dispatch for Gen'l Lane, informing him of his appointment, and forwarded it to Thos. J. Reed, P.M. at Louisville, with a request that he would send it to him by the first boat descending the River. This Telegraphic dispatch I delivered to Gen'l Bowman, the editor of the Bedford *Gazette,* who took it to the Telegraph office in the village of Bedford & sent it off to-night. Mr. Meek left in the Western Stage and proceeded on his journey. My orders are that the Governor, Marshall, and other officers of Oregon should, if practicable, proceed to Oregon this fall, & for this purpose a military escort has been ordered to be in readiness at Fort Leavenworth, Mo., to accompany them. If Gov. Lane and the other officers can leave Fort Leavenworth by the 15th of September, they can cross the Rocky Mountains before the snows of winter will obstruct their passage.

Tuesday, 22nd August, 1848, -- This morning was cool & fires were comfortable. It is almost too late in the season to visit this watering place. In the hot weather it must be a delightful spot. I rode two miles & visited Maj'r Watson at his house this morning. Major W. had invited me to do so. I was accompanied by a company of Gentlemen. When we arrived we met Judge Black, who is a candidate for the Democratic nomination for Governor of Pennsylvania. There was a cold collation and other refreshments. I returned to the Springs & after dinner rode to the village of Bedford at the invitation of several of the citizens. A party of gentlemen accompanied me. We stopped at a Hotel where many citizens of the village called and were introduced to me. We took supper and returned to the Springs. I spend my time very comfortably. Judge Laporte, Judge Black, Col. Black of Pittsburg, lately returned from Mexico, Mr. Magraw, & other Democratic friends are of the company at the Springs. The Hon. Job Mann, the representative of the District in Congress, Gen'l Bowman & others who reside in the village, spend a part of every day with me at the Springs. I use the water freely, & think the rest, mountain air, & water has invigorated and improved me. On returning from the village this evening I found the Hon. John McKeon of the City of New York, with whom I once served in Congress, had arrived. He very soon asked me to walk, and informed me that he had come especially to see me and to say that he would accept the office of Attorney of the U.S. for the Southern District of New York, if I removed Benjamin F. Butler, who now holds that office. The day before I left Washington Mr. McKeon called on me, and I informed him that I had intended to remove Mr. Butler and that I had thought of tendering the office to him. He at that time declined accepting it, and in consequence of doubts on his mind who should be appointed, he requested me to postpone making the removal & appointment until after my return from my contemplated visit to Bedford Springs & consult two friends, Mr. Cutting and Mr. Charles O'Connor, as to the proper person to be appointed. I agreed to postpone action as he requested. The Secretary of War was present during that conversation with him. He was to write to Mr. Marcy after his return to N. York. After he left I saw Mr. Marcy in the evening & told him that I would rely upon his opinion as to the person I would appoint. Now Mr. McKeon desires the appointment himself. I informed him of what I had said to Mr. Marcy on Thursday, after he left my office, & that I would not act until I saw Mr. Marcy, and that I would probably, after what I had said to him, appoint the person whom he might recommend.

Wednesday, 23rd August, 1848 -- Mr. John McKeon of New York, who arrived here on last evening, left here early this morning. About 11 O'Clock to-day accompanied by 8 or so gentlemen in carriages & in pursuance of a previous arrangement, I set out to ride to the village of Schellsburg, about 9 miles on the turnpike road in the direction towards Pittsburg. In passing through the village of Bedford I called a few minutes at the House of my friend, the Hon. Job Mann, the Representative in Congress from this District, & paid my respects to his family. Mr. Mann accompanied the party to Schellsburg. At Schellsburg the people from the village & many from the country called and shook hands with me at the tavern at which we stopped. Several ladies called. The people seemed to be much gratified. They said, and the people of the village of Bedford, that I was the first President of the U.S. who had ever visited them since the Whiskey insurrection in 1794, when troops had been collected there to suppress it, and when Gen'l Washington was there. The people seemed to be much gratified at my visit. We took dinner at Schellsburg and returned to the Springs, having had a pleasant ride & spent the day pleasantly. On my return I found Judge Longstreth who, as well as Judge Black who accompanied me to Schellsburg, is a candidate for the Democratic nomination as a candidate for Governor. He had arrived in the afternoon. The State convention to make the nomination will meet at Harrisburg on Wednesday next, the 30th Instant. I was informed that during my absence to (at) Schellsburg a fellow named Nugent, the correspondent of the New York *Herald* over the signature of *Galvienses*, and who has been calumniating me for the last two years in his letters to that paper, had arrived. He is the same fellow who was arraigned before the Senate for contempt at its last Session. He was pointed out to me, for I had never seen his person before to know him. He has, no doubt, followed me to the Springs to see what new slander he can invent for his employers to be published in the *Herald*. I informed Judge Laporte who he was, & took especial care not to speak to him & not to permit myself to converse in his presence. Though a writer of some smoothness I consider him an unprincipled scoundrel. I may expect to see some falsehood or other propagated by him in the *Herald*.

Thursday, 24th August, 1848 -- Intending to leave on to-morrow I spent a considerable portion of the day in writing in my room. Quite a number of persons from the surrounding country called to see me to-day. Judge Black and Judge Longstreth both left to-day. The weather is so damp and cool that most of the company speak of leaving in two or three days. In the evening a number of young persons, male & female, came out from the village of Bedford, and there was dancing in the Ball room. I was requested to walk into the Ball room. I did so, & after remaining a few minutes I retired. My nephew, Samuel P. Walker, did some copying for me to-day.

Friday, 25th August, 1848 -- After Breakfast this morning I set out in the Stage for Cumberland, Md., on my return to Washington. I was accompanied by my nephew, Sam'l P. Walker; Dr. Foltz, surgeon of the U.S. Navy; Col. James Polk of Maryland, who has been one of my party during my visit to Bedford; and by Col. Samuel Black of Pittsburg, and his wife. When the stage had proceeded about four miles, I was overtaken by a messenger with a Telegraphic dispatch from Gen'l Lane of Indiana, dated at Louisville, Kentucky, this morning, informing me that he had received the Telegraphic dispatch which I had sent through Thos. J. Reed, P.M. of Louisville, Ky., to him on the night of the 21st Instant and that he accepted the appointment of Governor of Oregon and would be ready to proceed to Oregon with Mr. Meek, the Marshall, this fall. This telegraphic dispatch is dated at Louisville, Ky., this morning, and reached me before 10 O'Clock A.M. The stage to Cumberland stopped at the half-way House between the Bedford Springs and Cumberland (Anderson's) where I found about twenty persons of the neighbourhood assembled to see me. I conversed familiarly with them. I stopped on the wayside to see an aged man named Cisney, who was and had been for many years a leading man of the neighbourhood. He told me he was 88 years old, that he had always been a Democratic (Democrat), & had voted at every election since he was entitled to vote. He is a remarkable person. We arrived at Cumberland about 5 O'Clock P.M. and remained there all night."

The diary entries provide a great deal of insight about the Bedford Springs of 1848: the accommodations, the activities, the water, and some of the notable persons who stayed there -- not to mention political intrigue. President Polk, while on vacation, conducted important business at the Springs. This example would be followed later by James Buchanan.

The Hotel ledger says President Polk stayed six days, in which time he spent $9.00 for board for himself, $4.50 for his servant's room, and 13 cents for postage -- his only expense. The ledger is marked "Paid in full, $13.63."

It is reported that General Zachary Taylor visited Bedford Mineral Springs where "one of the many balls and cotillions" was held in his honor. According to the Bedford County Historical Society, "Soon after the Springs ball, he was nominated for the Presidency by the Whig Party, and the following year, 1849, he was elected President."

In 1849 President Taylor again visited the Springs. His visit took place in August, accompanied by Governor Johnson. The President was ill, and he would die a year later. Known as "Old Rough and Ready", Taylor had a 40-year military career in the U.S. Army, serving in the War of 1812, Black Hawk War, and Second Seminole War before achieving fame leading U.S. troops to victory at several critical battles of the Mexican-American War. Taylor died of acute gastroenteritis just 16 months into his term.

This visit is described in an undated clipping from the *Bedford Gazette* in the Bedford County Historical Society collection: "They were met by the Committee of Arrangements at the Juniata Crossings, 18 miles east of the Borough, where they were the guests of George McGraw, Esq., and citizens of East Providence Township.

"They were conducted to our Borough by the Committee, passing through the village of Bloody Run where hundreds of the sturdy yeomanry had assembled to greet and take by the hand the Old Hero.

"At half past 11 o'clock their arrival in sight of our Borough was announced by the ringing of bells and music. A procession was formed and marched to the eastern part of the town. Upon the arrival of Gen. Taylor, Gov. Johnson and suite, the procession was again formed and proceeded to the Bedford Hotel.

"Upon their arrival the President was welcomed on behalf of the citizens by John Mower, Esq. After dinner, prepared by mine host of the Bedford Hotel, Daniel Crouse, Esq., the General and Governor Johnson were conducted to the Bedford Springs. They were received in handsome style."

In the 1840s one of the regular guests at Bedford Springs was John S. Lutz, who came for hunting excursions; on one such excursion he took along a bottle of brandy. While he was at the Springs, he ordered many mint juleps, an indication that he was from the South, possibly Loudon County, Virginia.

Many Bedford residents also patronized the Springs, enjoying the fancy balls, teas and for socializing. A group of ladies dined at the Springs on July 14, 1846, and on several subsequent occasions. They included Carrie Cessna, Lou and Mary E. Anderson, Mary E. Davis, Mary E. Hafer, Mary Lyon, Maggie and Lottie Watson, Eliza King, Ellie Hall, Emily Filler, Alice Getty, Etta Reamer, Beckie Russell, Nellie Hartley, Etta Reynolds, Jane Tate, Kate Johnson, Mary and Emma Barclay, Louise and Kate Washabaugh, Julia Montgomery, Tessie King and Mary Fyan.

Another visitor to Bedford Springs was George Bancroft of Massachusetts, who served as Secretary of the Navy under President Polk. Harriet Lane was a good friend of the Bancroft family, and often accompanied them on summer vacations at Rockaway Beach, Saratoga Springs and Bedford.

By 1850 many of Buchanan's old friends had passed away or no longer traveled to Bedford. This is noted in a letter from Bedford Springs dated August 4, 1850 to his niece Harriet Lane.

Buchanan writes, "I have found Bedford very pleasant, as I always do; but we have very few of the old set, and the new are not equal to them. I will not tell you how many inquiries have been made for you, lest this might make you vainer than you are, which to say the least is unnecessary."

Buchanan retired to Wheatland in 1849, but in 1852 President Pierce appointed him Minister to Great Britain. So he was off to the Court of St. James's. Harriet Lane would join him the following summer. During his years in London, his annual visits to Bedford were suspended.

His role as minister lasted from 1852 to 1856, during which time he helped to draft the Ostend Manifesto, which proposed the purchase of Cuba from Spain in order to extend slavery. However, this was a major blunder, as Congress refused to accept it, unwilling to upset the delicate balance between free and slave states.

The Democrats nominated Buchanan in 1856 largely because he was in England during the Kansas-Nebraska debate and thus remained untainted by either side of the issue. He was nominated on the 17th ballot. Although he did not want to run he accepted the nomination. Buchanan was seen as a great compromiser by people on both sides of the slavery issue. He was viewed as a person likely to bring the opposite factions together. As a result every slave-holding state except Maryland gave Buchanan its electoral vote in 1856. Buchanan and vice-president John C. Breckenridge were elected by a large electoral majority and took office the following year.

According to historian Helen Hill Greenburg, Buchanan visited Bedford Springs 16 times before he became President.

During Buchanan's absence in London, things were happening at the Springs. The resort was as busy as ever, but the Anderson heirs were trying to sell the property. At this time period, J. Edgar Thomson, chief engineer for the construction of the Pennsylvania Railroad, was looking for resort properties of this caliber. It was Thomson who skillfully coordinated the construction of the PRR through the Juniata Valley, over the towering Alleghenies, and on to Pittsburgh.

James Buchanan

At Huntingdon, Thomson purchased a tract of land near Warm Springs, a mineral springs resort, but was unsuccessful in buying the land on which the Warm Springs were located.

According to published reports, Thomson assembled a group of investors in 1854 with the intent of purchasing the Bedford Mineral Springs from the Anderson family. They put down $10,000 to hold the property. But due to some misfortune in western land speculation some of the investors backed out of the deal. The sale never materialized and the down payment was forfeited.

Thomson and his associates at the PRR never lost interest in mineral springs resorts. They purchased Cresson Springs in nearby Cambria County at the close of the Civil War.

Unable to sell, Espy L. Anderson agreed to revive the Bedford Mineral Springs Co. charter of 1816; the company had never been incorporated. Bedford Mineral Springs Co. was now incorporated with the following stockholders: Alexander King, William P. Schell, Espy L. Anderson, John Shoenberger, Wilson McCandless, Job Mann, Daniel Washabaugh, John Cessna, John McCaules, Henry K. Strong, Samuel Davis, William T. Daugherty, Dr. William H. Watson and Nicholas Lyons. The property was transferred to the new corporation on April 11, 1857 for $200,000.

Waterman-Watkins' History of Bedford County states that this company made many improvements around 1857, including the cottage (Swiss Cottage? -- the construction date of 1848 also has been suggested for this portion of the hotel) and two bathing houses. Philip Gossler was named president of the new company.

With the completion of the Pennsylvania

In the days of President Buchanan - 59

Railroad the Springs had been bypassed by this new -- and faster -- mode of transportation. This may have contributed to the financial difficulties facing the Bedford Mineral Springs Company.

The Baltimore & Ohio Railroad had reached Cumberland, MD in 1844, but passengers headed for the Springs had to board a stage coach for the trip to Bedford.

The popularity of mineral springs resorts is reflected in a notice published in the *National Intelligencer* July 17, 1858 by the Baltimore & Ohio Railroad, advertising rail passenger service to five resorts, namely, Berkley Springs, Jordan's Springs, Shannondale Springs and Capon Springs (all in northern Virginia, now West Virginia) and Bedford Springs. The item for Bedford Springs announces, "For Bedford Springs by the trains from Washington at 5:15 a.m., or at 6:30 p.m., for Cumberland, 210 miles; and thence by stages 23 miles to Bedford. The stage leaves Cumberland every morning at 6 o'clock, arriving in time for dinner at the Springs. Fare through, $7.75."

As early as 1846 the management of the Bedford Springs was expressing its disappointment that both railroads would bypass Bedford. A newspaper clipping dated July 3, 1846 stated, "Espy L. Anderson, Prop., Bedford Mineral Springs, fitted up and newly furnished, the above celebrated watering place will be placed under the superintendency of Messrs. Alden & Martin, Mr. G. W. Alden has experience at the Monongahela House, Pittsburgh, and more recently US Hotel, Philadelphia. Excellent band of music produced." Arrangements were to have been made with B&O and Pennsylvania Railroads to stop at Bedford and to sell tickets direct to the Springs, but Anderson reported that those arrangements had failed. "However, conveyances by carriage or stage to Cumberland could be made and the stage is comfortable."

The Huntingdon & Broad Top Mountain Railroad and Coal Co. was formally organized January 10, 1853 to construct a rail line from Huntingdon, on the PRR, to the Broad Top Coal Field. The first locomotive passed over this road on July 30, 1855. The line reached Hopewell in Bedford County, 31 miles from Huntingdon, the following year.

Although the primary aim of the railroad was to reach the coal region, it was not the only goal. H&BT resident engineer John Fulton stated, "The secondary design was to extend the railroad from Hopewell to Bedford, 20 miles, to accommodate the visitors to the Bedford Springs, and to develop the iron ores in various places of this locality. Whether the ultimate aim was to reach Cumberland, MD is not very clear, but doubtless it was remotely considered."

Eventually the line would reach both Bedford and Cumberland, but not until 1874, and in 1856 the Bedford Springs remained isolated from rail passenger service.

To help solve that problem, a stage line was established between Hopewell and Bedford. In 1857 a Notice promoting the Bedford Mineral Springs Co. proclaimed that rail passengers from Baltimore and Philadelphia could reach the Springs over the PRR and Broad Top Railroad in one day, "leaving but twenty miles of staging over a fine road."

Ironically, there was a railroad that passed very close to the Springs property, but it did not serve hotel guests, and it remained out of sight. It was the Underground Railroad, transporting slaves to freedom. From the Maryland line up to and beyond Bedford, a few sympathetic families operated "stations" at which escaped slaves could hide along the route. And bounty hunters were always hot on the trail. It is ironic that the Springs was so close to the Underground Railroad because the slavery issue would plague President Buchanan during his four years in office.

Dr. William H. Watson, like his father Dr. William Watson, was associated with the Bedford Springs. During his many years practicing medicine he observed first-hand the cruelty inflicted on captured slaves by bounty hunters.

One of the routes took the escaped slaves up Cumberland Valley. As stated in The *Kernel of Greatness,* "There were no stations in this valley, and their route was rather dangerous because the whole area was carefully watched by slave catchers. Often the fugitives had to leave the road and skirt Evitt's Mountain on either side in order to arrive at Bedford. This accounts for the two-pronged road. The western side brought them up through Centerville, behind the Bedford Springs Hotel. The trek along the eastern side brought them through Chaneysville, Rainsburg and along the present Route 326 to Bedford."

Dr. William H. Watson recounted an incident from the 1850s in which a family, consisting of an escaped mother and several children from Virginia, were captured. Settlement of an estate required the sale of these slaves. The mother, dreading separation, fled northward with her little ones and a horse.

They were captured about six miles south of Bedford on a frigid December day. Dr. Watson saw them in the hands of their captors at Centerville, where the bounty hunters had stopped at a tavern to warm themselves. Among the children was a lad of sixteen or seventeen, who had on his stockingless feet an old pair of tight boots that looked like a castoff pair of gentleman's boots. To secure him, his captors had bound his hands and feet under the horse's body. His feet were frozen; when his boots were pulled off, the skin and soles of his feet came off with the boots. Despite this horror no man dared to question the captors or interfere with them in any way.

On July 18, 1855, while working for the Pennsylvania Anti-Slavery Society, abolitionist Passmore Williamson helped Jane Johnson and two of her children escape from Col. John H. Wheeler, who was on a trip with his slaves from Washington, D.C. to Nicaragua, where Wheeler was to serve as ambassador. Williamson, along with a group of freemen, forcibly took Wheeler's slaves from his possession and helped them escape to freedom. All participants were charged with riot, forcible abduction and assault.

Williamson was later convicted of perjury by U.S. District Court Judge John K. Kane on a writ of habeas corpus for his refusal to produce Jane Johnson and her two sons before the bench (Williamson claimed he no longer knew Jane's whereabouts). He served his sentence between July 27 and November 3, 1855 in Moyamensing Prison. The story spread throughout the country.

Williamson's legal team initiated appeals, affidavits and statements regularly featured in the press, emphasizing Kane's use of the federal bench to bend state law (Pennsylvania law clearly did not recognize slavery) to the whim of a passing slaveholder rather than advancing antislavery arguments. The case was appealed to the Pennsylvania Supreme Court, which sat at Bedford Springs August 11, 1855 to hear arguments. Williamson's appeal was denied. This was a landmark case leading up to the Dred Scott decision a year and a half later.

It was ironic that Bedford Springs, which sat so close to the Underground Railroad, was the setting for the appeal.

Members of the Pennsylvania Supreme Court at Bedford Springs. At the far right is Springs manager Ed. H. Anderson. Courtesy Omni Bedford Springs Resort.

Both guests and staff members of the Resort brought black servants with them, and the urge to escape to freedom was always present. A notice published July 7, 1847 proclaimed, "A boy which is bound to the Subscriber, leader of the band at Bedford Mineral Springs, having made one attempt to run away -- should he run away, the Subscriber will give $5 if taken within 3 miles, $10 if taken within 10 miles; and $10 if taken over 10 miles. The boy is about 4' 9" high, dark brown complexion, 12 or 13 years of age, black, slightly curled hair. Lewis Clark."

President, James Buchanan, did not like slavery, nor did he like the Abolitionist movement. As early as 1836, Buchanan wrote, "Before this unfortunate agitation commenced, a very large and growing party existed in several of the slave States in favor of the gradual abolition of slavery; and now not a voice is heard there in support of such a measure. The Abolitionists have postponed the emancipation of the slaves in three or four States of this Union for at least half a century." And in predicting the War Between The States, he continued, if the abolitionists persist, "They will cover the land with blood." ... "The Union is now in danger, and I wish to proclaim that fact."

In 1847 in a letter written from Reading, PA Buchanan stated he did not expect northern Democrats to approve of slavery, but he did expect them to honor the U.S. Constitution that left the slavery question up to the individual states. Also, Buchanan did not believe that the Constitution gave individual states the right to secede from the Union. In this regard his position on slavery was clear.

Buchanan's new Secretary of the Treasury (former Speaker of the House) Howell Cobb was a slave owner from Georgia. Like Buchanan, Cobb disliked the principle of slavery and felt that it would slowly die from economic pressures. Both were correct. Had the Civil War never taken place, the industrial revolution and advances in agriculture would have accomplished that result.

Buchanan had a favorite desk that he used while at the Bedford Springs, and an anecdote about that desk is told in *The Old Furniture Book* by Hudson Moore. In Moore's own words, "It stood for many years in one of the little outside houses near the main hotel, and when, a number of years ago, a visitor asked to buy it, the proprietor told him the piece was known as the "Jimmy Buchanan desk."

"Mr. Buchanan was in the habit of spending his summers at Bedford Springs, and always occupied the room where this desk was. In 1857, when as President Buchanan he arrived at Bedford, the proprietors in his honor had refurnished his room.

"They were congratulating themselves that the President would be gratified at what they had done for him, when he suddenly came into the room and demanded in a rage what had become of the desk. If it was not forthcoming he would go elsewhere.

"He could use it, he said, to write on, and then the drawers were roomy and just suited

Jon Baughman poses with President Buchanan's desk in the Hotel lobby.

him for his clean shirts. It is needless to say that the desk was brought down from the garret, and was never removed from the room when President Buchanan visited there."

Today the Sheraton style desk used by President Buchanan is on display on the main floor of the Colonial Building, for all to see.

Another incident involving the President which took place at Bedford Springs is recalled by biographer Philip S. Klein. In those days Simon Cameron, a Republican, was one of Buchanan's political rivals and a bitter enemy. Cameron made a fortune in railways, newspapers and banking before seeking a political career. He was elected to replace Buchanan in the Senate in 1844. Cameron was President Lincoln's Secretary of War but resigned a year later due to scandal and corruption. And like Buchanan, Cameron was a regular at the Bedford Springs.

The President had become interested in a wealthy widow from Virginia, a Mrs. Bass. She and her children were frequent visitors at the White House. This incident took place in 1859.

As Klein writes, "Toward the end of July, Buchanan set out for his regular fortnight at Bedford Springs, taking the widow Bass and her three young children with him. The pleasant interlude was marred by only two incidents. Buchanan found himself placed in rooms next to Simon Cameron, and the abolitionists ran away with Mrs. Bass's Negro servant girl. People at the Springs generally assumed that Cameron had arranged the episode to spite Buchanan. Apparently some people of Bedford had persuaded the girl to leave and had given her money with which to travel farther North. But Mrs. Bass took it calmly, announcing that the girl was honest and capable, and had taken none of the money and jewels available in the rooms. She hoped only that others would care for her and treat her kindly, which she feared they would not." They returned to Washington on August 1.

It is odd that the girl was staying with Mrs. Bass in her rooms at the Springs, because it is generally believed that Negro servants were housed at a hotel in Bedford owned by the Harris family.

During one of the President's visits to Bedford he also met John Fulton, chief engineer of the Huntingdon & Broad Top Railroad. The visit is recorded in Fulton's diary which is preserved in the Johnstown Flood Museum. Fulton was in Bedford on business and met Buchanan at a hotel. He later visited him at the Bedford Springs.

Fulton wrote, "I told him by way of introduction that I wanted no office for myself or friends. His face lighted up and he cheerfully said, "Take a seat and let me offer you a cigar." We had a pleasant conference, as he was a descendant of Ulster Scots."

This was not their last meeting. Upon the death of her parents Harriet Lane had inherited certain lands in Bedford County. She could not obtain the inheritance until she became of age. The value of the property was uncertain and the boundaries needed to be surveyed. The land was located in Broad Top Township, near Hopewell, and contained some valuable seams of coal.

Recalling his previous meeting with Fulton, he summoned him to Bedford and asked him to survey the property. Needing money, Fulton readily accepted the assignment and made a complete survey of the tract, which was located along Sandy Run. When Fulton was paid for his work, he donated the majority of the funds to the Presbyterian Church.

Although unrecorded, it is possible that Buchanan took the stage from Bedford to Hopewell, accompanied by Miss Lane, to look at the property.

Development of this section of the Broad Top Coal Field did not take place until the 1870s when the railroad constructed a branch line up Sandy Run. After mines were opened on this property, Miss Lane (then Harriet Lane Johnson) became a wealthy woman.

Midway through 1857 the nation suffered a financial panic. Although the recession was brief, the recovery was uneven and not all areas of the country recovered at the same pace. The recession ended a period of prosperity that followed the Spanish American War. One immediate result of the panic was a loss of business at Bedford Springs. It came at a bad time for the newly incorporated Bedford Mineral Springs Company. The Springs Company would strug-

In the days of President Buchanan

gle until the outbreak of the Civil War when wealthy Southern patrons were no longer able to come north. Then things got worse, and on November 20, 1862, the Sheriff of Bedford County sold the property. Espy L. Anderson, the largest stockholder, was the buyer. He, in turn, died intestate May 29, 1866 and the ownership passed to his widow and children.

One of Buchanan's cabinet members, Judge Jeremiah S. Black who served as Attorney General, was also a regular at Bedford Springs. If you recall, he was at the Springs when President Polk stayed there. He was a native of nearby Somerset County and was keenly familiar with the Bedford area. An attorney, he was elected judge in 1842 and was highly respected as such. In 1851 he was elected to the Supreme Court of Pennsylvania and his membership is probably the reason why the high court met at the Bedford Springs to hear the Passmore Williamson case.

In 1860 he was named Secretary of State, and in that post, Black denied the constitutionality of secession and urged that Fort Sumter be properly reinforced and defended.

Perhaps the most notable event at the Bedford Springs during the Buchanan presidency was the transmission of the first message over the Trans-Atlantic cable, sent from Queen Victoria to President Buchanan at Bedford Springs, August 17, 1857. This historic event was re-enacted at Bedford Springs on August 17, 2008.

The cable was an attempt to speed up communications between North America and Europe with the formation of the Atlantic Telegraph Company in 1856. This was not an easy task. The laying of the cable by two ships, one starting in the mid-Atlantic and heading for Ireland and the other heading for Newfoundland, began in June 1857 but a total of five attempts were made due to the cable breaking. The fifth and final attempt was made in July 1858 and on August 5, both ships reached their destinations. The continents were joined.

President Buchanan was at Bedford Springs when the news came that the cable had been successfully completed. The entire town of Bedford celebrated at the news.

According to the history of the Transatlantic Cable, the first message was sent on August 16, not the following day as is commonly believed. That message stated, "Glory to God in the highest and on earth, peace, good will to men." The "test" transmission by telegraph proved that the cable worked.

The following day, August 17, Queen Victoria sent the first official message transmitted over the cable to President Buchanan at Bedford Springs. The Queen's message stated, "London, England. Come let us talk together. American genius and English enterprise have this day joined together the OLD and NEW worlds. Let us hope that they may be as closely allied in bonds of peace, harmony and kindred feeling. Victoria, R."

Buchanan answered the Queen, although not immediately, as he had to compose an appropriate reply. It stated, "Bedford Springs. NEW England accepts with gladness the hand of fellowship proferred by OLD England and if ever discord or diversity of interests should threaten this alliance let our language be 'entreat me not to leave thee or return from following after thee for the interests of thy people shall be the interests of my people and thy God shall be my God.' James Buchanan, President, U.S.A."

At this particular moment the Americans and British were embroiled in a controversy over European intervention in Central America, especially Nicaragua and Costa Rica. These nations had asked the British to intervene against "the barbarians of the United States." The Americans favored a "federal system ... resembling that of the United States" for Central America.

Sir William Ousley was named by the British to make arrangements with the Central American leaders for the acceptance of American demands. Ousley was to meet with Buchanan to discuss his plans before proceeding south. Ousley had been a close friend during Buchanan's service as Minister to Great Britain. He joined Buchanan at Bedford Springs in August, 1858 and was there when the first Transatlantic Cable message was received.

Buchanan biographer Klein talks about the controversy and how it affected the

Transatlantic Cable message. Klein writes, "Two weeks later (after Ousley's arrival at Bedford), Victoria sent to Buchanan the first official message to be carried by the cable. American newspapers which printed the brief, almost insultingly brusque text, thought that the queen had cast an intentional slur upon the nation, and they called on Buchanan to respond with indignation. Assuming that some mistake had occurred, he prepared a highly complimentary reply. For a time Americans grumbled about Buchanan's "toadyism" but it was announced a short time later that the cable had failed before the queen's communication was completed."

Victoria's reply to Buchanan's message was, "Valentia, Ireland, via Trinity Bay, N.F. to the Honorable president of the United States, Aug. 18. The Queen desires to congratulate the President upon the successful issue of this great international undertaking, in which the Queen has taken the greatest interest. The Queen is convinced the President will join her in fervently hoping that the electric cable which now connects Great Britain with the United States will prove an additional link between nations whose friendship is founded upon common interest and reciprocal esteem. The Queen has much pleasure in this communicating with the President and renewing to him her wishes for the prosperity of the United States. Victoria, R."

Klein adds, "Victoria was highly pleased that Buchanan had, by an act of trust, sustained the good will between the countries and saved her from personal embarrassment. The incident was small; yet it may be counted among the series that gradually diminished rancor and bred better Anglo-American relations. Perhaps the most significant development was their abandonment, in 1858, of the right of search on the high seas."

As for the cable, it soon failed. The engineer, William Whitehouse started applying high voltages, rather than the weak currents that had been tested during cable laying. Within three weeks the damage inflicted on the cable by the high voltages was becoming apparent and it ceased to work. A replacement cable was not completed until 1866.

One final incident regarding the President took place at Bedford Springs -- the announcement that he would not seek a second term in office. By that time Benjamin F. Myers was editor of the *Bedford Gazette*. General George Bowman had gone to Washington after 25 years as editor to serve as Public Printer in the Buchanan administration.

The renouncement took place in 1859. Years later, Myers recalled the incident vividly in his reminiscences:

"Late in July, 1859 the Pittsburg Post suggested, in an elaborate editorial, the nomination of Mr. Buchanan for a second term of the Presidency. When that article appeared the President was a sojourner at the Bedford Springs. He was greatly exercised over the matter . . . and as he knew he could announce his determination not to accept re-nomination, in the Gazette the next day after his receipt of the Post article, he sent a cab to my house late at night, with a request for me to come to him at once at his rooms at the Springs.

"The cabman could not give me any reason for the alleged request, and I at first doubted the genuineness of the invitation, being mystified by its coming at so unseasonable an hour. However, since the "cabby" insisted that he had come directly from the President, I concluded to go with him.

"On arriving at the President's quarters I found him sitting at a table, in his shirt sleeves, poring over a manuscript which he had apparently just finished. The hour was about one o'clock in the morning.

"Turning to me he said, "Your paper comes out to-day. I wish you to print this article (handing me the manuscript) in today's issue as your leading editorial."

"The article was a renunciation of all claims or desire for another term of the Presidency, and appeared as the leader in the Gazette, under the caption of "Mr. Buchanan and the Next Presidency." -- Benjamin F. Myers.

The following summer Buchanan made his last trip to Bedford Springs as president. The people of Bedford made plans for a grand celebration with food and music for dancing, at the Springs. The people waited for many hours for his stage coach, but it never arrived. Like

President Polk before him, he did not arrive as scheduled. Buchanan arrived the next day.

And so ended the Buchanan presidency. It would be Buchanan's last visit to the Springs as President, but not his last visit.

Top photo: The Bedford Springs Hotel as it appeared during the Buchanan presidency. The Colonial Building is at left; Evitt is hidden from view, but the Stone Inn and Swiss Cottage are visible at right.
Courtesy of Omni Bedford Springs Resort

Left: The Sulphur Spring as it appears today.
Photo by Jon Baughman

A nation divided: The Civil War years

In the years leading up to the Civil War, Bedford Springs was a busy place, and there are a number of published accounts that describe both the resort and the notables who stayed there.

Many of the Springs patrons were involved in the iron industry and included many of the leading families of Pittsburgh and of other iron producing regions of the state.

Dr. Peter Shoenberger, a medical doctor by training began to practice medicine in Pittsburgh in 1800. He took over the iron furnaces of his father, George Shoenberger in Huntingdon County, in 1815. Returning to Petersburg upon his father's death he had planned to manage the properties on a temporary basis. The iron industry whet his appetite and he soon abandoned his medical practice.

Having a keen eye for business, Dr. Shoenberger within a short time owned these industrial properties in Central Pennsylvania: Rebecca Furnace on Clover Creek, Rodman Furnaces at McKee, Allegheny Furnace at Duncansville, Sarah Furnace at Sproul, the Bloomfield mines and furnaces at Ore Hill and Elizabeth Furnace near Woodbury. Here a high quality of iron was produced.

The blooms were hauled to Pittsburgh where they were drawn into bars, then rolled into plates at Shoenberger's Juniata Iron Works, an extensive rolling mill. Shoenberger moved back to Pittsburgh in 1824 but retained his iron furnaces and forges in this region.

The United States military preferred Shoenberger iron for their armaments and large quantities of it were shipped to the Federal arsenal at Harper's Ferry, VA. This was the iron that made the Union strong during the Civil War. Although the old ironmaster died in 1854, his heirs continued the operations.

The Shoenberger family, including Dr. Shoenberger and his brother George, were frequent visitors to Bedford Mineral Springs, as is told in the book, *The Iron King,* by Calvin W. Hetrick, 1961. Hetrick provides numerous entries from the Bedford Springs ledgers and cash books that pertain to the Shoenbergers.

July 13, 1845: Dr. P. Shoenberger, Lady, Daughters & Servt. to tea. Club $3.85, sponge cake, $1.00. Dr. P. Shoenberger, 28th to tea.

July 30, to 3-1/4 days board for self, $4.87; 2 wks. & 3 ds. board Lady $24.29; Daughter $24.29; Servt. $12.15; 15 days livery of 2 horses, $15.50.

July 30, Miss M. (Martha) Shoenberger came to Bkfst., To 1 wks. Board, $7.00.

July 7, 1847, Mr. J. H. Shoenberger, Master Shoenberger & Servt. to tea; Post. 5¢, bar 12¢, Post 5¢, 10¢, Bar 25¢, Post 20¢, Club, $3.85. (Post. stands for postage).

July 8, to Carriage hire, $6.00, Post 5¢, music 37¢, Bar 37¢, Bar 50¢, Post 10¢, 2 juleps, 25¢; 1/2 Bot. Champ. $1.25, Bar 10¢, Post 5.5¢, cash $1.25.

July 23, To 2 wks. 1-3/4 days board, self $22.50; Livery 2 Horses $13.75, Board for Driver $11.25; Total $135.91.

July 9, 1846, Geo. Shoenberger, Son & Servt. with 2 horses & Livery. To 1 week's, 2 days Board for Self, Son & Servt., Livery for 2 Horses, 2 Bottles Champagne, Bottle Sherry, Bar Expenses, Concert Tickets, etc. plus $20.00 cash, $78.87.

These excerpts from the ledger give the reader an idea of the charges made for various items and services at the Hotel. And, as Hetrick noted, "At the Bedford Springs Hotel the guests were not burdened by carrying cash around; everything, postage, liquor, etc. was charged and settled for when the guests departed.... A fancy meal could be had for $1.00 then."

But wait. There's more.

July 16, 1846, Mr. John Duncan (Shoenberger's son-in-law) to Dinner; Candle 13¢, cash to Hack Driver 25¢, Corkage 50¢ (This was the charge by the Hotel for opening and serving liquid refreshments brought by the guests), Billiards 50¢.

"The above quotations are given," Hetrick said, "to illustrate the items thought necessary for that gracious way of living prevalent among wealthy and socially prominent people who could afford to make the Springs their summer home."

But the Shoenbergers were more than patrons of Bedford Mineral Springs. They also sold goods to the Springs, and not just iron products.

In 1842 during construction of the Colonial Building, the Bedford Springs paid to G. & J. H. Shoenberger & Co. $155.44 for "iron and nails for new house at Springs."

July 7, 1840: (paid to) G. & J.H. Shoenberger, by bill of Hams and Iron, $93.10; April 17, 1851: G. & J.H. Shoenberger, by bill of Hams, $403.20.

By the prices of that day this would be a lot of hams. And in his story, Hetrick asks, "It seems an odd circumstance that the Shoenberger brothers sold hams as well as iron to the Hotel..." He then offers this explanation "... but the explanation may lie in the fact that ironmasters bought huge quantities of provisions for sale in their company stores, and thus were enabled to secure favorable wholesale prices."

I would like to offer another explanation. In the manufacture of iron, charcoal was a necessary ingredient, along with ore and limestone. To make the charcoal, entire forests were cut down. The land that was not situated on steep terrain was then cleared of stumps and converted into very productive farms, many of which remain in agriculture today. It is more likely that the hams sold to Bedford Springs came from the hogs raised on the Shoenberger family's many farms.

Dr. Shoenberger in one of his final business ventures before his death, helped found the Cambria Iron Company in Johnstown in 1852. He died in 1854, before the Cambria company became a success, and before the nation was embroiled in a bloody civil war. His heirs would make a fortune selling iron to the Union for the manufacture of armaments.

In 1857, John Shoenberger, a member of this distinguished family, became a charter member of the Bedford Mineral Springs Company, which made him a stockholder in the resort.

Andrew Gregg Curtin, wartime Governor of Pennsylvania, was another frequent visitor to Bedford Springs in the period leading up to the war. In July, 1846 a number of items were charged to Curtin's personal account on the hotel ledger. Among them: July 11: "came to tea." July 16: post. 22¢, Ten Pins $1.00; July 17: 2 concert tickets, Ten Pins 50¢, Segars 13¢; July 19: Segars 13¢, Post. 5¢, Segars 13¢; July 21: Two Bottles Champ. $5.00, Segars 13¢, Bar 37¢, Segars 13¢.

July 22: Segars 25¢, Bar $1.00, Segars 13¢; July 23: Segars 13¢, Post. 5¢, 13¢, 12¢, 13¢, 12¢, 13¢, 12¢. Board, 15-1/2 days $22.13. Total $22.13. Curtin apparently liked to smoke, enjoyed alcoholic beverages, and mailed a lot of letters.

Still another of the famous visitors to the Springs in the period leading up to the war was Thaddeus Stevens. Generally well known for his role in support of public education, he was also a devout abolitionist, which would have made him an enemy of those Bedford Springs visitors who hailed from the deep South.

Stevens began to practice law in Gettysburg, where he defended runaway slaves for free. He served in the state legislature from 1833 to 1842, where he was an advocate of free public schools. Elected to Congress in 1848, he was an outspoken opponent of slavery who did not want to appease the South in any way.

He was also engaged in iron manufacture, like the Shoenbergers. His operation was called the Caledonia Iron Works, not to be confused with the forge of the same name that McDermott operated on the Bedford Springs property. Stevens' was located near present day Caledonia State Park in Franklin County, east of Bedford County.

Abraham Lincoln, whose election to the office of President was the spark that launched the War Between the States, had family ties to Bedford County through the Evans family. They shared a common ancestor, Evan Ap Evan, who brought his family to Pennsylvania from Wales in 1689.

His son, Cadwalader Evans, left the state and was the great-grandfather of Nancy Hanks, mother of the future President. Cadwalader's brother, Thomas Evans, was the great-grandfather of Amos Evans, who moved to Broad Top Township, Bedford County in 1791 and is the ancestor of the Bedford County branch of the family.

Nancy Hanks married Thomas Lincoln in 1806. Both had been born in Virginia, but their families ended up in Kentucky. Of his mother, President Lincoln wrote that she was from an "undistinguished family" of humble, ordinary people.

The Lincolns lived in poverty in Kentucky for about ten years where Thomas had problems with the titles to the various farms they lived on. Abraham was born in 1809. In 1816 they moved to Indiana where land could be purchased from the government. Nancy became ill of "milk sickness" and died. Her husband made a coffin and buried her on the hill behind the cabin, without ceremony or a preacher. The future President was nine years old.

In 1820 Thomas returned to Kentucky to visit. When he returned, he brought a bride, the widow Sarah Bush Johnson and her three children, in a wagon. Lincoln had a step-mother. But despite his humble beginnings, he would soon rise to prominence. There is not enough space here to detail his rise to fame, but in brief, he was a captain in the Black Hawk War, spent eight years in the Illinois legislature, and rode the circuit of courts for many years. His law partner said of him, "His ambition was a little engine that knew no rest."

He married Mary Todd, and they had four sons, only one of whom lived to maturity. In 1858 Lincoln ran against Stephen A. Douglas for Senator. He lost the election, but in debating Douglas he gained a national reputation that won him the Republican nomination for President in 1860.

People in the north saw the conflict as an anti-slavery issue; in the south it was viewed on the basis of states' rights vs. the powers of the federal government.

In 1858 Bedford Springs owner Espy L. Anderson became active in an organization whose purpose was to bring rail service to Bedford. The railroad construction boom in other parts of the state had left Bedford behind. Clients traveling to the Bedford Springs had to rely on stage coaches, which Anderson realized was a handicap to the Springs.

Anderson's close friend, William P. Schell, a state senator and business partner at the Springs, was elected chairman of the committee, which began meeting in Bedford in 1858. At Schell's urging, an Act of Assembly incorporating the Bedford Railroad Company was approved in Harrisburg March 19, 1859. That was the easy part. Money had to be raised.

The board, in addition to Schell and Anderson, was composed of John P. Reed, William G. Moorehead, Joseph Harrison, Jr., John H. Town, Jay Cooke, Frances Jordan, Nicholas Lyons, Valentine Steckman, James Burns Jr., John Sell, Michael Lutz and William

The Civil War Years - 69

T. Daugherty.

Many of these are Bedford names, but Cooke and Moorehead were investment bankers and partners in the private banking firm, E. W. Clarke & Company, of Philadelphia. Cooke resigned from the firm in 1858 to, according to a biographer, "reorganize abandoned Pennsylvania railways and canals and placing them again in operation." This three year effort brought him in contact with the Bedford Railroad project.

Schell, Anderson, Nicholas Lyons, and William T. Daugherty were all stockholders in the Bedford Mineral Springs Company. Another Bedford Springs stockholder, Attorney John Cessna, was not involved with this railroad project, but would become the driving force behind another Bedford railroad project 12 years later.

John Fulton, chief engineer of the Huntingdon & Broad Top line, was hired to determine a preliminary route between Hopewell and Bedford. To pay Fulton his initial expenses, all the committee could raise was $28 in gold pieces, an ill omen of things to come. The survey work began at Hopewell in November, 1858 and by December 2 a route had been selected.

Several years prior to this, the H&BTMRR had agreed to extend its line to Bedford if Bedford residents could raise $100,000 for the purchase of stock, but this effort failed.

Now, Anderson, Schell and others found themselves trying to raise $100,000 -- again. By September 1859 only $75,000 in stock had been subscribed and only $51,000 of that had been paid. The contractor, Collins and Dull, were found in default of their contract for not paying employees and causing the work to stop on the line. 1860 found the contractor and railroad company in litigation. An agreement was reached July 23, but then the contractor demanded another $8,400 in claims, which the stockholders did not have.

Schell resigned as president March 23, 1861 and was replaced by Samuel L. Russell. Attorneys were instructed to prosecute those persons who had subscribed for stock but failed to pay. Russell and the contractor again tried to reach an agreement.

In Harrisburg, many miles from Bedford, events were taking shape that would give new hope to the Bedford Railroad. The state legislature had placed a "tonnage tax" of five mills per ton-mile on freight the Pennsylvania Railroad hauled more than 20 miles. The tax was designed to help "protect" the state-owned system of public works (canals and railroads), particularly the Pennsylvania Main Line Canal, which was being hurt by the PRR. Historian and author Dennis McIlnay points out that the tax "was intended to punish the railroad for encouraging shippers to use its lines instead of the Pennsylvania Canal, thereby denying revenue to the Main Line of Public Works." PRR President J. Edgar Thomson, who with several others had entered into an agreement to purchase the Bedford Springs in 1854, unsuccessfully -- fought the tonnage tax and was a harsh critic of the legislature for passing it.

The tax was so high that, according to McIlnay, "coal from England shipped to Philadelphia was cheaper than coal mined in Central Pennsylvania" and transported by rail.

In 1861 the tonnage tax was lifted on the condition that the PRR invest the amount of tax

First train to Bloody Run (Everett)
The engine is a Ross Winans "Camel"
Collection of Jon Baughman

collected and unpaid ($850,000) in the bonds of eight railroad companies, one of which was the Bedford Railroad (slated to receive $100,000).

On April 27, the directors of the Bedford Railroad voted to comply by issuing bonds as required. But there was one hitch. To qualify, five miles of grading had to be completed at both the Hopewell and Bedford ends. The company hadn't even purchased a right-of-way near Bedford.

By June 30, 1862 the PRR had only picked up $25,000 in bonds, and with these limited funds the track was completed to Bloody Run (Everett) by May 26, 1863.

In a final attempt to have the line completed to Bedford the board floated a $240,000 bond issue, with three trustees named for the prospective bondholders. They were Thomson, Lewis T. Wattson (H&BT President) and William G. Moorehead.

Sale of the bonds met with limited success, and the railroad was extended another mile and a half to Mt. Dallas. Here the money ran out and construction stopped. The company could not afford a trestle over the Raystown Branch of the Juniata River. Soon the line was merged into the Huntingdon & Broad Top, and the people of Bedford would have to wait another decade to get rail service.

There was one small benefit for the Bedford Springs. Guests could now take the train to Bloody Run instead of Hopewell, and then take a shorter Stage Coach ride to the Springs. This would have increased the number of patrons to the Springs, except for one thing -- war.

The news of the outbreak of the war had caused much uncertainty in business circles. Mines, forges and factories were pressed into service to support the war effort, and business in Pennsylvania improved greatly. The only catch was the loss of patrons from the southern states who had loved to come to Bedford Springs.

Bedford Springs manager A. G. Allen advertised the opening of the Resort for the 1861 season on June 15: "...this well established and popular watering place is now open for the reception and accommodation of visitors and will be kept open until the first of October. Persons wishing Bedford Mineral Water, will be supplied at the Springs, at the following prices, viz: For 1 barrel (oak) - $3.00; For 1/2 barrel (mulberry) - $3.00; For 1/2 barrel (oak) - $2.00; Bottles, 1/2 pint, per dozen - $1.50."

Not all southerners avoided the Springs. A few managed to get to the Resort, as the following newspaper item reveals. *Bedford Gazette,* August 30, 1861: "Some three or four weeks since, a Mr. Parker, with a male companion, arrived and took lodgings, at Bedford Springs. They entered into the gaieties of the place, con amore, and seemed to enjoy themselves hugely. Parker was the best billiard player at the Springs, could 'discount' almost every other player, and was a very good hand at chess. One day last week Parker and friend concluded to pack up and leave. Having paid off their bill, Parker informed a gentleman whose acquaintance he had made, that he wasn't Parker at all, but Colonel Pegham, late of the Confederate Army, and now a prisoner of the United States. His companion was also a rebel prisoner. They were here on parole." And perhaps to spy, too?

In 1861 Jay Cooke and Moorehead formed the private banking firm of Jay Cooke & Company.

Cooke, who had invested money in the Bedford Railroad, was now collaborating with Secretary of the Treasury Salmon P. Chase in the sale of $500 million in Treasury Department bonds to support the war effort. Many of Lincoln's cabinet members visited Bedford Springs, and Chase, Cooke and Moorehead may have been to the Resort. Perhaps they discussed the sale of bonds on a visit to the Springs. One can imagine them seated on the veranda, discussing ways to finance the war effort.

Like the Shoenbergers, Cooke and Moorehead were also in the iron industry as the owners of an iron works, Pine Grove Furnace in Cumberland County, which Moorehead purchased in 1864. This furnace supplied iron for the war effort. They operated it as the South Mountain Iron Co.

The Panic of 1857 and the loss of tax revenue from the partial dismemberment of the Union had taken a massive toll on the finances of the federal government.

Also due to the panic and the loss of its lucra-

The Civil War Years

tive southern patronage, the Bedford Springs Company failed in 1862 and was sold by the Sheriff to Espy L. Anderson on November 20. The property was back in the hands of the Anderson family, whether they liked it or not.

For years historians have debated whether Lincoln stayed at the Bedford Springs, but no solid evidence of this has been found. There are also reports that the First Lady, Mary Todd Lincoln, was a guest at the Bedford Springs.

According to the Bedford County Historical Society, Mrs. Lincoln made a reference to Bedford Springs in her diary, but the Bedford Springs hotel registers do not indicate that she was a guest.

Bill Defibaugh pointed out that Mary Todd Lincoln's great-uncle and Revolutionary War veteran William Todd once owned a farm west of Bedford along present-day Route 30, and the future First Lady may have visited there as a child. The old barn is still standing and was restored in 2009 by current owners Priscilla and Charles Mackall.

The restored barn is now the home of the Bedford County Historical Society.

The day to day, week by week activities of President Lincoln and his family have been researched more thoroughly than that of any other figure in American history. If either the President or his wife had visited Bedford, it would have been documented.

It is safe to say that President Lincoln "almost" visited the Springs in the weeks that followed the Battle of Gettysburg. That information can be found in *Team of Rivals* by Pulitzer prize winning author Doris Kearns Goodwin.

Had Lincoln been able to get away from Washington, D.C. that summer, the resort would have still been there by a stroke of luck. For, you see, the Bedford landmark was threatened with destruction in the weeks leading up to the Battle of Gettysburg.

It all started in the Spring of 1863 with the defeat of General Robert Milroy at Winchester, VA and the retreat of the Union soldiers, in disarray, into Pennsylvania. The forces of General Milroy managed to re-unite at the village of Bloody Run (now Everett) -- tired, demoralized, and half starved.

Rumors circulated that General Lee's army was about to invade Central Pennsylvania. That left the entire line of the Pennsylvania Railroad from Altoona to Harrisburg vulnerable, as well as the iron industry located in Blair and Huntingdon Counties. These furnaces turned out the famous Juniata iron that was used to make the Union's armaments. Also threatened was the Huntingdon & Broad Top Railroad and coal shipments from the Broad Top mines. It was feared that General Lee could cripple this important region with one blow, while his main divisions held the mountain passes to the east against the Federal army.

To counter the threat, Col. Jacob Higgins stepped forward to organize a volunteer army of former soldiers and ordinary citizens who were assigned the task of fortifying the mountain gaps at Loysburg, Waterfall, McKee, Mt. Dallas, Piper's Run, St. Clairsville, Shade Gap, McConnellsburg and other strategic locations.

Col. Higgins fought bravely at Antietam in the 125th Regiment but had been discharged in 1863, soon to be recalled to defend the region from invaders.

*Photo, opposite page: At the turnstile.
Above, looking from the bridge toward the Colonial Building.*
Courtesy of Omni Bedford Springs Resort.

A rag-tag army of volunteers answered the call, but were later mocked as "chicken raiders" for their habit of raiding farmers' hen houses to obtain food.

At Bloody Run, Gen. Milroy was relieved of his command to Col. Lewis Pierce. A court of inquiry was brought against Milroy, which eventually exonerated him. As for Col. Pierce, he was dismissed from the service for conduct unbecoming an officer, including his actions or lack thereof while at Bloody Run. With Pierce in charge, a Confederate fighting force could have easily been over-run and the Rebels could have advanced to Bedford.

Harrisburg was General Lee's objective but another unit of the Confederate Army west of Tuscarora Mountain was moving northward. Imboden's cavalry, having completed the destruction of the B & O Railroad, crossed the Potomac at Hancock and was advancing in two columns. One moved towards McConnellsburg; the other towards Mercersburg. Unopposed, they could push their way towards Mount Union, Altoona and Bedford.

One of the heroes of the day was Capt. William Wallace, who had served under Col. Higgins and who had been discharged from the service. He organized a "Call to arms" in Huntingdon County. A skirmish led by Capt. Wallace and his scouting party, Col. Szink (who was digging trenches on top of Cove Mountain in Fulton County), and Col. Moss, one of Milroy's officers, who commanded 300 cavalrymen, were able to stop the Rebel advance. It took place when their combined forces ambushed a unit of Confederate cavalry along Cove Mountain. The Confederates were forced to halt and fight, uncertain of the number of men in front of them. After probing the mountain for several hours the Confederates proceeded down the mountain and occupied McConnellsburg for two days before moving eastward. This act alone may have spared the Bedford area from invasion. Keep in mind that Bedford Mineral Springs would have been a target due to the number of high ranking political figures who stayed there, and whose capture would have been advantageous to the Confederate cause.

Confederate General Imboden's cavalry had been drifting in and out of McConnellsburg. On one such visit they met some resistance from a group of Union soldiers under the command of Capt. Jones. Two Confederate soldiers were killed and 32 captured; the prisoners were taken to Bloody Run. The citizens of McConnellsburg buried the two dead soldiers along the Mercersburg Pike. Two granite markers were erected over their graves in 1929.

The Confederates, who had assembled at nearby Mercersburg, were forced to turn east, then joined General Lee's army for the battle of Gettysburg.

While Bedford and the Mineral Springs were spared, one landmark was not. Thaddeus Stevens' Caledonia Forge, just east of Chambersburg, was destroyed by Gen. Jubal Early's Confederates in late June, 1863. Even though General Lee had issued his famous General Order Number 72 which prohibited damaging or destroying private property, Early justified burning both the Stevens iron works and property at Gulden's Station because Stevens was so outspoken in his condemnation of the Confederacy. Early claimed that this action was in direct retaliation for Stevens' perceived support of similar atrocities by the Union Army in the South.

The Civil War Years - 73

The summer of 1863 was one of the hottest in many years. In the nation's capital, it was especially miserable. One resident reported, "The garments cling to the skin, shirt collars are laid low; moisture oozes from every object, standing in clammy exudation upon iron, marble, wood, and human flesh." All who could leave Washington, did, for cooler locales such as Bedford Springs. Mrs. Lincoln, with sons Tad and Robert, left for Philadelphia, Vermont and the White and Green Mountains.

Initially, the invasion of Pennsylvania had prevented some government officials from leaving, and the First Lady lamented that she was not at her husband's side during the emergency. But following the victory at Gettysburg, those who had not left, soon did.

There is little wonder that Washingtonians would want to escape from the city for weeks, even months, to places like Bedford. At the time of Buchanan's inauguration (and Lincoln's also) the city of Washington was a southern town, without the picturesqueness, but with the indolence, the disorder and the want of sanitation ... Fish and oyster peddlers cried their wares and tooted their horns on the corners. Flocks of geese waddled on Pennsylvania Avenue, and hogs of every size and color, roamed at large, making their muddy wallows on Capitol Hill. ... People emptied slops and refuse in the gutters, and threw dead domestic animals in the canal. Most of the population still depended on the questionable water supply afforded by the wells and by the springs in the hills behind the city. Privies, in the absence of adequate sewage disposal, were plentiful in yards and dirty alleys, and every day, the carts of night soil trundled out to the commons ten blocks north of the White House (Margaret Leech, *Reveille in Washington 1860 - 1865,* pp 11 - 12). It wasn't just the heat that the people were trying to escape.

One who remained behind, for a time, was Secretary of War Edwin Stanton. His wife, Ellen and children had left for Bedford Springs where they would spend the summer. Stanton, writing to her, remarked that "all is silent and lonely, but there is consolation in knowing that you and the children are free from the oppressive heat and discomfort of Washington."

According to historian Doris Kearns Goodwin, "All summer, Stanton harbored hopes that he and Lincoln might escape to the mountains of Pennsylvania. "The President and I have been arranging to make a trip to Bedford," he told Ellen, "but something always turns up to keep him or me in Washington. He is so eager for it that I expect we shall accomplish it before the season is over." In fact, though Stanton finally joined his wife during the first week of September, Lincoln journeyed no farther that summer than the Soldiers' Home."

The President never did make it to the Bedford Springs. The Soldiers' Home was one of Lincoln's favorite outings. As for those who felt sorry for the President for being stuck in Washington, Lincoln enjoyed the solitude, the freedom from office seekers, and the interference from friends and family in his work. Despite the heat, he became refreshed.

The summer of 1863 was not the last time during the War that Bedford Mineral Springs faced the threat of destruction. The second took place in 1864, when a Rebel force again crossed the border into Pennsylvania. The sudden thrust, initially into Maryland, had President Lincoln concerned that Washington, D.C. might be surrounded and isolated. Destruction of property was on the minds of the Confederate soldiers as they advanced.

Rumors of the movement of Confederate troops north were heard the first week of July. General Lee had sent General Jubal Early northward with 15,000 troops to threaten Washington. They were met by a smaller Union force led by General Lew Wallace at Monocacy River near Frederick, MD on July 9. the Federals were routed, giving Early's men a clear path to the north. As the Rebels ranged through the countryside they destroyed railroad tracks, stores, mills and houses.

At Silver Spring, MD two mansions belonging to Postmaster General Montgomery Blair's family were looted and dismantled by the soldiers. One mansion was torched; the other would have been, but the arrival of Gen. John Breckenridge put a stop to it. He made the soldiers put everything back, and gathered up documents and important papers for safekeeping. Asked by Gen. Early why he was making

The Magnesia Spring and Pavilion. Each guest was given a turtle shell to use to drink the water from each spring, and a cane to walk with on their daily constitutional to the various mineral springs. The turtle shells and canes are next to the large tree.   Courtesy of Omni Bedford Springs Resort.

such a fuss, Breckenridge replied that the Blair family had taken him in during a difficult period in his life, and he wanted to return the favor.

As this was taking place, reinforcements sent by General Grant had arrived in Washington, saving the capital, but it did not prevent the Rebels from launching a second invasion of Pennsylvania. Early sent Gen. John McCausland on a mission that had two objectives. One was to get revenge for Union General "Black" David Hunter's burning buildings and towns in the Shenandoah Valley and especially the Virginia Military Institute in Lexington, VA. The second was to get Federal currency and gold by holding northern cities and towns for ransom, and burning them to the ground if they did not comply.

Of course, the Confederate soldiers also needed supplies, and they could get them by looting.

McCausland left Winchester, VA, protecting the left flank of Early's army. He demanded a ransom of $20,000 at Hagerstown, and receiving it, moved on to Frederick, demanding a $200,000 ransom from the citizens. During this same period the main line of the Baltimore & Ohio Railroad was torn up, and on July 9, McCausland's forces took part in the Battle of Monocacy River.

Word traveled fast. In Bedford County the leading merchants of the town of Bloody Run (Everett) got together and on July 13, drafted an agreement in the form of a letter, which stated, "We the undersigned merchants and storekeepers of Bloody Run, in consideration of the invasion of the North and the threatening of our National Capital by an armed force of Rebbels - do promise - agree and bind ourselves to close all our stores and places of business and sell no goods, nor do any business, nor any one of us in the way of buying and selling goods until the said Rebbel force be defeated and driven back and these of our number who volunteer for the insurgency and go to aid their Country in this hour of peril have returned, excepting the Post Office may be open during office hours to hand out news, but no one to enter inside and for the full and true performance of the above named agreements - we pledge our swords - our Sacred Honor and our all."

(Signed), J. M. Barndollar & Sons, J. B. Williams & Brothers, Jeremiah Baughman, William Masters, J. A. Gump, Thomas Ritchey, States and Steckman.

The merchants removed their money and goods to safe locations, and it also looked like they planned to mobilize to help defend the region.

If they refused to do business until the threat had passed, their stores would have been closed for nearly a month.

On July 12, General Hunter resumed his campaign of burning towns in the Shenandoah Valley.

Proceeding north into Pennsylvania, McCausland's men continued to raid the countryside for supplies, and upon reaching Chambersburg in Franklin County, a ransom of $100,000 was demanded. Over the mountain in McConnellsburg, Confederate troops occupied the borough for the second time in just over a year. The Rebel forces were getting uncomfortably close to Bedford County.

McCausland's forces threatened to burn McConnellsburg if not provided with needed rations. Private homes were robbed and citizens were stripped of their valuables in the street. In nearly every instance money was demanded and secured through threats of burning or a cocked revolver pointed to a citizen's head. All of the town's merchants suffered a considerable loss.

Over the mountain in Chambersburg, the citizens failed to raise the $100,000 and on July 30, the town was set afire and many valuable records were destroyed in the Courthouse, banks and businesses. The old office and records of the Chambersburg and Bedford Turnpike were also destroyed. It is believed they were in possession of Turnpike president T. B. Kennedy, as his home was also burned.

Harry Gilmour and Col. Dunn were ordered by General McCausland to burn the Bedford Springs if no ransom was paid.

An amusing story is recalled from this period involving the Turnpike. Confederate Col. John Mosbey was scouting the countryside a few miles west of McConnellsburg when they reached the Pike, now the Lincoln Highway. Heading east they came to a toll gate. Riding up to the gate keeper, a rugged mountaineer, and feeling they were safe as they were disguised in blue uniforms, the leader asked, "Have you seen any Johnny Rebs about here lately?"

The tollkeeper answered, "Yes, sir."

"Where are they?" asked Col. Mosbey.

Right there in that saddle," said the gatekeeper, pointing toward him.

"How did you know?" asked Mosbey when he recovered his breath.

"I can tell by your horses," was the reply. "Our men don't ride such wiry animals."

This story reveals that some of the Confederate raiders were dressed in Union blue in an apparent ruse to allow them to travel undetected.

On the return trip south from the burning of Chambersburg, Harry Gilmour of the 2nd Maryland Confederate Cavalry, states in his memoirs that he and Col. Dunn were ordered by General McCausland to burn the Bedford Springs if no ransom was paid. Since the raiders were disguised as Union soldiers, they could have easily made their way to Bedford. Fortunately for the Springs the Confederate rear guard was attacked by Union Cavalry, so they moved down the valley from McConnellsburg to Hancock, MD after relieving the citizens of McConnellsburg of their valuables.

Bedford Springs would have been an ideal target as the former Summer White House of President Buchanan and the burning would have been very symbolic to the Confederate cause. Who knows how many Union officials and politicians might have been captured, had the raiders reached Bedford in 1863 or `1864?

The capture of notable persons was certainly on their minds, and in fact did take place the following year. In 1865, an operation to kidnap Union officers was planned and executed by McNeill's Partisan Rangers. Pvt. John B. Fay, one of McNeill's men and a resident of Cumberland, MD suggested scouting Union troop positions to find the locations of and kidnap Generals George Crook and Benjamin Franklin Kelley.

The two Generals were staying in a Cumberland hotel, only 23 miles from Bedford, and were successfully captured on February 1, then taken to the headquarters of General Early. They were transported to Libby Prison where they were quickly exchanged.

Unbeknownst to the raiders, two future presidents, Major - General Rutherford B. Hayes and Major William McKinley were guests in the same hotel but were not taken.

During the Lincoln presidency, former president James Buchanan continued to frequent the Bedford Springs. Even before he left office, the former president was attacked in the press and was the target of character assassinations. Almost all of the claims were false or exaggerated.

As Buchanan biographer Klein wrote, "Congress abolished the franking privilege of ex-presidents in order to gag him. The abolition papers reported that Buchanan was in constant correspondence with foreign governments, urging the recognition of the confederacy ... and even on one occasion, announced, on successive days, that the ex-president was in Leamington, England, selling Confederate bonds, and at Bedford Springs plotting with spies. Suspicion mounted so high that his incoming and outgoing mail was opened and sometimes pilfered."

Other than at his Wheatland estate, it was well known that Buchanan preferred being in Bedford. He continually suffered from gout, an ailment caused by his "serious drinking." He never revisited Washington after Lincoln's inauguration, but as Klein reported, "He went regularly to Bedford where he thoroughly enjoyed himself, for the ladies still made a great fuss over him, and the "waters" seemed to ease his gout. Once he tried a New Jersey seashore resort, but the experiment proved a dismal failure. The gout struck while he was there, and for the first time in his life, he could not drink a drop of wine."

Had Buchanan been at Bedford Springs in the summer of 1863 he would have made a high profile target; his capture by Confederate troops would have boosted Confederate morale. Was he a target? In the final months of his presidency there was Confederate plot to kidnap him. It was long rumored that Senator Louis Wigfall of Texas was responsible for the plot to kidnap Buchanan and to install the southern - leaning vice-president Breckinridge in the White House, and to hold the captive President as a hostage until terms of compromise could be proposed. When approached by Wigfall to assist, Secretary of War Floyd rejected the scheme in anger, refusing to have anything to do with it. Floyd himself was later accused by Congress of a plot to ship huge quantities of arms from Pittsburgh to the south; after a thorough investigation the accusation was dropped.

By January the Capital was not only abuzz with the kidnapping rumors, but also of a southern conspiracy to take possession of the city before Lincoln's inauguration and declare Breckenridge president, and make it the capital of the southern states. Buchanan stopped both by bringing extra troops into the city.

Were they rumors or fact?

In 1879 the *North American Review* published in serial form *The Diary of a Public Man.* It was billed as the Secret History of the American Civil War, but the author was never identified. Historians are still trying to determine his identity but it is obvious that he was an insider during these turbulent times. One of the things he confirmed was the plot to kidnap President Buchanan, which would have left Breckinridge, a secessionist, as chief executive.

There were also rumors of plots to kidnap Lincoln, and in 1862 the Union was planning to kidnap Jefferson Davis. Neither happened.

Just prior to the Battle of Gettysburg, Buchanan was not at Bedford He remained at Wheatland, despite the pleas of his friends to vacate. The Rebels came within ten miles of Wheatland. The demolition of the Susquehanna bridge at Wrightsville was the only thing that stopped them. Had they crossed the river, they would have likely burned Buchanan's home and captured him.

He was probably at Bedford during the 1864 invasion of Pennsylvania, but his biographer does not say.

In May, 1868 Buchanan took seriously ill of the complications of a cold. Klein stated, "He knew his end had come." On June 1, he died at Wheatland of the various complications of old age. The people of Bedford would miss him.

During the war, the Virginia widow, Mrs. Bass, who had accompanied Buchanan to Bedford Springs, and who frequented the Resort, suffered greatly. An outspoken Unionist, she "had seen her Virginia estate destroyed by the rebels, and had with great difficulty escaped through the lines under federal military escort to get medical care in New York."

Simon Cameron, Buchanan's adversary, and a frequent visitor to Bedford Mineral Springs, joined the Lincoln cabinet as Secretary of War. He only served a year before resigning amidst corruption. He was then appointed Minister to Russia.

As Secretary of War he was replaced by Edwin Stanton, also a frequent patron of Bedford Mineral Springs. Stanton served as Attorney General under President Buchanan. He disliked Lincoln, but only for the good of the country agreed to work as a legal adviser to the inefficient Secretary of War, Cameron. When Cameron was removed from office, Stanton got the nod for Secretary of War and was very effective in administering the huge War Department. Stanton became a Republican and apparently changed his opinion of Lincoln. At Lincoln's death Stanton remarked, "Now he belongs to the ages," and lamented, "There lies the most perfect ruler of men the world has ever seen."

Stanton and his family continued to frequent Bedford Mineral Springs during and after the war.

During the conflict many Union officers were guests at the Bedford Mineral Springs. The hotel guest ledgers also indicate that the wives of officers were registered while their husbands went off to fight, leaving the wives to visit the Springs alone.

Bill Defibaugh examined the Bedford Springs Hotel guest ledger No. 9, dated 1860 through 1866, and compiled a list of the names of Army and Navy officers who registered during that period. Here are some of the names:

Commodore Cadwalader Ringgold.

Generals: John Williams, Selles Green, J. L. Perry, Edward Schriver, John B. Todd, August Kautz, James T. Thurston, Eugene Asa Carr, William Hickey, W. Ettinger, Hiram George Berry, and D. B. McKibben.

Major (later General) Don Carlos Buell.

Colonel: R. H. Miles, Chapman, Billingsley, M. J. Cohen, William Selden, A. Edwards, B. Parker, Joseph Darr, P. G. Washington, A. W. Denison, George Leonard, George Andrews, Wharton, William B. Fordley, J. B. Murray, William Slater, Warwood, Bowie, Nailer, W. A. Sullivan; and Lt. Col. L. K. Barnes.

Captains: Glendy, Banon, Pendigrat, L. M. Powell, McInkey, J. K. Casey, L. D. Shaw, Queen, Perry, Weems, R. L. Parker.

This ledger also shows Benjamin Chew Howard and wife staying at Bedford Mineral Springs in 1866. He received a A.B. and an A.M. from Princeton University in 1809 and 1812, respectively. His study of law was interrupted by his service in the War of 1812 in which he attained the rank of brigadier general. A Democrat, he served on the city council of Baltimore in 1820 and both houses of the Maryland legislature. He was elected to the Twenty-first and Twenty-second United States Congress, serving from March 4, 1829 to March 3, 1833. In 1835, President Andrew Jackson named Richard Rush and Howard to arbitrate the Ohio-Michigan boundary dispute.

He returned to Congress in the Twenty-fourth Congress and was re-elected to the Twenty-fifth, serving from March 4, 1835, to March 3, 1839. He chaired the House Foreign Relations Committee for four years. From 1843 until 1862 he was reporter for the United States Supreme Court.

In 1861, he was one of the emissaries sent by President James Buchanan to try to secure peace with the Confederacy.

John Jay Knox was registered at the Bedford Springs in 1860. A prominent banker, Treasury Secretary Salmon P. Chase appointed him to a clerkship position at the Treasury department after reading an essay Knox wrote in 1862 that called for a national banking system. Knox held several positions before being named Deputy Comptroller of the Treasury in 1867. President Grant appointed Knox Comptroller of the Treasury in 1872.

Prior to and following the assassination of President Lincoln, Thaddeus Stevens was the leader of the Radical Republicans who had full control of Congress after the 1866 elections. He largely set the course of Reconstruction. He wanted to begin to rebuild the South, using military power to force the South to recognize the equality of Freedmen. When President Johnson resisted, Stevens proposed and passed the resolution for the impeachment of Andrew Johnson in 1868.

Stevens' harsh views of Reconstruction were not only due to his views of the Confederacy, but also because General Early had destroyed his iron works in 1863. He was the principal author of the Fourteenth Amendment and also the Reconstruction Acts, which initially remanded the Southern states to military rule.

Stevens spent the summer and fall of 1866 at Bedford Mineral Springs, and also was here in the summer of 1867. On September 4, 1866, while at Bedford, Stevens made a famous speech where he stated that all men were created equal, and that the nation could not have different laws for whites and other races.

The book *Sketches and Reminiscences* by William Hall recalls an incident involving Stevens at the Bedford Springs in 1867.

"The guests of the house had all departed and Mr. Stevens remained almost alone. There were none to talk to and none with whom to play euchre or whist. While walking one afternoon I observed six or eight small boys (the little peddlers of flowers and maple sugar who frequent the resort) running races around the circle about the fountain. Some old gentleman sat on the brick porch near a column, to whom at the end of each race they had run for their reward ... Mr. Stevens was amusing himself. He gave each winner a quarter of a dollar, and so spaced the boys that eventually each one won a race. A merrier or more joyous crowd was seldom seen."

In the days of Buchanan, Stevens, Cameron, Polk, Stanton and other notable guests at the Bedford Springs, there was another side to the famed watering place. Yes, life was different back then, and most modern conveniences that we take for granted today, did not exist.

It is essential that a few paragraphs be devoted to those ordinary folk whose daily labors made the resort function. Back in October 1982, historian Winona Garbrick, writing for "The Pioneer," touched on that aspect of life at the Springs.

Notes Garbrick, in the early 1850s the number of employees at Bedford Mineral Springs varied very little from year to year. In 1851 there were 46 employees listed in the ledger. Five years later, the number was still 46. She added that the names changed but the jobs remained the same.

She explained, "The buildings had only the barest minimum of indoor plumbing -- a few water taps here and there. A chamber maid carried the water for drinking and bathing to each occupied room; likewise, she had to empty the "slops" not once, but several times daily. These chores she did in addition to changing the bed linens and towels, and keeping the rooms tidied up, with numberless trips back and forth, up and down stairs."

In that period, 12 hour work days were the rule, and that didn't leave much time for rest or relaxation. But housekeeping was only one job; there were many others.

Ms. Garbrick continues, "In the kitchen, cooks labored over immense cast-iron stoves that required constant firing with wood or coal. There had to be always a supply of hot water on hand. They prepared innumerable meals for the "regulars" as well as all the goodies

The Civil War Years - 79

for special teas and parties. Refrigeration -- such as it was -- came via fifty-pound cakes of ice from the hotel's ice house.

"Pity the cooks, but don't forget the lowly kitchen help who washed, pared, and cut up fresh vegetables and fruit; kept the fires going; brought in the ice; washed dishes, silverware, and glasses; kept the pots clean and shining -- and at the end of the day's work, scraped the butcher block and scrubbed the kitchen floor."

The work was hard, the hours were long and the pay probably seemed very low, but do not get the impression that it as all drudgery. As Ms. Garbrick adds, "Actually, back in those days, the hotel offered better working conditions than many other summer resorts. To have worked there was a good recommendation for one seeking a job elsewhere.

"Besides that, employment at the Bedford Springs Hotel conferred a measure of prestige that in part made up for the long hours, low pay and hard work. You see, in conversation one could say, *Well, out at the Springs...* and command respectful attention."

Some of the names, job descriptions and compensation, for the years 1851 to 1856, should be of interest. Some of the jobs are unusual or colorful:

Elizabeth Booher, 3 weeks scrubbing @ $1.00 per week, 9 weeks chamber maid - $9.75.

Lewis Miller, knife cleaner - $25.00.

Harriat Henry, service in kitchen, 3 weeks - $4.50.

Violet Calahan (a "free" negro), 1 week, 2 days - $2.00.

John McDevitt, head cook - $171.00.

James Graham, hostler - $14.65.

John Boxer, ten-pin setter, 7 days - 75¢.

Polly Brown, washer woman - $16.15.

Jerry Bolen, chicken picker - $14.99.

W. Drenning, pantry helper - $14.85.

Emily Thompson, 2 mo. chamber maid and nurse - $16.75.

Eliza Rekard, cook at $1.12 per wk. - $9.95.

Mrs. Rooney, housekeeper - $56.50.

Mary Morris, clean water closets and bath house & scrubbing - $8.00.

Mary Hartzhiser, milk maid, 9 wks. - $18.00 (the Springs apparently had their own cows).

John Owens, barkeeper - $100.00.

Frank Owens, billiard room, $5.00 per mo., 2 mo. 2 days - $14.40.

Margaret Gordon, washing & ironing @ $2.00 per wk. - $10.58.

? Miller, woodcutting @ .62-1/2 and .50 - $16.87-1/2.

Sarah Borden, scrubbing, 8 wks. @ .75 per week - $9.40.

Camilla Koontz, scrubbing, 9 wks., 1 day - $18.75.

Peter Reily, head waiter, 7 days - $86.00.

William Filler, ten-pin setter @ $4.00 per week - $5.75.

Nancy Marshall, made soap & maid of all work - $20.50 owed; minus $5.00 paid for a coffin, $15.50.

Mary Morris, 2 days scrubbing baths and privies - $2.00.

Many of those holding the higher paying jobs were not from Bedford County, but hailed from such places as Cumberland, Baltimore, Washington, D.C., Philadelphia and Pittsburgh. Nearly all of these were men. In addition to their wages, they also received travel fare, mostly by stage coach.

Espy L. Anderson, who got the Bedford Springs back at a Sheriff's sale on November 20, 1862, died intestate May 26, 1866. The title to the property then became vested in his widow and children. Despite efforts to sell the Hotel, the Andersons would own the property for another 18 years through good times and bad. The Springs was under the management of Espy's son, Ed. H. Anderson.

80 - The Bedford Springs Resort

The rich and famous flock to Bedford Springs

The end of the Civil War brought many changes to the nation and to Bedford County. The southern states were devastated, and a long period of reconstruction was beginning. Since the south lay in ruins, Bedford Mineral Springs would no longer enjoy the lucrative patronage from that region. The Bedford Mineral Springs would have to reinvent itself.

The Industrial Revolution was now gaining momentum in the United States. The rise of industry meant that in the coming decades, vast fortunes would be created and spent, especially in New York, Philadelphia, Baltimore and Pittsburgh. The Springs management had to attract the "newly wealthy" if the Resort were to prosper. Industrialists, bankers, financiers, and politicians would flock to the Springs.

Bedford Mineral Springs was now facing competition from a new resort, located northwest of Bedford at the top of the Alleghenies at Cresson Springs. Started before the war by a doctor named Robert Montgomery Smith Jackson, the main attractions were the iron springs and the pure mountain air. Jackson's goal was to establish "the place of restoration for all forms of human suffering."

Jackson was a friend of J. Edgar Thomson of the Pennsylvania Railroad, and the PRR soon took over Cresson Springs, erecting a hotel. Jackson, in his spare time, tended bar at the hotel. David McCullough, in *The Johnstown Flood,* noted that Jackson was best remembered "for the two jars he kept prominently displayed on one shelf, flanked on either side by whiskey bottles. In each jar, preserved in alcohol, was a human stomach. One had belonged to a man who had died a natural death and was, according to all who saw it, an exceedingly unappetizing sight. But it was, nonetheless, an improvement over its companion piece, which, according to its label, had belonged to a man who had died of delirium tremens." As a result the bar became the most patronized in the region; the the jars, a major attraction.

Jackson served in the Civil War as a surgeon in the 3rd Pennsylvania Regiment, and died in 1865.

Cresson Springs became a favorite retreat for Pittsburgh industrialists, among them Andrew Carnegie, who constructed a cottage there. Cresson was a stone's throw away from the PRR main line, and this close proximity to the railroad provided easy access by rail, which the

Bedford Mineral Springs did not have. Other patrons felt the railroad was too close; the constant train traffic, day and night, was a big distraction to those seeking peace and quiet.

The PRR constructed a much larger hotel at Cresson in 1881, and for a time it was very busy. But Cresson had its drawbacks. The walks in the woods, the spectacular scenery, cool breezes in the summer and curative powers of the iron springs were not enough. Patrons wanted to combine recuperation with recreation. According to historian Cindy Aron, "Savvy resort proprietors learned quickly to cater to clients who hoped to combine recreation with recuperation. It was not difficult for health resorts to serve, equally well, as pleasure spots."

Bedford had everything that Cresson lacked, and more. Even before the war, Bedford Springs offered billiards, ten pins, cards, hiking trails, balls, concerts, orchestras, and other leisure activities. In the latter part of the 19th Century, more activities would be added.

Helen Hill Greenburg wrote for the July 1982 issue of *The Pioneer,* "General activities consisted of weekend balls, with ticket prices varying, from $1.25 to $2.75. Card games were popular; there were afternoon teas and concerts with tickets costing $1.00 to $2.50. For lovers of the outdoors there were hiking and horse-back riding over the mountain trails, ten-pins, or boating..." Ten pins was enjoyed on the outdoor bowling greens across the creek at the promenade at the base of Constitution Hill.

At one time there was a small lake with an artificial island in front of the Resort buildings, formed by the old mill dam at Dr. Anderson's Mill, on which Springs patrons could launch small boats. The Springs patrons "sailed pleasantly" around the lake. Later, the stream at the Black Spring was dammed up, creating Lake Caledonia, and boating on Lake Caledonia became a popular pastime.

Billiards may have been the most popular activity for men, Greenburg said. Many men participated at 25¢, 50¢ or $1.00, depending on the number of games played. "One registered guest, the Honorable DeFiganier, was an excellent billiard player. There can be no doubt of this because of the guest accounts telling the men who indulged in the pastime challenging this billiard hot-shot."

In the bar, champagne was very popular at $2.00 a bottle, claret was a close second at from $1.25 to $2.00. Other prices: Madeira $3.00, Port $2.50, sherry $2.00, grape $2.00. Whiskey was $1.50 a bottle; a flask of whiskey cost 50¢ at the bar. "Segars" were purchased with almost every order of spirits and cost 25 to 50 cents.

Guests had to purchase their own candles, made from sperm whale oil, which were two for a quarter.

Over at Cresson Springs, there was no room for construction of a lake. As boating became popular, the Pittsburgh businessmen who patronized Cresson (and Bedford) decided to establish their own private retreat, making use of an abandoned reservoir at South Fork that was restored for fishing and boating. The eventual failure of this impoundment would cause the tragic Johnstown Flood of 1889. I will return to that subject shortly.

The Anderson Heirs, owners of the Bedford Mineral Springs, now consisted of Louisa H. Anderson, widow of Espy L. Anderson and a daughter of the first Dr. William Watson, and her children. They were John, of Bedford; Major William W., who died in service to his country near Harper's Ferry in 1865; Dr. J. Ross; G. Espy of Cumberland, MD; Mary E. Middleton of Bedford; Eliza W. Beatty of Harrisburg; and Edward H. of Bedford, manager of the Springs. It was no secret that the "Heirs" desired to sell the resort, but there were no takers.

Fortunately for the Heirs, the United States was enjoying a prolonged period of prosperity that began during the Civil War and extended into the post war era. Business was good, and now that the conflict was over, patrons who had stayed away during the war were flocking back to Bedford.

During these years the Springs was self-supporting to a large degree, with a farm and dairy operation that offered fresh milk, butter and smearcase (cottage cheese). The resident farmer raised poultry and had fresh eggs; fresh vegetables from the garden and fruits in season from the orchard. Nearby farmers provided additional produce, fruits and beef.

A boom in railroad construction was also under way. The first transcontinental railroad, completed on May 10, 1869, was followed by the construction or expansion of numerous rail lines in the eastern United States to meet the needs of business and industry. Between 1850 and 1890, the total mileage of railroad track increased from 9,000 miles to an incredible 163,000 miles. Unfortunately, Bedford was still isolated from rail service. While other major resorts were conveniently located along the major rail lines, Bedford Mineral Springs was not.

Many miles from Bedford, events were unfolding that would have a profound and lasting impact on the Bedford Mineral Springs. In the Georges Creek area west of Cumberland, MD vast deposits of coal had been discovered and were being mined as early as the 1830s. When the Baltimore & Ohio Railroad reached Cumberland in 1842, the development of the coal region became economically feasible. The B & O began coal shipments in 1846, and coal also began moving by boat over the Chesapeake & Ohio Canal when that waterway, following the Potomac River, reached the city in 1850.

Huntingdon & Broad Top passenger train crosses the Raystown Branch of the Juniata River at Mt. Dallas. Photo courtesy of Dick Spargo.

Several independent railroad and mining interests joined forces to form the Cumberland & Pennsylvania Railroad in 1850. The new company soon developed into a transportation monopoly in a major portion of the Georges Creek coal field and delivered coal to both the B & O and the canal for shipment to eastern markets.

During the Civil War, Confederate raiding parties as well as invading armies tore up the B & O tracks on many occasions, interrupting badly needed coal shipments destined for Baltimore, Washington and other eastern cities. The use of coal was also gaining favor as a heating fuel in New York and New England. To reach these destinations it had to be loaded onto ships at the Port of Baltimore.

When constructed in 1854 - 1855, the Huntingdon & Broad Top Railroad had three goals, the primary one being to reach the Broad Top coal region in Bedford and Huntingdon Counties. The secondary goal was to reach Bedford and the Bedford Mineral Springs; the third, to extend the line to Cumberland. In 1870, only the first goal had been attained. The main line ended at Mt. Dallas, near Bloody Run (Everett).

On March 8 of that year the railroad's board of directors voted to make a survey from Mt. Dallas, following the Raystown Branch of the Juniata River to Bedford, a total of eight miles. Engineer John Fulton made the survey and estimated the cost of the extension to be $84,098 for bridges, grading and masonry; $3,000 for engineering; and $90,478 for ties, ballast and rails. The Bedford terminus, Fulton suggested, would allow for some future extension of the road to connect with the Pittsburgh & Connellsville Railroad at Bridgeport (Hyndman).

In 1855, Pittsburgh & Connellsville Railroad inaugurated train service between Connellsville and West Newton. It reached Pittsburgh in 1857.

Finally, on June 14, 1871, the line from Cumberland, Md., to Connellsville was completed by the B & O. When combined with the Pittsburgh & Connellsville, it provided what became the B & O main line to Pittsburgh.

The H&BT management was not aware that

The rich and famous - 83

The Pennsylvania Railroad depot, Bedford, served patrons of the Bedford Springs Hotel
Photos above, and at right, courtesy of Bedford Springs Historical Society

"other parties" were already planning a new rail line to stretch from Mt. Dallas to Bedford, and on to Bridgeport. The "other parties" were led by John Cessna, Bedford attorney and former state legislator, who had been elected to Congress in 1868. Cessna was one of the incorporators of the Bedford Mineral Springs Company in 1857, but lost his investment in the Springs when the company went bankrupt and the Anderson Heirs took the property back during the Civil War.

Cessna had not been involved in the ill-fated Bedford Railroad project a decade before, but there is no doubt that he was "a leading spirit during the inception and construction of the Bedford & Bridgeport Railroad." Beginning in 1870 Cessna served as president of the company for 15 years.

Cessna and other backers began selling stock in 1870 and purchasing rights-of-way, which were surveyed by John Fulton. Stock sold slowly until the Pennsylvania Railroad, recognizing the importance of the new line, purchased $308,950 of the capital stock and all of the first mortgage bonds ($1,000,000), assuring its success. George B. Roberts, PRR third vice-president, took an active role in the construction of the new line, which was completed in the summer of 1871. The first train rolled into Bedford September 23.

The Bedford & Bridgeport was leased to the H&BT for one year; after that the operation was assumed by the PRR. As the Bedford & Bridgeport had no physical connection to the PRR, all traffic was exchanged with the H&BT at Mt. Dallas as the bridge route to Huntingdon and the PRR main line.

In 1872 a physical connection was made with the Cumberland & Pennsylvania just north of Cumberland. From that time on, and continuing for nearly 40 years, tremendous volumes of Georges Creek coal would pass over the new railroad. It was now the shortest route for coal shipments to New York and New England from the Georges Creek mines. The volume eventually reached 2 million tons of coal a year.

The benefit to the Bedford Mineral Springs was felt almost immediately. By the end of 1872 passenger trains were running daily between Huntingdon, PA and Cumberland, MD. The Bedford & Bridgeport established a depot at Bedford, which was located on the opposite side of the river from the Bedford business district. The Bedford Springs provided a horse-drawn hack to shuttle guests between the hotel and the railroad station.

Gone were the days when visitors to the Bedford Springs had to endure lengthy stage coach rides over bumpy, dusty roads. Pittsburgh, Cumberland, Baltimore, Washington, Philadelphia, New York, Harrisburg and other cities were within easy access to Bedford. This convenient form of travel gave Bedford Springs a new lease on life -- just in time to help the resort weather the next recession.

In May, 1873 a financial panic started in Berlin and Vienna, and it soon spread across Europe. On September 18, the firm of Jay Cooke & Co., of New York and Philadelphia, which had been financing the expansion of industrial enterprises in the United States, went under. Four days later, the Panic of 1873 hit Pittsburgh. A number of banks failed within a few months. The panic ended the prolonged prosperity of the Civil War and post-war era.

Those persons fortunate enough to keep their jobs were forced to accept substantial cuts in wages. It would take the nation nearly a decade to fully recover from what was then being called the "Great Depression of the 19th Century."

Railroad travel made it possible for the Bedford Mineral Springs to weather the storm. As the recovery gained momentum, visitors again flocked to the Springs.

The cycle of boom and bust would continue to impact the Bedford Springs into the 20th Century and beyond.

In Pittsburgh, Judge Thomas Mellon, owner of T. Mellon & Sons bank (the forerunner of Mellon Bank) was observing the economic cycles, trying to make sense of them. Judge Mellon developed the principle of "five up and five down" years and that, "Any boom was bound to go bust " eventually, due to natural business cycles and also due to "dishonest speculators." Judge Mellon observed that "the American economy was liable to spurts and spasms, to booms and busts, which could be neither moderated nor eliminated, but which must be endured." Nor could they be precisely predicted, he added. Mellon also knew that recessions could be beneficial to business by ushering in creativity, efficiency and innovation, which in turn hastened a return to prosperity.

By 1878 a recovery was well under way, and bankers, business leaders and industrialists like the Mellons would invest in a number of new enterprises including real estate, coal and steel.

One of the upstarts funded by Mellon was young Henry Clay Frick, who had entered into the manufacture of coke to feed the growing steel industry of western Pennsylvania. As Harvey O'Connor wrote in *Mellon's Millions*, "It was an age of giants in Pittsburgh ... The insatiable maws of its blast furnaces

Passengers board the private coach of Stephen Elkins of Elkins, West Virginia, parked at the Bedford depot.

gulped tons of coke at one feeding and cried for more." Frick would become a "regular" at Bedford Springs, Cresson, and other spas.

But Frick was just getting started and not yet 21 years of age when he presented himself at T. Mellon & Sons Bank in Pittsburgh, looking for a loan. The Judge was impressed by Frick's confidence and by his knowledge of the coal and coke industries. Mellon had a feeling that Frick would succeed. When Frick left the bank he had $10,000 in his pocket.

The failure of Jay Cooke made it impossible for Frick to borrow money from any source, including the Mellons. Judge Mellon helped Frick sell a short line railroad to the Baltimore & Ohio, saving him from bankruptcy.

As the recovery began, Frick went to T. Mellon & Sons in 1876 where he met young Andrew Mellon, future Secretary of the Treasury under three Presidents, for the first time. This was the beginning of a long business relationship between T. Mellon & Sons and the H. C. Frick Coke Co., and the beginning of a life-long friendship between Frick and Andrew Mellon.

The Mellons gave him a $100,000 line of credit, which he used to gobble up distressed coke companies at bargain basement prices -- another benefit of the depression. By 1878 he controlled the Connellsville coke industry and the price of coke soared from 90¢ a ton to $5.00; of that, $3.00 was profit. Frick was a millionaire by age 30.

Many such stories could be told about the rise of Pittsburgh. The rising stars of Pittsburgh industry would flock to the Bedford Springs in the coming decades. Before the end of the century, they would purchase the resort.

But that was yet to come.

During the recovery of 1878 - 1882, the Anderson Heirs were still trying to sell the Springs.

Harriet Lane, the darling of Washington during the Buchanan presidency, was back in Bedford County, this time as Harriet Lane Johnston of Baltimore. As the Civil War drew to a close, she had met a wealthy Baltimore banker, Henry Elliott Johnston, during a visit to Bedford Springs. Harriet was then approaching the age of 36, considered by many to be an "old maid." They were married in Baltimore in January, 1866.

James Buchanan lived to enjoy Harriet's new family and to fondle her first-born son on his knee at Wheatland. He also visited the Johnstons on one occasion at their Baltimore home before his death June 1, 1868.

The couple had two boys, who died at the ages of 12 and 14.

In March 1877 the Huntingdon & Broad Top Railroad completed a new branch line up Sandy Run to open up a large body of coal land east of Hopewell, Bedford County. Mrs. Johnston closely followed these developments, as she was the owner of a large tract of valuable coal property in this region. Numerous trips were made to Bedford in 1876 and 1877 so that she and her husband could personally supervise the leasing and development of mines on this prop-

The Bandstand at the Bedford Springs. The Ladies' Bath House is in the background.
Courtesy Omni Bedford Springs Resort

86 - The Bedford Springs Resort

erty. Thus, the reason why the Johnstons were back at the Springs. The first of these mines was named "Harriet Lane Mine" in her honor.

Another Bedford Springs supporter, John Cessna, had also acquired coal lands in this area, amounting to 675 acres.

Over the next several decades, Cessna and the Johnstons would make a small fortune from these leases. Harriet, wealthy from her marriage to Johnston, was now a successful business woman in her own right.

Following the death of the eldest child the Johnstons began planning for an institution that would research the cause and treatment of childhood diseases. in those days, pediatrics was unheard of, and was only later grudgingly accepted by the medical profession. Before the plan could be carried out, Henry passed away after 18 years of marriage. In her grief, Harriet moved back to Washington.

Back in Baltimore a group of brilliant young doctors at Johns Hopkins Hospital conceived the idea of separating young patients from adults, and the hospital assigned them a small space in an existing clinic to test their new ideas. In a short time, the small space was jammed with patients, and it became obvious that a new building was needed to house the children's clinic.

Harriet threw herself into the fundraising effort, donating a great deal of her own money which came from her Bedford County coal mines; sought money from friends, and from anyone who would listen. The new facility was appropriately named the "Harriet Lane Children's Clinic of the Johns Hopkins Hospital."

One of the early medical breakthroughs that took place at the new Harriet Lane Children's Clinic was when Blalock and Taussig, after years of hard labor, devised a new technique for the "blue baby" operation, previously considered hopeless.

Upon her death in 1903 Harriet left an estate worth $1 million which was divided among public projects and charities. Her will also founded St. Albans School, a preparatory school for boys in Washington, D.C.

In 1863 a charter was issued by the state to the South Pennsylvania Railroad Company, which wanted to construct a rail line across the southern section of the state from Harrisburg, through Bedford County, and to eventually reach Pittsburgh. This little railroad with big dreams never seemed to get off the ground. In 1880 Franklin B. Gowan became interested in the "South Penn" because it could become an extension of his railroad, the Philadelphia & Reading, in building a line west to compete with the PRR.

Gowan needed to raise funds for the project and turned to William H. Vanderbilt whose own railroad, the New York Central, was a fierce competitor of the PRR. Vanderbilt, who was also an occasional visitor to the Bedford Springs, helped Gowan put together a syndicate to take over the South Penn.

In Pittsburgh, the steel industry had recovered from the Panic of 1873 and the "steel titans" felt their companies could do even better were it not for the high freight rates being charged by the Pennsylvania Railroad. The South Penn project immediately caught the attention of Andrew Carnegie, Henry Oliver, Henry Clay Frick and others who saw it as a way to break the monopoly of the PRR. The syndicate soon raised $15 million, with the funds coming from Vanderbilt, Gowan, Carnegie, Oliver, Frick, John D. and William Rockefeller and other investors.

Plans were made to run a double track main line through the southern counties. The advantage was obvious. From New York to Pittsburgh over the PRR, the mileage was 445; over the Reading and South Penn, 396 miles.

In 1880 George B. Roberts, who had been in charge of the Bedford & Bridgeport Railroad and other PRR - backed projects, became president of the Pennsylvania Railroad. As the South Penn project moved forward in 1883, he publicly announced that he would "smash the South Penn like a bubble."

Bedford was on the route of the new railroad. John Cessna became an avid supporter of the South Penn, even before construction began. Some might think that, since Cessna was President of the Bedford & Bridgeport, this might be a conflict of interest. The Pennsylvania Railroad certainly thought so. Cessna did not see the two rail lines as com-

The rich and famous - 87

petitors, since the South Penn would run east to west, and the B. & B. went north and south.

Cessna also saw the South Penn as an economic boost to the county in general and the Bedford Springs in particular.

Oliver W. Barnes was hired as chief engineer to oversee the survey of the route of the new line. Barnes was no stranger to the Bedford County area. In 1855 he had been placed in charge of laying out the route of the Pittsburgh & Connellsville line, of which he later served as President and Superintendent. In 1881 he was also the chief engineer, along with Anthony Bonzano for the construction of the Kinzua Viaduct in northern Pennsylvania, then the highest railroad bridge in the world.

Barnes, then living in New York City, made a topographical survey covering nearly a thousand square miles, and ran five thousand miles of location lines. The work took two years and is considered the most complete railroad survey in American history.

On September 6, 1883 a contract was entered into by the South Penn for construction of a double track main line between Harrisburg and Port Perry, near Pittsburgh. The route passed through Fort Littleton, Ray's Hill (Breezewood), Everett and Bedford. There was a great deal of excitement in the region as armies of construction workers were employed. The route also included nine tunnels. Work on the tunnels began in 1884.

In Bedford County, the representatives of the line were calling it the "Harrisburg & Western" in an apparent effort to confuse the Pennsylvania Railroad into believing that more than one railroad was involved. The "locals" in Bedford knew that it was the Vanderbilt interests who were buying up rights-of-way and supervising the grading of the new road.

While Oliver Barnes supervised the work from offices in New York City and Harrisburg, the chief engineer on the Bedford division is identified in the records as Edward H. Barnes, who was here in 1883 and 1884. His presence in Bedford could not have been kept a secret from the PRR. The author believes that Edward was a son of Oliver W. Barnes, but has not been able to establish this as fact.

Another Barnes who came to Bedford was Reon Barnes, a New York City attorney in the employ of the South Penn. The exact relationship between Reon, Edward and Oliver has not been established.

South Penn researcher Russell Love has spent hours trying to determine the exact relationship between the three men, without success. Love believes that Oliver and Reon Barnes were related.

As indicated on existing maps of the railroad route through the Bedford area, Love pointed out that the main survey took the railroad through downtown Bedford, then followed the approximate route of the Pennsylvania Turnpike to New Baltimore and over the Alleghenies.

Love went on to explain that there was an alternate route under consideration in 1882, which turned south at a point near the old red barn that is still visible at the east end of Bedford. The track passed 100 feet behind the barn and went up Shober's Run past the Bedford Springs, and then south of the Springs turned west. It passed through several water gaps in the mountains to reach Buffalo Mills, then followed present-day Route 31 to a point south of New Baltimore. This southern route would have taken the new railroad directly in front of the Bedford Springs Resort. Had a depot been established there, the Springs would have enjoyed easy access, but the day and night noise from passing freight trains would have been a major disruption from the customary peace and quiet of the hotel grounds.

According to Russell Love, the route through Bedford Borough was selected, sparing the Bedford Springs from the noise and smoke of locomotives. The South Penn did plan to build a spur line to the Mineral Springs which would have left the main line near the old barn, mentioned above. The barn is, in fact, clearly shown on South Penn survey maps. The spur would have provided passenger service directly to the Resort with a depot to be located near the Anderson Mill.

Copies of two letters written by Oliver Barnes in 1882 on South Pennsylvania Railroad letterheads, in the possession of Love, provide a time line for what Barnes called the Wills Mountain route past the Bedford Springs. The first letter, dated June 20, 1882, is addressed to F. A. Dietz, engineer, at Bedford:

"Mr. Reon Barnes & some friends with him left Harrisburg yesterday for Bedford via the located line. They will probably be with you on Thursday & Friday, possibly longer. Please show him around the located lines & explain the Maps & Profiles to them.

"I do not advise that you present the new Bedford Springs line to them, as it is as yet very uncertain how it will look on the profile. If it should prove successful it will be a pleasant surprise at some future time, but if not successful would be a disappointment. You can allude to it as a necessary topographical exploration to enable me to report why we did not locate via Bedford Springs." (signed) Yours truly, Oliver W. Barnes, Chief Eng.

The second letter, dated July 11, 1882, is also addressed to Dietz: "Do not do anything more on the Wills Mt. route except to have the topography properly taken; show it on your maps & on the 1200' scale map -- The position of the Bedford Springs and the houses around them also the roads leading from various points to the Springs must be shown within a scope of 2 miles around the Springs. Please also have the position and contour of the hills adjacent to your "M" line of survey shown giving their height, etc. as near as a skillful topographer can take them by observation."

(signed) Oliver W. Barnes

Love explained that the survey crew had to plot out the Shober's Run spur by "observation." No survey transits were set up so that the Wills Mountain line could be kept a secret from the Pennsylvania Railroad, lest the Bedford & Bridgeport be tempted to build their own spur to the Bedford Springs.

The letters seem to indicate that Reon Barnes and friends were in Bedford to address legal issues concerning the acquisition of rights-of-way for the new railroad, but as the Wills Mt. route was still tentative, Barnes instructed Dietz not to "show" it to them, just allude to it. Oliver Barnes, in his second letter, seemed to consider the Bedford Springs as an important destination. Still, it would be hard to imagine that Reon Barnes did not visit the Bedford Mineral Springs during his trips to Bedford. He must have loved the property because the following year he tried to purchase it.

In the approved route the track went through what is now the East End service station and followed the river on the south side. The track would have gone through the site of Fort Bedford, Love said.

The Wills Mt. route was dropped from consideration because there was no suitable water gap in Wills Mountain to eliminate steep grades.

In 1882 there were published reports that George W. Mullin, proprietor of the St. Cloud Hotel, Philadelphia, had attempted to buy the Bedford Springs from the Anderson Heirs. For one reason or another, the deal was not finalized.

In late 1882, Reon Barnes, legal counsel for the South Penn, returned to Bedford and after meeting with Ed. Anderson, he paid $10,000 down on an option

Ladies with bicycles.
Courtesy Omni Bedford
Springs Resort

Miss Ford's Hayride, 1893. Courtesy Omni Bedford Springs Resort.

to purchase the Bedford Mineral Springs. In an article the *Bedford Gazette* speculated that Barnes was acting on behalf of the Vanderbilt interests. Perhaps he was. The Vanderbilts certainly had the money to buy the Resort, but Barnes did not. He was trying to get enough investors on board to raise the money.

Soon after the option was signed, Anderson was offered $250,000 for the property by telegram from a businessman in Philadelphia, but it was too late. Barnes had his option.

On February 6, 1883 the Huntingdon & Broad Top Railroad's "Annual Report for 1882" indicated that the Bedford Mineral Springs property had already changed hands, which was not exactly correct. The report stated, "Bedford Springs property has lately changed ownership and the purchasers propose to form a company with a capital sufficient to make the proper improvements to accommodate a large number of guests, and to market the water throughout the country."

In 1883 Barnes shared with the *Bedford Gazette* his plans for the property. All of the buildings except the Colonial Building would be demolished. It would be made part of an immense hotel, with a wing at each end running east, and in front of the main building and wings a spacious plaza. Among the modern features to be incorporated into the building would be elevators, gas, steam heat, and other conveniences. It would accommodate 4,000 guests.

But the centerpiece of the Barnes plan was a "mile" race track with a club house in the center to compete with Saratoga Springs in New York, known for its horse racing season. Frank S. Heissinger, landscape architect, would be in charge of the project.

By the time the option expired, Barnes had failed to raise the money. He put down $5,000 for an extension of time, but he had no better luck. The purchase failed.

In downtown Bedford, the *Bedford Gazette* reported in 1883 that A. B. Carn who lived on the north side of Pitt Street had voluntarily offered a right-of-way across his property to the railroad. As the rights-of-way were signed the South Penn asked Bedford Borough Council to open a street 80 feet wide along the rail line on the south side of the river. Several meetings were held, and the issue divided the community. Many favored the street, others were opposed to the street but wanted the railroad. Some wanted neither, fearing that all of the smoke and dirt from the locomotives would cause property values to go down. But none of the arguing could stop the railroad.

The project was moving along nicely. In March 1884 the South Penn advertised in the *Bedford Gazette* for proposals for construction of a "bridge of 2 spans of 140 ft. each over the Raystown Branch of the Juniata River" with bids for masonry to be accepted by March 1 and for iron, March 15. The bridge was located in "the Narrows" east of Bedford. Completion of the railroad was eyed for the Autumn of 1885. In May, 1885 the completion date was changed to July, 1886.

The nation was hurt by another recession which lasted from 1882 to 1886, but in Bedford County it was somewhat moderated by the construction of the South Penn, which employed hundreds of men. As with the Panic of 1873, the wages of workers in many industries were cut, but this time, those working for less were mainly immigrants from Poland, Hungary, Russia and Italy.

The demise of the railroad boom across the southern counties of Pennsylvania came suddenly, and without warning, in July 1885. It was arranged by one of the nation's wealthiest men, J. P. Morgan, New York banker and financier. Morgan was very concerned about the fierce struggle between the Pennsylvania Railroad and the South Penn. He believed that cut-throat competition between railroads would lead to financial ruin for all involved. He arranged a meeting between Vanderbilt and Roberts on his private yacht, the Corsair, during which time both parties were pressed to resolve their dispute. By the end of the meeting, Vanderbilt agreed to pull out of Pennsylvania in exchange for concessions from Roberts, who agreed to buy the South Penn to dispose of in any way he saw fit. Roberts also agreed to transfer $5,600,000 in Bedford & Bridgeport Railroad bonds to pay off the minority shareholders of the South Penn.

By September 16, most contractors had walked off the job, and the work would never resume.

In Everett, a newspaper cried, "The people should have some rights," especially the landowners who had granted rights-of-way on the condition that the railroad would be completed and placed in service by 1887. A petition of Bedford County residents was sent to the state Attorney General objecting to the sellout and demanding that the minority South Penn shareholders take control of the railroad and complete it.

In reality, the minority shareholders were furious. These men, including Carnegie, Oliver and Gowan felt double-crossed by Morgan and Vanderbilt. Gowan went to Harrisburg and was able to get an injunction preventing the PRR from taking over the South Penn. It was not enough to save the project. The branch line to the Bedford Springs, like all other portions of the South Penn, was dead.

Rumors persisted for years that the minority shareholders would complete the line, but there was not enough financial backing to make this a reality.

Eventually, in the 1930s, much of the old South Penn was reopened as the Pennsylvania Turnpike.

Since the death of Espy L. Anderson the Heirs had continued to make improvements to the Bedford Springs property. A new gazebo at the Magnesia Spring was built in 1865. As documented by Bill Defibaugh, 1880 saw the Heirs making a number of improvements to the property, perhaps upgrading the resort in an attempt to interest potential buyers. The biggest improvement made in 1875 was the demolition of the old frame Evitt building and the construction of a new, 4 story Evitt House, which is still standing and in use. The work also included a band stand in front of Evitt, a gazebo at the Sulphur spring, and a bridge across Shober's Run to the Limestone spring. A short time later a new bridge was built to reach the Magnesia and Iron springs.

In 1885, the open space between the new Evitt House and the Colonial Building was closed in with a "fill-in addition," Defibaugh said. The area filled in is the location of the Sweet Spring, long famous as the source of "table water" for the bottling plant. At one time there was a hillside garden at the location of the Sweet Spring, but it was difficult to maintain due to the steep bank.

These would be the last improvements made by the Anderson Heirs. Within two years of these final improvements, the hotel was sold -- finally. Since Bedford had become a favorite vacation spot for the growing Pittsburgh aristocracy, it was only fitting that the buyers were from that city.

The rich and famous - 91

*The Anderson House, at right, was new when this photo was taken.
Courtesy Omni Bedford Springs Resort.*

This time the buyer was Attorney Philander C. Knox. Along with James H. Reed, he had organized the law firm of Knox & Reed in 1877. Knox had connections. He was a close friend of industrialist George Westinghouse, and of Robert Pitcairn, Pennsylvania Railroad executive. All three were members of the exclusive Duquesne Club. As an attorney, Knox also represented the Mellon interests, specifically brothers Andrew and Richard Mellon in their banking and business deals.

In the summer of 1887 Knox came to Bedford to work out the details of the purchase with the Anderson Heirs. Knox told the *Bedford Gazette* that he was not representing anyone, only himself, in the purchase. He might interest some other gentlemen in the property. He added that he liked the Bedford Springs and thought it was a good investment.

The timing was right. The recovery of 1887 - 1893 was beginning, and business prospects were rapidly improving in Pittsburgh and other industrial centers. There was no reason why the Bedford Springs could not prosper.

Referring to the Pittsburgh elite who patronized the Springs, Knox added, "I have frequently heard of the noted people who make Bedford their summer home, but I didn't believe it until I examined the register at the hotel. It was a real surprise. There is certainly no other resort in the country which entertains so large number of solid and prominent men."

Knox paid $50,000 in cash, and had agreed to a $200,000 mortgage held by the Anderson Heirs -- the same purchase price that the Andersons had demanded of Reon Barnes.

The deed, as recorded at the Bedford Courthouse, is dated Sept. 14, 1887. The sellers are listed as John Anderson, Edward Anderson, Edwin Middleton, Mary E. Middleton, Louisa Hickok, G. Irwin Beatty, Eliza W. Beatty and Rebecca Anderson, and the buyer, Philander C. Knox.

It turned out that Knox was busy selling stock in the Bedford Springs Company, and on January 6, 1888 he and his wife, Lillie, sold the Springs property to the Company for $290,000.

Although the new stockholders of the Bedford Springs Company are not listed, the deed does contain an interesting clause that "ten acres of the ground hereby conveyed is to be set apart and conveyed ... to the parties hereafter named

92 - The Bedford Springs Resort

... J. W. Dalzell, John H. Dalzell, Maxwell K. Moorhead, W. E. Schnertz, D. T. Watson, John W. Chalfant, William Hartley, James M. Bailey, Jesse W. Lippincott, and P. C. Knox, ... shall each choose and designate one acre of ground" so as not to interfere with the springs, or with any future improvement the company may choose to build on the hill in back of the present buildings.

It appears that these are the ten stockholders of the Bedford Springs Company. The Dalzells, prominent Pittsburgh attorneys, were regular visitors to Bedford Springs.

Some of these same men, particularly Knox and Moorhead, were already in the resort business, not publicly but in the form of a private hunting and fishing club. The South Fork Hunting and Fishing Club was formed in Cambria County, southwest of Cresson in 1878 due to their dissatisfaction with Cresson Springs Resort.

Among the incorporators were Andrew Mellon, Frick, Knox, Pitcairn, Phipps, Westinghouse, Andrew Carnegie, Benjamin Ruff, and others -- 16 in all. Each member purchased one share in the club at $200, except for Frick, who bought three shares; Ruff had four. The charter was approved November 15, 1879.

The distinguished group of gentlemen included a future Secretary of the Treasury (Mellon), future Secretary of State and Attorney General (Knox), future Congressman (George F. Huff), America's first ambassador to Turkey (John G. A. Leishman) and future president of the PRR (Samuel Rea).

The club purchased an old earthen dam above the village of South Fork that had previously been used as a reservoir, supplying water to the Pennsylvania Main Line Canal. The dam was completed in 1850; from 1857 on, the year the Pennsylvania Railroad purchased the state's Main Line of Public Works, the dam was unused and not maintained. On June 10, 1862, following heavy thunderstorms, the dam broke. When the club purchased it, there was no lake, just a large pond. Under Benjamin Ruff's supervision, the dam was rebuilt and the lake was filled and renamed Lake Conemaugh.

A club house was constructed, as well as a group of cottages where the individual members stayed, two boat houses, boardwalks and docks. The members and their families, many of which were also members of the Duquesne Club, gathered there socially on weekends and for summer vacations. But many of the wives still preferred Bedford and Cresson because there was more to do there.

The disastrous Flood of 1889 is remembered in history books as one of the state's worse natural disasters. The unusually heavy rains that continued for 38 hours forced

On the Anderson House porch: Note the water pails at left, and the faucet, at right, where guests obtained water for their rooms. The young man in the back row is identified as Joe Thropp, son of Joseph E. Thropp, owner of the Iron Furnace at Everett, Bedford County. He was Thropp's son to his first wife, Carolyn F. Moorehead. Thropp later married Miriam Scott, daughter of Thomas A. Scott, who became president of the Pennsylvania Railroad.
Courtesy Omni Bedford Springs Resort

streams over their banks. The main line of the PRR between Huntingdon and Pittsburgh was out of service. Every highway bridge between Hollidaysburg and Duncannon was washed out, except one in Huntingdon. The Huntingdon & Broad Top Railroad suffered extensive damage in the form of wash-outs. All passenger service to Bedford was halted, just as the summer season at Bedford Springs was getting under way. At the Springs, Shober's Run became a torrent, but the buildings were spared due to their distance from, and elevation above, the creek. This was fortunate because many of the guest rooms were already occupied for the Memorial Day holiday.

On the day after Memorial Day, the South Fork dam failed for the second time, pouring millions of gallons of water into the narrow valley of the Conemaugh River. The wall of water roared unannounced into the City of Johnstown. Some 1800 buildings were destroyed, and 2,029 people lost their lives.

There was an immediate outcry against those privileged rich whose private club had caused the devastation and loss of innocent lives. Ruff was accused of being careless in the reconstruction of the dam, and the club was sued for negligence in its maintenance. The club was defended in court by Knox, who successfully argued that the flood was an act of God and that the club could not be held responsible. Knox & Reed successfully fended off all lawsuits that were filed against the club.

Of the members of the South Fork club who were verbally attacked following the Johnstown Flood, the criticism of Frick was especially harsh. Over the decades Frick has been singled out for being especially callous during the disaster.

Frick was not at South Fork during the flood. Research conducted by Bill Defibaugh confirmed that Frick was staying at the Bedford Springs at the time of the flood. Even if he had desired to leave Bedford for the disaster area, swollen streams, washed-out bridges and roads clogged with mud prevented it.

Defibaugh was approached by Frick's great grand-daughter a few years ago. She wanted to clear his name, and Defibaugh confirmed that the industrialist was staying at Bedford. "She was very grateful for this information, and had worked hard to find the evidence. When she found it, it did my heart good to see the relief she felt," Defibaugh said.

A relief fund was established in Pittsburgh for the Johnstown flood victims. Frick donated $5,000; the Mellon family, $1,000; Carnegie Steel, $10,000. One club member, S. S. Marvin, even traveled to the devastated city to provide aid. But Frick refused to talk to the press, nor at any other time following the disaster did he made any public comment. It was his nature. He distrusted the press, and did not talk to reporters on any topic, ever. For this, he was vilified.

Bedford Springs recovered quickly from the flood, which did not hurt that year's patronage. On July 26, 1889 the *Bedford Gazette* reported, "A big boom has at last struck Bedford. There are to-day at the Springs hotel two hundred more people than were ever there before at one time. All the other hotels are full, and the steady stream of arrivals shows no evidence of slacking."

The continuing popularity of Bedford Mineral Springs with the Pittsburgh crowd is noted in a newspaper clipping dated 1891 *(Bedford Gazette)*: "Bedford Springs has shared the honor of entertaining fashionable Pittsburghers for the past 10 days with Cresson. Quite a large party of the Cresson colony has taken possession of the springs, and during last week not only drank religiously of the health-giving waters, but also indulged in a great deal of gaiety. In the early part of the week Miss Margaret Graham gave a tally-ho party, which was participated in by Mr. and Mrs. McKee Graham, Miss Lyon, Miss Darlington, Miss Williams, Miss Warden, Miss Holland, Miss Negley, Miss Taylor, Miss Bailey, Miss Lois Bailey, Miss Huselton, Miss Halderman, Mr. Leonard Graham, Orville Hickok, Ross Hickok, Charles Hickok, Brady Halderman, Mr. Huselton, Mr. Deull, Mr. Moorhead, Mr. Van Kleek, Mr. Graff, Dr. Pitcairn, Mr. Wallace, Mr. Murray and Mr. Marvin.

"Friday evening Miss Darlington and Mrs. Louis Dalzell gave a german (an intricate, improvised group dance intermingled with waltzes), which was largely attended. The

*The new tennis courts, with the Dormitory Building in the background.
Courtesy Omni Bedford Springs Resort.*

Darlington party, with Mrs. Dalzell, returns tomorrow to Cresson, and will be present at the tournament of the Golf and Gun Club, which takes place Thursday, Friday and Saturday of this week. Immediately after the tournament the Darlingtons leave for Watch Hill, where they remain for the month of August. They will be accompanied east by Miss Martha Dalzell, who joins a house party of Farmington school friends. Mrs. Dalzell will remain at Cresson for the balance of the season."

The Pittsburgh owners of the Bedford Springs, led by Knox, were making improvements to the property to keep up with the times. The sport of tennis was conspicuously absent from Bedford Springs until 1890 when the owners dismantled the Crockford building and reassembled it adjacent to the Colonial Building kitchen annex. A third floor was also added. In photographs of the tennis courts from that period, this building is shown with a gambrel roof. Within a few years it was converted into a dormitory building where hotel employees could live during the busy tourist season.

The Crockford, according to newspaper articles, was considered an eyesore, another reason for its removal.

This opened up a spacious area in front of the Colonial Building where four tennis courts were installed, complete with a judge's stand and a reviewing stand. Soon the hotel staged tournaments and exhibitions, and professional players were hired to provide personalized instruction to the guests.

Also in 1890, the large Anderson building was erected to provide additional guest rooms and Evitt was remodeled to match it's facade.. An old ice house was demolished to make way for the new building. Knox enlarged the mineral water bottling plant in front of the hotel.

A July 11, 1891 article in the *Bedford Gazette* proclaimed, "Every train that now arrives here brings summer visitors, and all the places of entertainment are rapidly filling up. Never before was Bedford so well prepared to accommodate those who come to spend the summer

The rich and famous - 95

with us. Of course, the Springs has taken the lead, the removal of the Crockford building being the most noticeable of the transformation. Marked improvements have been made in all directions....Passenger elevators and a new system of electric bells are among the principal additions to the comfort of guests."

The article continued, "J. Pierpont Morgan, a member of the banking house of Drexel, Morgan & Co., famous in Europe and America, paid his first visit to Bedford last week. He traveled by tallyho to all the surrounding points of interest and expressed himself as delighted with his trip. He is said to have salted away $50,000,000 for a rainy day. A few weeks ago he sent a check for $25,000 to Yale College.

"Another man at the Springs whose millions run into two figures is William H. Kemble of Philadelphia. He never misses a season at Bedford. He rarely indulge in riding, driving or other amusements. He comes here simply to loaf, and his most violent exercise is a game of cards.

"Samuel Joseph is another contribution to Bedford by the Quaker City. Mr. Joseph is famous as a Democratic politician. He wears a benevolent face and a high white hat. Whole in repose no one would imagine him to be the fierce warrior that he is. If Philanthropist Childs were as gray, he would be taken for Joseph's twin brother, and probably neither of them would like that.

"Governor Pattison left yesterday to make a tour of the military encampments. His family remain here and he will return on the 25th."

The H&BTRR Annual Report dated Feb. 3, 1891 stated, "It is intended to establish better facilities for passengers in hopes of adding largely to this branch of the business and particularly in view of the extensive improvements and additions that are being made at Bedford Springs to accommodate the largely increasing tide of travel to that point."

The following year, the H&BTRR stockholders were informed of the purchase of "A modern high-speed passenger locomotive, new combination car and passenger coach which are used on the express train, which runs from Huntingdon to Bedford without stops and which has been very successful during the year in making the journey to Bedford Springs more quick and accessible. Other improvements are contemplated in the passenger service as travel to Bedford will undoubtedly increase from year to year."

For the year 1893, the H&BT records indicated "a decrease in travel to Bedford Springs due to the Chicago World's Fair."

As was customary, the owners of the Bedford Springs leased the property to an operator, although in many instances the historical record does not indicate who the various operators were. However, in the *Press and Leader,* published in Everett, October 22, 1892 the new operator of the Bedford Springs was named as L. B. Doty. The details of his contract were also given in great detail. This gives a glimpse into the specific details of the lease.

The newspaper states, "Mr. L. B. Doty has leased the Bedford Mineral Springs property for a period of fifteen years, the consideration being five percent of the net income arising from the management of the hotels and the sale of the water. The expenses of all necessary repairs and improvements in and about the premises are to be paid by the company, who also agree to keep all the departments well furnished for hotel purposes. Mr. Doty has the privilege of having all the servants needed, and he may terminate the lease on three months notice before April 1st of any year before the term expires. The hotel is not to be used as a sanitarium nor is it to be sub-let. Firewood is allowed the lessee, and he has the privilege of giving out certain parts of the farm land of the property to be farmed on shares. Under this lease Mr. Doty has the exclusive management and contract of the Bedford Mineral Springs property for fifteen years on condition that he pay over to the board of directors of the company 95 percent of the gross proceeds accruing during each year after all the expenses have first been paid."

The Tally-ho, so often mentioned in connection with the Bedford Springs, was a stage coach pulled by four horses and used for excursions and outings. A favorite pastime was for hotel guests to pile on board (on top of the coach, if possible) and the coach would then race through the streets of Bedford. The blaring bugle gave warning to clear the road. Sometimes the passengers used instruments and noisemakers to create as big a racket as possible.

Bill Defibaugh notes that a favorite destination of the tally-ho was the Defibaugh Tavern east of Bedford, a 20-minute ride from the Springs, for a great chicken dinner. "The tradition lasted at least 100 years to the beginning of the twentieth century," Defibaugh explains. The Tavern, in later years, became known as The Willows.

On July 26, 1889 the *Gazette* proclaimed, "The tally-ho coach, driven by James Corboy, made its first appearance on Wednesday. It carried a party of twenty ladies and gentlemen to the Willows for supper. It is a very handsome vehicle."

Helen Hill Greenburg recalled, "As a girl I was fascinated by a skillful bearded man handling the four horses as the Tally-ho went down Penn Street. The dust flew as the four horses galloped along. The women held their hats, ribbons streaming, and the bugle brought children running to watch the Tally-ho go by.....As he turned off Richard Street onto Penn at the Corle House, the bugler sounded his bugle and residents along the street came out to wave and bid them on their way."

She continued, "It was looked upon as an exciting adventure; such was the drive on the Bedford - Chambersburg Pike to a little village Willow Grove, and dinner parties at the well-known Willows Inn, halfway between Bedford and Everett, and operated by Mrs. Mortimore and her daughter, Amanda Clark.

"This well established inn, from the late 1700's, became a rendezvous for travelers and drovers, the food excellent. There were accommodations, especially for the drover transporting stock overland. If he remained overnight, there were fenced pens for the animals and pure, sparkling water that was brought from the spring and piped under a huge elm tree, to a roadside trough. Many a man and beast quenched his thirst."

Golf came to Bedford Springs less than a decade after it was first played in the United States, and only a year following the formation of the United States Golf Association in 1894. In 1888, native Scotsman and iron manufacturer John Reid and a friend played the first game of golf in the United States in Reid's cow pasture in Yonkers, New York. In a short time the "pasture," dotted with apple trees, grew to six holes and St. Andrews Golf Club, the first modern course in the U.S., was founded. The first 18 - hole golf course in the U.S. was the Chicago Golf Club at Wheaton, Illinois, founded in 1893.

The Pittsburgh owners of the Bedford Springs were quick to bring golf to their resort. They didn't want to be left behind. Baltimore, Md. golf professional Spencer Oldham was called upon in 1895 to design the original 18 - hole golf course at Bedford Springs. It was opened to the public in 1898. The 6,000 - yard course was huge for its time; most courses in those early days of the sport were 4,000 or 5,000 yards. Oldham's style has been described as belonging to the "primitive American era" of golf course layout, characterized by geometric or "steeplechase" features.

Some features from Oldham's original course still exist, including chocolate drops, geometric S - curves and donut bunkers. This course remained unchanged for 14 years.

For the year 1895, the Huntingdon & Broad Top Railroad reported that they were operating "additional and express trains in the summer to accommodate the travel to Bedford Springs..."

The Defibaugh Tavern, later called The Willows.

The Pittsburgh partnership had invested heavily in the Bedford Springs, with the golf course being their biggest -- and final -- project. It was also bad timing. In 1890 Baring Brothers, a famous British investment bank whose clients owned a lot of American stocks, went bankrupt. This caused a sell-off of American stocks owned by Europeans and investment capital from abroad was drying up in the United States.

A Panic began in April 1893, caused by many financially unsound railroad lines and too many parallel, competing lines (just as the South Penn would have been, had it been completed). Also contributing to the Panic was a growing trade deficit that produced a drain on U.S. gold reserves.

The election of Grover Cleveland as President contributed to the Panic. There were doubts about Cleveland's competence in economic matters. As the President's term started in 1893, the New York Stock Exchange collapsed. Businesses, banks and railroads failed across the nation.

As the Panic swept the country, the owners of the Bedford Springs were also having financial problems caused by an inability to borrow money. Hundreds of national and state banks and mortgage companies had gone into receivership. The famed resort seemed to be as busy as ever, but the Bedford Mineral Springs Co. defaulted on the interest due on 6% bonds due February 1, 1896. The bondholders requested Merchants Trust Co. of Philadelphia to sell the property. Plus, the Anderson Heirs still held a $200,000 mortgage on the Bedford Springs.

The Tally-Ho coach prepares to depart from the Miller's House for The Willows.
Photos courtesy Omni Bedford Springs Resort

98 - The Bedford Springs Resort

The Bancroft years

Not much is known about golf course designer Spencer Oldham of Baltimore.

It is known that Oldham was a friend of Jesse Hilles, also from Baltimore, and that Hilles and Samuel Bancroft, Jr. of Delaware purchased the Bedford Springs property in 1896.

A newspaper clipping surfaced in 2009 that confirmed that Hilles and Bancroft owned stock in the Bedford Springs prior to 1896. It stated, "The Bedford Springs Company has been reorganized by the withdrawal of the Dalzells and Baileys of Pittsburgh and the substitution of Jesse Hilles of Baltimore; Samuel Bancroft, Jr. of Wilmington, Delaware; C. P. Dull of Harrisburg; Robert McNee of Mifflin; E. S. Doty of Bedford; Rev. L. M. Colfelt of Philadelphia, and others. The Company has purchased the water lease from Jesse H. Lippincott, and will hereafter have control of the sale of water." -- November 20, 1890.

Hilles was born in Baltimore in 1828 and died in that city in 1914. He was a Baltimore businessman and a Quaker. Samuel Bancroft, Jr. was his friend and business associate. Together, they would operate the Bedford Springs Resort during its golden years, and they would make it a first class destination.

The Bancroft family was in the textile business. Samuel's father, Joseph had been apprenticed in his uncle's cotton spinning and weaving mill in Manchester, England before coming to America in 1824. He opened his own spinning and weaving mill in an abandoned grist mill at Rockford (now part of Wilmington, DE) in 1831. He returned to Manchester in 1854 to learn the latest processes in spinning, weaving and finishing, thus laying the foundation for the family's wealth.

His two sons, William P. and Samuel, Jr. joined the company, which was from then on known as Joseph Bancroft and Sons. The two became sole owners after their father's death in 1874. They were able to enlarge the mill, largely due to the excellence of the finishing and dyeing processes that had been added to the manufacturing operation.

Samuel and William acquired and operated Todmorden Mills, near Media, PA. prior to 1878.

Company records indicate that Samuel had a second residence at Media after 1881.

With plenty of funds to spend and invest, Samuel Bancroft, Jr. purchased a number of stocks. In the late 1890s he invested heavily in

"Fun at the Springs!"
Check out the facial expressions on these guests.

Anger

The photos were taken on Sept. 5, 1892 by Lois Bailey, photographer, who took many of the photos from the 1890s that appear in this book.

Hilarity

Left to right: Capt. Barber, Regina Barber, Mr. Olmstead, Vinnie Pattison, Ollie Richardson, Isabel Boarman and Columbus Lee.

Surprise

Photos courtesy Omni Bedford Springs Resort

100 - The Bedford Springs Resort

the Huntingdon & Broad Top Railroad and on February 3, 1891 was elected to the railroad's board of directors along with Baltimore businessman Johns Hopkins, which met in nearby Philadelphia.

His interest in the H&BTRR brought him in contact with the Bedford Mineral Springs, and he and his family began to visit the resort during that time period in which he began to buy railroad stocks. He eventually acquired his own private railroad car.

Samuel Bancroft, Jr. began collecting art in 1889, particularly Pre-Raphaelite art. He made his first major purchase in 1890, a painting by Dante Gabriel Rossetti titled "Water Willow." He continued to add to the collection until his death in 1915. Today, the Bancroft collection belongs to the Delaware Art Museum in Wilmington.

Samuel and Mary Bancroft had two children, son Joseph Bancroft and daughter Elizabeth (Mrs. John) Bird. Joseph joined his father on the Huntingdon & Broad Top board of directors Feb. 2, 1909, and by that time was already active in the management of the Bedford Mineral Springs.

In the Spring of 1896 the Sheriff of Bedford County advertised the Bedford Mineral Springs Company for sale, on behalf of the trustee, Merchants Trust Company, Philadelphia. The property offered included 1,500 acres, a 3 story brick building, large 4 story frame building (Evitt), 3 story stone building, 3 story Swiss Cottage, 3 story frame building (Anderson), all in use as a summer hotel with accommodations for 600 guests; brick kitchen, laundry, separate building for servants' quarters, ice house, stabling for 50 horses, tool shed, bottling house and storage, mineral bottling houses, gardner's house, six tenant houses, barn, stables and out buildings.

Bancroft, Hilles and A. M. Neeper (of Pittsburgh) purchased the property for the $212,203.67 mortgage still owed to the Anderson Heirs, plus costs, for a total bid price of $280,000, being the highest bid received.

Three separate deeds were issued by the Sheriff. One was a Levari Facias deed and the other a Fieri Facias (Fi. Fa.) deed; both were related to the mortgage held by the Andersons.

The Fi. Fa. deed was a writ giving the buyers control of the property once the judgment of the Andersons was satisfied; the Levari Facias was used to sell lands of a mortgagor once a judgment had been obtained by the mortgagee.

Hilles and Bancroft had been negotiating to buy the property before the company went into default. They may have already been in control of the property because the Sheriff's deed lists them as the "tenants" of Knox.

The three men formed a "Limited Partnership" to operate the Bedford Springs, with Hilles and Bancroft each contributing $80,040 and Neeper, $39,920. Bancroft and Hilles each got a two-fifth interest, and Neeper, a one-fifth interest. The agreement is dated September 5, 1896.

The value of the property was listed on the agreement:

* 1,500 acres of land, $288,450.00.
* Morris property, one acre and one and one-half story log house, $350.00.
* Drenning tract, one acre and two-story log and frame house, $$400.00.
* Bates House, one and one-half story log house and stable, $100.00.
* One stone and log house, two-story, $200.00.
* One two-story house frame kitchen (Peck house), $350.00.
* One two-story log house and kitchen (Caledonia house), $400.00.
* One frame barn, 44 x 60 ft., $3,000.00.
* One frame ice house, 22 x 30 ft., $800.00.
* One two-story frame tool house, 14 x 20 ft., $250.00.
* One two-story frame laundry and engine house, 26 x 70 ft., $2,000.00.
* One three-story and attic brick hotel building 65 x 160 ft., brick kitchen 80 x 60 ft., $30,000.00.
* One four-story frame hotel building, 36 x 165 ft., including hydraulic elevator therein contained, $35,000.00.
* One two-story stone and one-story frame hotel building, 35 x 140 ft., $8,500.00.
* One three-story frame hotel building, 36 x 160 ft., $20,000.00.
* One one-story frame bowling alley, 22 x 80 ft., $150.00.

The Bancroft years - 101

* One one-story frame bath house, 40 x 70 ft., $1,800.00.
* One old stone mill, $250.00.
Total value: $400,000.00.

The above is subject to a "mortgage debt of $200,000 for part of the consideration on purchase money thereof, and secured to be paid by a mortgage executed by said Bedford Springs Company Limited, to Alexander King, Trustee, of Bedford Borough, Bedford County, Pa." It is interesting to note that the recently completed Anderson House section of the Hotel is not listed.

Another deed was issued Sept. 9, 1896 by the Sheriff to Hilles and Bancroft for the sum of $40.00, to clear up the title to what is referred to as the Lizzie Morris property.

Within days of this deed, the three partners sold their holdings to the Bedford Springs Company for $400,000. Signing the deed were Jesse Hilles and wife Mary, Samuel Bancroft Jr. and wife, Mary, and A. M. Neeper and wife Margaret. From then on, the Bedford Springs Company would be a stock company, owned by shareholders.

Knox, after acquiring the Springs property in 1887, had stated that he did not plan to run the hotel. "That is not my business and I don't know anything about it." He brought in professional managers. Bancroft and Hilles also brought in professional, highly skilled managers. This tradition has continued to the present day with the Bedford Springs capably managed by Benchmark Hospitality in 2007, and currently by Omni Hotels & Resorts.

In 1896 the Springs opened for the season as always, and in June some 400 guests were staying there. Work continued on the golf course, which was being laid out by Hilles' friend, Spencer Oldham but not yet completed.

Not holding a grudge over losing the property Knox arranged to hold the Pennsylvania Bar Association's annual convention at the Bedford Springs that summer. Knox was sworn in as the Association's new president.

A copy of the Menu, copied from the *Bedford Inquirer*, and found in the files of the Bedford County Historical Society, gives an idea of the banquet fare being served at the Bedford Springs. Note that the spellings below are the same as they appeared in the newspaper: Little Neck Clams, Consomme Princess, Salted Almonds, Olives, Radishes, Broiled Kenebec Salmon, Shrimp Sauce, Sliced Cucumbers, Potatoes Chateau, Sweetbreads, Glace and with New Peas; Asparagus, Hollandaise Sauce; Tenderloin of Beef, larded with mushrooms; New Potatoes, Marquis; Roman Punch, Broiled Squabs on toast, au Cresson; Lettuce and Tomato Salad, Nesselrode Ice Cream, Fancy Cakes, Roquefort and Cream Cheese, Crackers, Coffee Noir.

Four hundred patrons may seem like a lot, but the travel industry was hurting. The H&BTRR annual report for 1896 noted "... a general falling off in travel due to demoralization of this business," and a year later, reported for the year 1897, " ... a general demoralization among all industries." Bancroft and Hilles were in the hotel business for the long haul. Things had to improve.

It took a war to end the Depression. In January, 1898 a riot broke out in Havana, Cuba, then a territory of Spain. There were fears for the lives of Americans living in Havana, and the USS Maine arrived in Havana on January 25, 1898. On February 15 at 9:40 p.m. the Maine sank in Havana Harbor after an explosion, resulting in the deaths of 266 men. The Americans claimed that the explosion was caused by a mine in the harbor. Even today, this cause is disputed; it was probably caused by coal combustion inside the ship. Within months Spain and the United States were at war.

The Spanish - American War decisively ended the Depression as the nation geared up for the war effort. The period 1898 to 1900 fostered in an exceptional economic boom, and the United States soon had the world's most powerful economy.

The tourist trade was no exception, as prominent visitors from all over the United States again flocked to Bedford. Bancroft's wealth was being invested in improvements to the Bedford Springs, which would usher in a new era for the famed Resort. In 1901 Thomas Parkes, of the Hotel Bristol in New York City, was brought in as the new manager of the Resort.

Travel was made more accommodating with

The Colonial Building as it appeared during the Bancroft years.
Courtesy Omni Bedford Springs Resort.

the addition of Pullman service from Philadelphia to Bedford. George Pullman started the company in 1862 after spending a restless night sleeping in his seat on a train trip from Buffalo to Westfield, New York. His new company provided luxury sleeping cars to the traveling public, which became very popular. The cars featured carpeting, draperies, upholstered chairs, libraries and card tables plus washrooms at each end of the car for men and women.

Upon Pullman's death, Robert Todd Lincoln, son of the late President, became head of the Pullman Company in 1897 and guided it into the next century.

Bedford Springs patrons could board a Pullman coach in Philadelphia, which traveled directly to Bedford.

In addition to this service the Pennsylvania Railroad and Broad Top line jointly offered parlor car service from Philadelphia to Bedford and on to Cumberland, MD.

The parlor car passengers could take advantage of a stop in Saxton, climbing the steps from the depot to Church Street to enjoy a quick lunch at the Grandview Hotel.

Saxton native Walter Fink of Adelphia, MD recalls hanging around the depot in his boyhood days, where the platform was lined with mail and baggage trucks, all in use. Fink said it was a favorite place to loaf, hear the latest news, or to see the passengers getting off the train -- hoping to spy a famous person traveling to the Bedford Springs Hotel. Some of the rich and famous came in their own private cars.

Another option available to travelers was to book a railroad excursion. Summer Railroad Excursions were popular and were listed in annual guide books. In 1899, for example, a trip to Gettysburg Battlefield, Luray Caverns or Washington, D.C. cost $35 from Boston or $22 from Philadelphia (per person).

The 1899 guide book listed excursions to Bedford. The route was over the PRR to Huntingdon and the Huntingdon & Broad Top to Bedford. The principal hotels in and around Bedford, and the capacity of each, were listed as follows: Arandale Hotel - 200; Bedford House - 60; Bedford Springs Hotel - 700; Chalybeate Hotel - 150; Corle House - 50; Hotel Arlington - 50; Hotel Waverly - 100; Union House - 50; Washington House - 75.

As you can see not every visitor to Bedford went to the Springs. If the Springs was fully booked, the other hotels and resorts took the overflow.

The guide book offers a very detailed description of Bedford Mineral Springs: "Bedford Springs are located in a beautiful valley on the eastern slope of the Alleghenies at an elevation of over a thousand feet above tidewater. Enthusiasts have declared that no medicinal water in the world is equal to that obtained from these springs. However this may be, it has certainly effected many wonderful cures. It is used for dyspepsia; for hepatic affections; for diseases of the stomach and intestines; for secondary diseases of the lungs; for skin diseases; for rheumatism; for kidney diseases; for gout; for Bright's disease; and countless other ills; and is especially efficacious in building up a system worn out by overwork or illness. The pure mountain air of this locality is a most valuable assistant to the waters in restoring health and energy. There is also an abundant opportunity for out of doors exercise, as the roads in this section of the State are good, and the rambles are picturesque and romantic.

"Besides the great turnpike thorofares, running west to Somerset, north to Hollidaysburg, east to Chambersburg and south to Cumberland, with taverns and inns located in quaint old towns at frequent intervals, there are numerous excellent country roads through beautiful valleys rich in agricultural development and picturesque scenery, affording unsurpassed opportunity for riding, driving and coaching parties. For thirty miles or more in all directions, these roads penetrate the surrounding country, far removed from the annoyance and danger of trolley or cable cars which are rapidly annihilating, all over this great continent, the healthful recreation and pleasure of horsemanship.

"If the wonderful medicinal waters found here were the invention of man, the inventor could not have selected a more lovely spot in which to locate them. On two sides rise the mountain

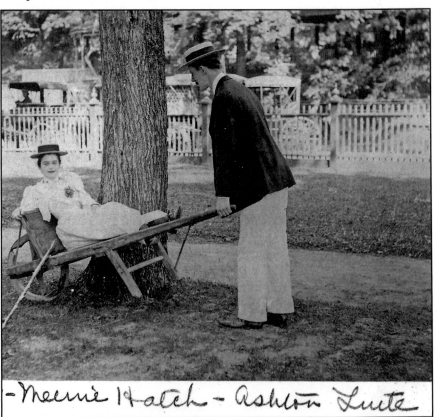

Photo taken August 2, 1893. Courtesy Omni Bedford Springs Resort.

spurs covered with luxuriant forests. In the valley between stands the hotel, and at short distances from it gush forth nature's healing waters -- the famous mineral spring, the iron spring, the sulphur spring, the chalybeate spring, the remarkable sweet-water spring, and the immense limestone spring.

"Bedford is easily and comfortably reached by the main line of the Pennsylvania Railroad to Huntingdon, thence by the Bedford Division."

Fares: Round-trip from Altoona to Bedford - $4.35; Hollidaysburg - $4.75; Baltimore and Washington - $11.80; Cumberland $1.85; Philadelphia - $12.75; New York - $16.75. "If you purchase a special form ticket which requires the purchaser's signature at the time of purchase and in the presence of the ticket agent, you receive a discount." The Washington, D.C. discount fare was $9.55 and the Altoona discount fare was only $3.50.

White Sulphur Springs, west of Bedford, was listed in the 1899 guide as a separate excursion. The round-trip fare from Pittsburgh was $7.05; Johnstown - $5.45; Cumberland - $1.35 and from Bedford - 50¢. Stage coach transportation to the hotel and back to the railroad station was not included in the train fare.

"The fine local reputation heretofore enjoyed by this health-creating resort has now become universal. It is located in Millikins Cove, one and one-half miles from Sulphur Springs Station and ten miles southwest of Bedford. The location is exceedingly picturesque and romantic. The water contains a combination of iron, sulphur and other mineral ingredients of medicinal value." The principal buildings at the Sulphur Springs were the Colvin House, capacity 200 and the May House, 40.

The publishers of the guide book didn't think highly of trolley lines. Bedford was free of the annoyance and danger of these contraptions. Ironically, in 1910 a proposal surfaced in the newspapers to expand the Altoona city trolley system, which ran to Hollidaysburg. A right-of-way for an electric railroad was surveyed in 1910 from Altoona to Bedford and on to the Bedford Springs. The survey indicated that it would have an overhead crossing of the PRR tracks east of Bedford, then pass through Bedford on Richard Street to the Springs.

The advent of the automobile doomed this project from the very beginning. Had it been built, it would have been a financial disaster for its investors.

1905 was a signal year in the development of the automobile, marking the point when the majority of sales shifted from the hobbyist and enthusiast to the average user. In 1908 Henry Ford introduced the Model T, which would prove to be very popular with the working class. But in 1900, the automobile was still no threat to the railway passenger business. For the next 20 years

Photo taken at the Colonial Building, second floor, August 1, 1892, "Six Handed Euchre." From left are Ruth Bailey, R. Barber, Ollie Richardson, Mr. Olmstead, Isabel Boarman, Capt. Barber and Regina Barber.

The Bancroft years - 105

An early parking lot at the Springs. The management provided tarps to protect the automobile interiors from the elements. Courtesy Omni Bedford Springs Resort.

the Broad Top rail line reported an annual increase in passenger revenues which was due, in part, to the increasing popularity of the Bedford Springs under the ownership of the Bancrofts.

Many roads in the Commonwealth suffered due to a lack of improvements. Most were dirt roads, which became muddy in wet weather and were marked with deep ruts in the Spring of the year. The various turnpike companies, such as the Chambersburg and Bedford Company, did not have sufficient toll revenues to properly maintain the roads. Railroads were still the way to travel.

Samuel Bancroft, Jr. left his mark on the Springs. In 1902 the order of meals was changed. It was now breakfast, luncheon and dinner, instead of breakfast, dinner and supper.

The first big change took place in 1903, when the original two-story kitchen building, constructed in 1842, was demolished. Immediately behind this structure was a second, brick structure, also constructed in 1842, and used as a lodging and meeting building. Both were annexes to the Colonial Building. Bancroft converted the second annex into a new kitchen between 1903 and 1905.

The new kitchen building also had a laundry facility, and in one end of the building two boilers were installed which provided steam for heating purposes and hot water for kitchen and laundry use.

The razing of the old kitchen made way for the construction of one of the first indoor swimming pools in the United States. The pool was meticulously restored for the official reopening of the Resort in July, 2007.

The application for National Register of Historic Places designation for the Bedford Springs describes the indoor pool this way. "The brick and wood Colonial Revival style building features a wrap-around veranda on the first story, and a low clerestory with a semi-octagonal solarium on the second. The semi-octagonal end has a series of twelve light French doors topped by a single light transom with sunburst muntins. The gable end has a fanlight window with delicate muntins. The impressive interior features a large swimming pool, galleries and a shallow vaulted ceiling."

From the time of its completion the pool, fed by mineral spring water, proved to be very popular with guests. The most daring would dive into the pool from the upper balcony. The pool itself was 63 ft. by 28 ft. The building also featured the solarium and individual hydrotherapy rooms. The pool water was heated.

Under Bancroft's direction, all of the buildings including stables and the old bottling house were removed from the lawn. The bottling operation was moved into a new, larger addition at the Anderson Mill. The grounds were laid out with flower gardens and paths, neatly landscaped. In 1905 a colonnade was constructed from the office and dining room floors of the Colonial Building to the bridge over Shober's Run leading to the mineral springs. New tennis courts and bowling alleys were installed.

They also installed a new pump house over the magnesia spring and constructed a small pool nearby.

That year the Pennsylvania Bar Association returned to the Resort for its annual convention, and was impressed with the changes and improvements being made.

The interior of building E had been completely renovated, with larger rooms and with private baths and ample toilet facilities added. H. E. Bemis was the manager and Corle H. Smith the chief clerk. The golf pro was George Baldrick.

William P. Schell of Bedford, writing in the *Bedford Gazette* on March 9, 1906, proclaimed, "Mr. Samuel Bancroft has so greatly and extensively improved the buildings and grounds that today there is no more superb, comfortable and delightful watering place in the United States. They have been patronized by presidents of the United States, senators and congressmen innumerable, cabinet officers, generals of the army, admirals and commodores of the navy. In fact, the public men of many states, in all callings, with most beautiful and accomplished ladies of the country have met here time and time again; and today as never before do they pay their annual visits."

In those days, gazebos dotted the lawns, and ornate gate houses guarded the drive-way entrances. Atop Constitution Hill, opposite the Colonial Building, a little summer house provided a resting place for those who used the bridle paths. On Federal Hill behind the Hotel was a wooden fire tower or observation tower, surrounded by a grassy open space. The old tower was a favorite picnic spot until, decrepit with age, it was finally torn down.

Bancroft became president of the Huntingdon & Broad Top Railroad Feb. 6, 1906.

On June 23, 1910 the Bedford Board of Trade enjoyed a dinner given to the organization by the Bedford Springs Hotel. A newspaper clipping described it this way:

"Promptly at the hour of 7:30 upwards of 80 members of Bedford's boom organization gathered around the tables in the spacious dining room of the historic hostelry, the guests of the management. The dinner was excellent in its every course, and was served as perfectly as it was delicious. The well-known Sykes Orchestra discoursed music during the progress of the feast.

"Speeches were made by John L. McLaughlin, President of the organization; Assistant Manager H. M. Wing, Hon. J. H. Longenecker, D. C. Reiley, Esq., Prof. J. A. Wright, A. C. Blackburn, O. W. Smith, A. Hoffman, E. A. Barnett and B. F. Madore, Esq. Every speaker expressed its appreciation of the entertainment and assured the hotel management of the hearty co-operation of the Board of Trade in everything that makes for the welfare of the Springs.

"Under the present management Bedford Springs has made great advancement, and the erstwhile popularity of this historic resort increases from season to season.

'A new era of good feeling between the Bedford Springs Company and the people of Bedford has been instituted and a more congenial fellowship has been called forth among the men who are striving for the betterment of our community." -- *Bedford Gazette,* July 1, 1910.

This era of cooperation between the Bedford Mineral Springs Co. and the community was a blessing, because the Resort, according to Bill Defibaugh, was becoming a "snooty place" where the "locals" were looked down on. This caused some resentment among the staff, especially staff members performing the essential menial tasks, and among residents of the County as well.

Bancroft brought in A. W. Tillinghast in 1912 to redesign the original 18 hole golf course. Albert Warren "Tillie" Tillinghast (1874 – 1942) was one of the most prolific architects in the history of golf; he worked on no fewer than 265 different courses. He was a native of Philadelphia. He laid out his first course, Shawnee-on-Delaware, in Pennsylvania in 1907.

Five years later, Tillinghast left his mark on Bedford Springs. To meet the growing popularity of golf, Tillinghast changed the course to nine holes by placing some holes on the main road that passes in front of the Resort, and others on the Resort side of the road. This included three holes in the vicinity of Lake Caledonia and the Black Spring. Those three were later discontinued. Tillinghast designed "Tiny Tim," one of the most famous holes in all of golf architecture. A clubhouse for golfers was also constructed.

Tillinghast was so pleased with the design of the "Tiny Tim" hole that he tried to incorporate it into all of the 150 golf courses he designed later.

Tiny Tim is discussed by Tillinghast in the book, "Gleanings From The Wayside," a collection of his essays published in 2001 as the third volume in a series. The essays include Tillie's analysis of some of his greatest designs, such as Tiny Tim, and some by other designers. As he stated, "During forty years I have probably trod as many golf holes as any man in the world, many of my own creation and many, many more designed by others. I know a good hole when I see one and I think I know a bad one, too."

Today, holes and greens No's. 1, 14, 16, 17 and 18 show the handiwork of this noted golf course designer.

Although the golf course is well known, the "golf court" at the Springs is not. In 2009 a scrapbook was given to Bill Defibaugh, and inside was found the original blueprint and photos of a "Golf Court" that was located in front of the main hotel building and dormitory. Two of the photos are reproduced here.

The golf court was arranged in a circle, with players putting from the central point through a number of obstacles to reach the holes, which were located various distances away. The distance in feet to each hole is noted on the blueprint. The layout resembles modern day miniature golf.

It is noted that the Bedford Springs' sister hotel, at Ormond Beach, FL, also had a golf court.

A Bedford Springs brochure from the 1920s proclaims, "Court or lawn golf, on the convenient hotel course attracts many of the guests, especially the ladies."

The golf course expansion was the last big project overseen by Samuel Bancroft, who passed away in 1915. His interest in the Springs was left to his widow and two children. Joseph Bancroft then became the driving force behind the improvements at the Springs.

Bedford Mineral Springs was truly a place where America's wealthy families and the socially prominent could spend the summer enjoying themselves, and the health - giving benefits of the mineral waters had taken a back seat to recreational pursuits.

In the 1920s, with the appointment of Dr. William Fitch as medical director, the mineral springs again became the focus of attention. Fitch was the author of "Mineral Water of the US and American Spas," published in 1927. He was one of a small group of physicians leading an effort to place water therapy, including mineral baths and ingestion of mineral waters, on sound scientific footing, calling for a redesign of American spas as health sanitaria along European lines.

In 1930 Dr. Fitch established a regimen which was called the "Bedford Cure," a three-week physician supervised treatment program of mineral waters and baths, regulated diet and supervised exercise. The "Bedford Cure" required the patient to imbibe each type of water (or a specific type of water depending on the individual's ailment) on a daily basis during their three-week stay.

A Hotel brochure of this time period proclaims "The Bedford Cure is a rational, scientific course of treatments of three weeks' duration, consisting of prescribed drinking of the mineral waters combined with carefully regulated diet and exercise, baths and massage.

"The waters are available to all guests of the Bedford Springs Hotel, and every convenience for their comfort is provided, under the supervision of a well-known physician and expert attendants.

"Eminent physicians throughout the country have endorsed the health-giving qualities of Bedford Springs and chemical analyses have proved the curative value of the waters."

The Hotel management was actively soliciting physicians across the country, in the form of the mass mailing of letters, to send their

*Court Golf, also called Lawn Golf, was popular, especially with the ladies.
Courtesy Bedford Springs Historical Society.*

patients to Bedford for the Cure.

The onset of the Great Depression limited the number of people who could afford a three-week stay at Bedford, and the number of guests coming for the "Cure" gradually diminished.

Across town at the smaller Chalybeate Springs Hotel, another "cure" was being made. Blackburn's History of Bedford County (1906) reported that "Mr. J. Harper Hafer, one of the proprietors of the Bedford House, and whose father at one time owned and conducted the Chalybeate Springs, is the manufacturer of the Celebrated Chalybeate Cure, or Iron Salve, which is compounded by the sediment thrown out by the spring with other healing ingredients, which is now having a large and well deserved sale. Its curative powers as a skin medicine are attested by many leading physicians who have been long using it in general practice."

As the Roaring Twenties began, business at the Springs was booming. The famed hotel never had enough rooms to meet demand. His father gone, Joseph Bancroft took the lead, embarking on two major projects. One involved a redesign of the Tillinghast golf course. The other was a major expansion of the hotel.

The Bedford Springs was showing its age; some of the main buildings were over 80 years old. Bancroft agreed that some newer facilities were needed.

In 1923 he employed contractor Walter S. Arnold to erect what is known as the Barclay House on Federal Hill, behind the Colonial Building. The Barclay House, when completed, was five stories high, with 203 guest rooms. It was expected to accommodate 400 guests, alleviating the room shortage.

In May, 1924, Joseph Bancroft arrived in his private railroad car to personally inspect the work on the new hotel building, accompanied by hotel manager Martin Sweeney. A newspaper article explained that the new building should be ready for occupancy by June 1, just in time for the 1924 season.

That newspaper article also hinted that the Barclay House was the "first section" of a new hotel, which would face the golf course.

Bill Defibaugh has in his collection the architect's drawings of this "new hotel," by architect Eric Fisher Wood. That same year Wood, in collaboration with Henry Hornbostel and Rutan and Russell, designed Schenley Quadrangle, a cluster of University of Pittsburgh residence halls that is a National Historic Landmark. Originally, the Schenley Apartments were home to Pittsburgh's well-to-do before being purchased in 1955 by the University. No doubt many of the residents of Schenley Apartments were Bedford Springs patrons.

Wood was studying architecture in the Ecole des Beaux-Arts at Paris when World War I erupted in 1914. He became an Attaché at the American Embassy in Paris and made four different trips to the front, covering territory which extended along the battle-line from Vitry-le-François in the east to a point near Dunkirk in the west.

On February 14, 1915 he sailed for home out of Liverpool, England to take up his career as an architect. His notebook describing his experiences in the war were later published in a book, "The Notebook of an Attache: Seven Months in the War Zone."

The Grant Building, completed in 1930 and a noted Pittsburgh landmark, was also designed by Wood and Henry Hornbostel.

The drawing in Defibaugh's collection depicts a massive hotel with 400 guest rooms with private baths, a grand lobby, 100 by 75 feet, a two-story kitchen, and a large dining room that could seat 750. The front entrance was framed by six massive pillars in the center. It was similar, but much larger, than the entrance to the Colonial Building below. The entrance faced and overlooked the golf course.

We can only speculate as to why this project was not started. Perhaps the Springs Corporation hesitated in spending that kind of fortune on the Resort. Had they completed this project, would the older, historic portions of the Bedford Springs been closed? Would they have been torn down?

A newspaper article in the *Bedford Inquirer* dated June 11, 1926 called the Barclay, "The new hotel's east wing," a "new five-story building of steel, brick and tile, with accommodations for 400 guests. All of the rooms in this new building face the outside, and each has a private bath."

The new Barclay Building, above; Dormitory, below.
Courtesy Bedford Gazette.

That article further stated, "The famous Bedford Springs Hotel announces its opening for the 110th consecutive season next Friday, June 18, with its excellent 18 hole golf course, new standard professional tennis courts, and its famous baths in operation.

"On the opening of the House, the 315th and 316th Infantry Officers will hold their usual annual get-together. The annual professional golf tournament, in which participate the leading professional golfers, not only in Pennsylvania but in surrounding states, will be held on the Bedford Course during the later part of July, and the annual invitation tournament, participated in by leading golfers and society people generally, is scheduled for the year."

The Barclay was apparently named for Dr. Francis B. Barclay of Bedford. Barclay owned a large tract of land behind the main hotel buildings, which Samuel Bancroft, Jr. had purchased from his estate in November, 1912. This tract remained in the possession of the Bancrofts until January 3, 1921, when Mary R. Bancroft and children conveyed it to the Bedford Springs Company for $1.00.

The construction of the Barclay House coincided with a complete redesign of the golf course back to 18 holes and an expansion of the clubhouse. Noted golf course designer Donald J. Ross was the mastermind behind the project.

Born in Scotland in 1872, Ross learned his trade in the country that invented the sport, serving an apprenticeship with Old Tom Morris in St. Andrews before investing his life savings in a trip to the U.S. in 1899. He also enjoyed a successful career as a golfer.

At his death in 1948, he left behind a legacy of 413 courses, including such gems as Pinehurst No. 2 in North Carolina, Seminole in Florida, and the site of the 1996 U.S. Open, Oakland Hills outside Detroit. Over 100 U.S. national championships have been played on

The Bancroft years -

his designs.

According to the Donald Ross Society, of all the courses that bear Ross' name, either as original designs or as renovation projects, he probably never even saw a third of them, and another third he visited only once or twice. So it is possible that Ross visited Bedford only a few times.

Work on the redesigned course was under way in Bedford in 1923, and it is generally believed that it opened to the public in 1924.

Ed Stone writes in "GoGolfandTravel.com" that Ross configured the course to have all 18 holes on the Resort side of the road. He said there are six holes "where Donald Ross's mark is not part of them. There are four holes where Ross and Oldham's work comes together and one hole with that of Ross and Tillinghast."

Some of the greatest golfers of the 20th Century played this course, among them, US Open Champions Francis Ouimet, Walter Hagen, Gene Sarazen, Sam Parks, Jr. and Arnold Palmer. Sam Parks, Jr. enjoyed the Bedford Springs course so much that he played it for three decades, from the 1930s into the 1950s.

The advent of the automobile didn't have much impact on the Bedford Springs during the first decade of Bancroft ownership because the condition of the state's network of roads was deplorable. Many of the toll roads suffered from a lack of upkeep, and a road trip by auto could be very challenging. By 1900 it was apparent that turnpike companies were no longer capable of maintaining the roads.

On May 31, 1903, Pennsylvania established a state highway department which was given the responsibility of addressing the problem. Not long after that the Sproul Act was passed, which gave the highway department authority

The Huntingdon & Broad Top Mountain R. R. & Coal Co.

Time Table in Effect SUNDAY, NOVEMBER 7, 1909.

FOR THE INFORMATION OF THE PUBLIC.   EASTERN TIME.

SOUTHWARD / NORTHWARD

9 Le. Sundays Only P.M.	7 Le. Sundays Only A.M.	MAIL 3 Le. Daily Ex. Sunday P.M.	BEDFORD SPECIAL 5 Le. Daily Ex. Sunday P.M.	EXPRESS 1 Le. Daily Ex. Sunday A.M.	Dist. from Hunt.	STATIONS	Dist. from Mt. Dallas	MAIL 4 Ar. Daily Ex. Sunday A.M.	BEDFORD SPECIAL 6 Ar. Daily Ex. Sunday P.M.	FAST LINE 2 Ar. Daily Ex. Sunday P.M.	10 Ar. Sundays Only A.M.	8 Ar. Sundays Only P.M.
S 5 40	S 9 05	S 5 40	S 2 00	S 8 35	0	HUNTINGDON	44.1	S 11 00	S 3 45	S 6 40	S 11 20	S 4 50
S 5 49	S 9 14	S 5 48	S 2 08	S 8 45	4.5	McCONNELLSTOWN	39.6	S 10 50	S 3 36	S 6 31	S 11 10	S 4 40
S 5 53	S 9 18	S 5 52	S 2 12	S 8 49	7.1	GRAFTON	37	S 10 46	S 3 32	S 6 27	S 11 06	S 4 36
F 5 57	F 9 22	F 5 56	F 2 16	F 8 53	9.5	BRUMBAUGH	34.6	F 10 41	F 3 27	F 6 22	F 11 01	F 4 31
S 6 02	S 9 27	S 6 00	S 2 21	S 8 58	11.2	MARKLESBURG	32.9	S 10 37	S 3 23	S 6 18	S 10 57	S 4 27
S 6 09	S 9 34	S 6 11	S 2 29	S 9 06	14.7	ENTRIKEN	29.4	S 10 29	S 3 15	S 6 11	S 10 50	S 4 20
S 6 15	S 9 40	S 6 16	S 2 34	S 9 11	17.8	HUMMEL	26.3	S 10 22	S 3 08	S 6 03	S 10 44	S 4 14
F 6 19	F 9 44	F 6 20	F 2 38	F 9 15	20	COVE	24.1	F 10 17	F 3 03	F 5 58	F 10 40	F 4 10
S 6 30	S 9 55	S 6 32	S 2 51	S 9 27	24.2	SAXTON	19.9	S 10 07	S 2 53	S 5 48	S 10 30	S 4 00
F 6 34	F 9 59	F 6 36	F 2 55	F 9 31	26.7	CLARK	17.4	F 10 00	F 2 44	F 5 41	F 10 24	F 3 54
S 6 42	S 10 06	S 6 44	S 3 04	S 9 40	29.5	RIDDLESBURG	14.6	S 9 54	S 2 38	S 5 35	S 10 18	S 3 48
S 6 47	S 10 13	S 6 48	S 3 08	S 9 49	31.6	HOPEWELL	12.5	S 9 49	S 2 34	S 5 30	S 10 13	S 3 43
F 6 55	F 10 21	F 6 57	F 3 17	F 9 58	35.8	CYPHER	8.3	F 9 39	F 2 25	F 5 20	F 10 04	F 3 34
F 7 00	F 10 26	F 7 03	F 3 23	F 10 03	38.2	BRALLIER	5.9	F 9 34	F 2 19	F 5 14	F 9 59	F 3 29
F 7 04	F 10 29	F 7 07	F 3 27	F 10 07	39.9	TATESVILLE	4.2	F 9 30	F 2 15	F 5 10	F 9 56	F 3 26
S 7 12	S 10 37	S 7 16	S 3 36	S 10 16	43.1	EVERETT	1	S 9 23	S 2 08	S 5 03	S 9 48	S 3 18
S 7 15	S 10 40	S 7 20	S 3 40	S 10 20	44.1	MT. DALLAS	0	S 9 20	S 2 05	S 5 00	S 9 45	S 3 15
S 7 30	S 10 55	S 7 40	S 4 00	S 10 40	52	BEDFORD		S 9 00	S 1 50	S 4 40	S 9 30	S 3 00
		S 8 25		S 11 28	75.1	HYNDMAN		S 8 10		S 3 50		
		S 8 55		S 12 00	89.1	CUMBERLAND		S 7 40		S 3 20		
P.M.	A.M.	P.M.	P.M.	NOON				A.M.	P.M.	P.M.	A.M.	P.M.

SHOUP'S BRANCH.

SOUTHWARD				NORTHWARD	
EXPRESS 41 Le. Daily Ex. Sunday A.M.	MAIL 43 Le. Mondays and Saturdays Only P.M.	Distance	STATIONS	EXPRESS 42 Ar. Daily Ex. Sunday P.M.	MAIL 44 Ar. Mondays and Saturdays Only A.M.
S 9 35	S 6 35	0	SAXTON	S 5 00	S 9 00
S 10 00	S 6 50	3	COALMONT	S 4 45	S 8 45
S 10 20	S 7 05	5.2	DUDLEY	S 4 30	S 8 30

CONNECTIONS.

MIDDLE DIVISION.—P. R. R.

Trains leave Huntingdon Westward, Daily: (F) 2:08 a. m., 5:44 a. m., 1:29 p. m.; 1:48 p. m.; 4:58 p. m., 5:22 p. m., 7:54 p. m., and (F) 9:52 p. m. Daily except Sunday: 6:10 a. m., 8:10 a. m., 10:03 a. m., 11:26 a. m., 12:48 p. m. and 4:25 p. m. Sunday only: 8:30 a. m., 9:34 a. m., 10:14 a. m., 11:40 a. m. and 5:30 p. m.

Trains leave Huntingdon Eastward, Daily: (F) 1:10 a. m., 7:17 a. m., 11:52 a. m., 12:26 p. m., 2:42 p. m., 4:08 p. m., 5:32 p. m., 6:51 p. m., 7:16 p. m. and 10:07 p. m. Daily except Sunday: 6:00 a. m., 8:25 a.m and 11:15 a. m. Sunday only: 6:17 a. m. and 9:02 a. m.

H. & B. T. Trains Nos. 1, 5 and 3 will wait at Huntingdon 30 minutes when necessary, for connection with P. R. R. Trains Nos. 30, 15 and 1, respectively.

B. & O. R. R.
Trains leave Hyndman West 1:54 p. m. and 3:21 p. m.
Trains leave Hyndman East 11:47 a. m., 12:14 p. m., and 5:35 p. m

W. M. R. R. (W. VA. DIV.)
Trains leave Cumberland at 7:00 a. m., and 3:00 p. m.
Trains arrive at Cumberland at 12:45 p. m., and 7:50 p. m.

G. C. & C. R. R.
Trains leave Cumberland at 7:00 a. m., and 1:00 p. m.
Trains arrive at Cumberland at 11:30 a. m., and 6:00 p. m.

F—Stops to let off or take on Passengers, upon Notice being given to Conductor or on Signal.   S—Regular Stop.

CARL M. GAGE, V. Prest. & Gen'l Manager.   A. E. YOHN, Superintendent.   J. A. GREENLEAF, Gen'l Passenger Agent.

to take over the old turnpike companies and develop and maintain a system of roads at state expense. The old Chambersburg & Bedford Turnpike was the first toll road to be taken over and it was opened to the public, toll free, in June, 1913. This marked the beginning of the Lincoln Highway, which began in New York and eventually crossed the United States. It went through the center of Bedford.

But the state and local roads, which were mostly dirt, were plagued with potholes, washouts, and especially deep ruts during wet weather. It was not unusual for the early automobiles to become stuck in deep ruts, which required several men using pry bars and planks to free the wheels.

The Lincoln Highway remained a dirt road until the Federal Highway Act of 1921 was passed. It allocated $75 million in matching funds to states to build "primary routes," which in most states, including Pennsylvania, the Lincoln Highway was the obvious choice. Federal funding allowed the road to be rebuilt using concrete. By 1926 the Lincoln Highway, now Route 30, had been paved to a point near Pittsburgh. Visitors to the Bedford Springs now had access to a "modern" highway. The number of guests driving to the Bedford Springs dramatically increased during this period. For the first time, parking areas were a necessity at the resort.

This increase in highway travel resulted in an expected decrease in rail passenger business. In the Huntingdon & Broad Top Railroad's annual report for the year 1927, it is noted, "The steady decrease in the number of passengers carried during the past eight years, due to the increased travel by automobile, from which all railroad companies are suffering, is constantly before your management..."

One of the steps taken by this railroad was the formation of a bus line, the Huntingdon & Broad Top Transit Company, which operated a number of routes including a route between Huntingdon and Bedford. This was one of the first bus companies to serve Bedford Springs patrons. It was no coincidence, as Joseph Bancroft was president of the Huntingdon & Broad Top Transit Company and the Bedford Springs Company.

The decade of the 1920s in America has generally been known as the Roaring Twenties, marked by increased consumer spending and economic growth under three Republican administrations -- those of Warren Harding, Calvin Coolidge and Herbert Hoover. Andrew Mellon of Pittsburgh served as Secretary of the Treasury under all three administrations. Under Mellon the federal government's intrusion into private business was restricted, and as a result the captains of business and industry became very wealthy.

Many of the wealthy and their families came to Bedford Springs each summer. Among the notable guests who stayed at Bedford with their families during this period were Henry Ford, Jay Gould and Henry Wannamaker.

Writes Scott D. Heberling in *More Than Mineral Water*, "The well heeled, genteel guests who frequented the Springs could engage in a full schedule of leisure activities from first light well into the night. These activities -- dancing, golf, tennis, bowling, lawn games, walking, riding, bicycling, swimming, or just simple sociability around a billiard table or card table -- may have done more to promote good physical and mental health than plunge baths or the thirty half-pints of mineral water that some guests routinely drank before breakfast each

A road trip by automobile could be very challenging, especially during wet weather when the rural roads were filled with ruts.
Courtesy Adam L. Watson.

day."

Many of these guests annually enjoyed what was then called the "springs circuit," a route traveled by the affluent residents of Baltimore, Philadelphia, Pittsburgh and Washington, D.C. In addition to Bedford, the circuit included enjoying the waters at The Greenbrier at White Sulphur Springs, WV and The Homestead in Hot Springs, VA.

One traditional activity that Bedford Springs guests could not enjoy, at least openly, was drink alcoholic beverages.

In 1920, the manufacture, sale, import and export of alcohol was prohibited by the Eighteenth Amendment to the United States Constitution which came to be known as "Prohibition". During this period, the Bedford Springs management could not legally sell beer, wine or mixed drinks to its patrons. Much to the ire of prohibitionists, Treasury Secretary Mellon believed that enforcement of Prohibition was a low priority, and this made it possible for many establishments to obtain liquor and beer from various sources. It is hard to imagine that Bedford Springs was completely "dry" during the Roaring Twenties. After all, it was still legal to "consume" alcohol.

Prohibition was not repealed until 1933.

No history of the Bedford Mineral Springs would be complete without mentioning author Hervey Allen, a frequent visitor to the famed watering place during his lifetime. Although his name is no longer well known among literary circles, he remains a favorite author in Bedford County where out-of-print copies of his four volume "historical fiction" series on Colonial America are still in demand. The books incorporate tales from the early history of Bedford County and the Western Pennsylvania region.

William Hervey Allen, Jr. was born December 8, 1889 in Pittsburgh, a son of William Hervey Allen, Sr. and Helen Eby Meyers Allen. His father was an inventor and businessman. The future writer was a young man when his father's fortune was greatly diminished by what was called "dubious business ideas." One biographer stated that the young Allen "grew up very distant emotionally from his father."

From the time he was a young man the family came to Bedford Springs each summer for vacation. After Hervey Allen left home to seek his own career, he continued to return to Bedford each year.

Hervey Allen qualified for admission to the United States Naval Academy in Annapolis, MD but was forced to leave because he suffered serious sports injuries. He received a degree in Economics from the University of Pittsburgh in 1915 and joined the Pennsylvania National Guard the following year, serving in El Paso, TX when the United States attempted to intervene in the Mexican Revolution. Three months after he returned to Pennsylvania, he was called to active duty, promoted to First Lieutenant and shipped off to France. Allen served in combat

Photo taken August, 1895. From left are Steve Elkins, Bessie Baccus and Dan Dull.
Courtesy Omni Bedford Springs Resort.

and was gassed, and suffered from shell shock. During an extended period of hospitalization, he began writing poetry which described his war experiences.

His war poetry found a wide audience among millions, and in the next decade he wrote poetry while taking graduate courses at Harvard; was a high school English teacher at Porter Military Academy in Charleston, SC; taught English at Pitt and lectured on American Literature at both Columbia University and Vassar College. In 1926 he published a biography of Edgar Allen Poe, titled "Israfel."

Having shifted from poetry to prose, his epic novel, "Anthony Adverse," published in 1933 became one of the biggest sellers of the 1930s. This novel is the tale of a young man born in 1775 in unfortunate circumstances and raised by a Jesuit priest in Auvergne, France. The main character eventually ends up in the American West. The novel presents a series of adventures by one central character, and is actually composed of three sets of three books each.

While teaching he met Annette Andrews, one of his pupils at Pitt. They married after Annette's graduation. This caused something of a scandal, since the bride was 19 years younger than Allen. For a time the couple lived in Bermuda, then New York after "Anthony Adverse" became a financial success.

Having fallen in love with Bedford, he continued to return every year except during World War II. Hervey Allen made many friends in Bedford, among them, Clarence "Judge" Davidson, who operated a small antique shop in a corner of the Pennsylvania Hotel. Through Davidson and many others he began to know quite well the pioneer history of the region. Two of his most favorite characters were Col Henry Bouquet and Captain Simon Ecuyer from the French and Indian War days. In fact he rated them superior to Forbes, Washington and Braddock.

For many years he maintained a home at 6215 Fifth Avenue in Pittsburgh, but moved to Dade County FL in his later years when he was working on a non-fictional series titled "Rivers of America." These popularized the environmentalist movement years before it was commonly known or accepted.

The Colonial America series of books had been envisioned by Allen as five volumes in all, although he was never able to complete all of them. The first, "The Forest and the Fort," (1943) had Ecuyer and Bouquet as the main characters. It was followed by "Bedford Village," (1944) and then by "Toward the Morning," (1948).

He began writing "The City in the Dawn," but upon his death December 28, 1949 at The Glades near Miami, it remained unfinished. Allen died of a heart attack while taking a shower. Annette found him dead; he was a few weeks shy of his 60th birthday. He was buried in Arlington National Cemetery. Annette died in 1976 and was buried alongside her

Photo taken August, 1891 on the second floor veranda of the Colonial Building. Courtesy Omni Bedford Springs Resort.

Mrs. Bancroft's "German"

Photo taken in the Ballroom by Lois Bailey, August, 1895.

Practicing dance steps: The young man at right is Joseph Bancroft; next to him is Carrie Hilles, daughter of Jesse Hilles. The others are Steve Elkins, Mr. Olmstead, Mary Latrobe, Dan Dull, Mary Linn and Don Haldeman.

Making German favors: From left are Mr. Olmstead, Mary Latrobe, Mary Colket, Don Haldeman and Carrie Hilles.

Courtesy Omni Bedford Springs Resort.

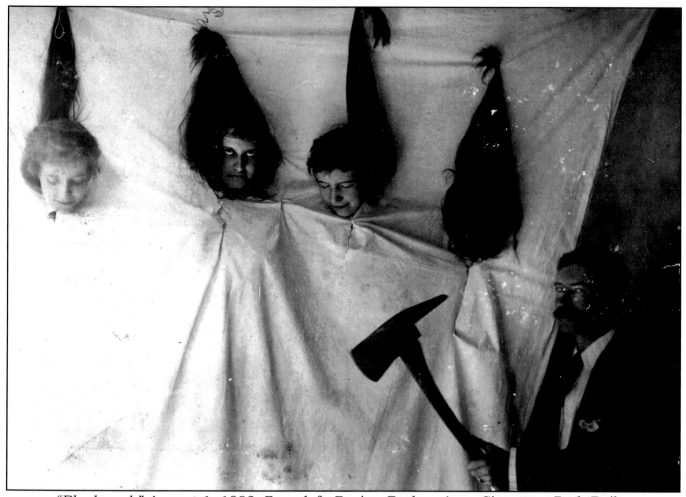

"Bluebeard," August 1, 1892. From left, Regina Barber, Anne Simonton, Ruth Bailey and Anne Barber; with the axe is Mr. Olmstead, a chaperone at the Springs.
Courtesy Omni Bedford Springs Resort.

husband.

After his death, the first three books and the unfinished fourth were combined and published in one large volume in 1950 which was titled, "City in the Dawn." The fifth book, to be called "Richfield Springs," was never started.

Much credit is given to Hervey Allen for his role in popularizing the early history of Bedford. In his day he was one of the most popular guests to stay at Bedford Springs.

It seemed like the good times would last forever, driven by consumer spending and easy credit. Throughout the 1920s the Federal Reserve expanded credit, by setting below-market interest rates and low reserve requirements that favored big banks, and the money supply increased. The phrase "buying on margin" entered the American vocabulary at this time as more and more Americans over-extended themselves, borrowing money to take advantage of the soaring stock market.

In 1929 Federal Reserve officials realized that they could not sustain the current policy of easy credit and started to raise interest rates. Stock prices had been wildly erratic since September. On October 29, also known as Black Tuesday, stock prices on Wall Street collapsed. This was the beginning of the Great Depression.

That same week, on November 1, 1929 Bedford County's largest employer, the Colonial Iron Company's iron furnace at Riddlesburg in the Broad Top went out of blast, putting 350 men out of work. Like the economic downturn itself, many thought the iron works would be closed for only a short time, but the iron furnace did not resume operation for nearly a decade (May, 1937).

The Bancroft years - 117

Under the presidency of Herbert Hoover, construction of new homes declined rapidly, automobile sales fell, and since car assembly plants were a major buyer of iron and steel, many mills closed. Consumer spending declined and business inventories went up. By 1932 industrial production in the United States was half of what it was in 1929. By 1933, 11,000 banks had failed and the jobless rate had reached 25 percent.

The Great Depression was especially difficult for the management of the Bedford Mineral Springs. Joseph Bancroft, who remained on the Bedford Springs board of directors through the 1930s, found himself in the unenviable position of guiding both the Huntingdon & Broad Top Railroad and the Hotel through hard times. What today is known as the travel industry was especially hard hit. Both routine maintenance and additional improvements were delayed because of a decrease in revenue. According to Bancroft, "Due to the decrease in revenue, expenditures of considerable amount, which under ordinary conditions should have been made, have had to be postponed."

In 1930 the railroad eliminated two passenger trains daily, primarily due to the falling off in passenger travel. The number of passengers carried in 1930 was 28,268, a decrease of 32,582 from 1929. But the transit company bus lines carried 39,260 passengers in 1930, an increase of 6,678 and earned the railroad a small profit.

Bancroft stepped down as President of the railroad company on September 1, 1934, and was made chairman of the board of directors. He would no longer be engaged in the day to day operation of the railroad.

It is known that at one point, the Hartley National Bank of Bedford was holding the Springs property for $75,000.

It is not known when the Florida East Coast Hotel Company became associated with the Bedford Springs. For several decades the Hotel Ormond was considered the sister hotel to the Bedford Springs.

The company was founded by Henry M. Flagler, who made his fortune as a partner with John D. Rockefeller in Standard Oil Company. He turned his attention to developing the Florida east coast as a resort area, after spending the winter there in 1876 on advice of physicians for treatment of his ailing wife. He constructed his first hotel, in St. Augustine, in 1885. It opened in 1888 with 540 rooms.

The Royal Poinciana in Palm Beach was one of Flagler's best known hotels, as was the Hotel

On the porch of the Anderson House, August, 1895. From left, back row, are Miss DeValesco, Mr. Milliken and Stephen B. Elkins, founder of Elkins, West Virginia; and in front, Stephen B. Elkins, Jr. and Bessie Baccus.

Ormond, which was built in 1888 and purchased by Flagler in 1890.

The Florida East Coast Hotel Company continued to operate after Flagler's death in 1913 and was also known as the Flagler System. The Royal Poinciana was badly damaged by a hurricane in 1928 and restored, only to become a victim of the Great Depression when Victorian hotels were going out of style. It was torn down in 1934.

An analysis of the water at the various springs at Bedford, dated September 30, 1905 by chemist Henry Leffman, is addressed to H. E. Bemis, Manager, Bedford Springs, PA.

Since Mr. Bemis was associated with the Flagler System for many years, this raises the likelihood that the Florida East Coast Hotel Company was managing the Bedford Springs Hotel as early as 1905.

In the 1920s, even prior to construction of the Barclay Building, Bemis was vice-president of the Florida East Coast Company (Flagler System) and the Bedford Springs Company, and also manager of the Royal Poinciana, while L. R. Johnson was manager of both the Bedford Springs and the Hotel Ormond. It appears that Joseph Bancroft was president of the Bedford Springs Company and that the Flagler interests owned stock in the Bedford Springs.

There is an undated brochure in the files of the Bedford County Historical Society, titled "Conventions at Bedford Springs Hotel, Bedford, PA." On the reverse panel, the Bedford Springs' affiliated hotels are listed. The Hotel Ormond is listed as the "Sister Hotel," while Royal Poinciana and Whitehall in Palm Beach, Hotel Ormond in Ormond Beach, and The Berkshire in New York City are named as associated hotels. This dates the brochure prior to 1934, when the Royal Poinciana was dismantled. L. R. Johnson is named as the manager at Bedford.

During the winter season, when Bedford closed, many of the staff members including chefs, chef's helpers, managers, and bellhops went south and worked at the Hotel Ormond until spring, when they returned to Bedford. This allowed them to be employed year-round.

The brochure proclaims the Bedford Springs Hotel to be "An ideal meeting place for all bodies, large and small, with every facility for business and pleasure." It continued, "Two large meeting halls, located in the hotel, will comfortably care for 500 to 600 people, at one sitting. Dining room facilities are ample to take care of the same number,"

The Bedford Springs, it said, offered "accommodations for approxi-

Foot bridge near the Old Mill, July, 1895. Young Joseph Bancroft is seated on the bridge; third from left is Carrie Hilles. Note the hose that ran from the limestone spring to the nearby bottling plant.

mately 500 guests, largely with private baths ... under one roof." ... "Unlimited facilities for entertainment are offered, with the decided advantage of having the gathering under one roof, and not scattered as they would be in a city with its counter attractions.

"A most excellent 18 hole golf course is available directly at the hotel. Two double tennis courts are also provided. Largest enclosed swimming pool of any resort hotel in the state is constantly available. Special out-door dancing parties on warm evenings on a first class platform, beautifully lighted and decorated. Saddle horses, good music, finest of food and service may be had."

The fee schedule is also interesting. "Rates are All American Plan. Single room, without bath - $7.00 per day, one person. Double room, without bath - $6.00 per day each person. Double room, exclusive use of private bath - $9.00 per day each person. Suites of two rooms with private bath to accommodate three or more persons - $8.00 per day each person."

Even during the Great Depression the Bedford Springs could boast about hosting a large number of conventions, among them, Pennsylvania Electric Association, Pennsylvania Bar Association, Pennsylvania Bakers' Association, 315 Infantry Officers' Association, Pennsylvania Confectioners' Association, National Freight Traffic Golf Association, Homeopathic Medical Society of Pennsylvania, National Tube Company Golf Association, Carnegie Steel Company Golf Association, New York Life Insurance Company, Pennsylvania Daughters of American Revolution, Pennsylvania Refractories Association, Pennsylvania Pharmaceutical Association, and others.

The Hotel Ormond was operated in conjunction with Bedford Springs until the Bedford property was sold. At the outbreak of World War II, some Pittsburgh investors bought the Bedford Springs. Hotel Ormond was finally demolished in 1992, despite its status as a National Historic Landmark.

Some believe the Florida interests were using the Bedford Springs as a tax write-off.

In a scrapbook given to Bill Defibaugh, a four page brochure offering the Bedford Springs for sale was discovered. The brochure is undated, but it appears to date to 1929 or 1930. The brochure is reproduced in this book.

A search of deeds in the Bedford County Courthouse failed to turn up any evidence that the hotel was sold. Since the property did change hands several times through 1945, it must have taken place through the sale of stock in the Bedford Springs Company, making it difficult to trace.

Leap Year German, in the Ballroom, July 20, 1896.
Courtesy Omni Bedford Springs Resort.

*Miss Weiss' Morning German at the Sulphur Spring Pavilion, 1895.
Courtesy Omni Bedford Springs Resort.*

Even during the hard times, the Bedford Springs remained open each year for the summer season, and that gives testimony to the popularity of the place.

Despite the Great Depression, America's love affair with the automobile was growing and could not be stopped, even though fewer Americans could afford new cars. Out of the Great Depression was born America's first four-lane limited access highway. It passed through Bedford and like the Lincoln Highway that preceded it, the new road would make it easier for the traveling public to reach the Bedford Springs. Autos were in fashion; rail passenger service was out.

As part of President Roosevelt's federal job creation programs, the Pennsylvania State Planning Agency was instructed to propose projects that could lower unemployment through public works.

In 1934 planning board member Victor Leqoc, William Sutherland of the Pennsylvania Motor Truck Association, and newly elected State Representative Cliff S. Patterson were discussing the idea of turning the old South Penn Railroad roadbed and tunnels into a toll highway, hoping to get a share of the Roosevelt administration public works funding.

Patterson felt that the Lincoln Highway was hazardous, since he drove it from his home in Monongahela to Harrisburg on a regular basis. It was icy in winter, foggy in summer, and steep all year long. A new toll road could correct these problems, Patterson believed. A federal planning grant was awarded January 27, 1936, and soon survey crews poured into the mountains and valleys to document the old South Penn right-of-way and to make recommended changes in the route.

The Pennsylvania Turnpike Commission was formed the following year, but the actual construction depended on federal financing. Roosevelt agreed to provide $25 million; he was convinced of the strategic military value of the

The Bancroft years - 121

new road for the movement of troops and supplies. After all, war clouds were gathering in Europe. Final approval of financing came from Washington on October 10, 1938.

It took two years to complete the original toll road from Carlisle to Irwin (It was later extended to Philadelphia on the east, and Ohio on the west). The details surrounding this massive construction project can be found in *The Pennsylvania Turnpike* by Dan Cupper, 1990. Opening day, October 1, 1940 created a huge traffic jam as throngs of excited motorists tried to be the first to use the new super highway.

Bedford County had two Turnpike interchanges, Bedford and Breezewood, which soon sprouted motels, gas stations, restaurants and long-haul trucking terminals. At Bedford, two service plazas were constructed so that motorists did not have to exit the Pike to get fuel and meals.

An early promotional map of the Pennsylvania Turnpike depicts several Bedford area attractions with the Bedford Springs prominently displayed. The Turnpike wanted to cater to the traveling public. The travel industry was changing. Now the average family could drive to parks, museums, resorts, amusement parks and roadside attractions. Summer vacations were no longer the sole privilege of the rich and famous.

From the day the Turnpike opened, newspaper headlines were filled with reports of war. World War II had a profound negative impact on the travel industry, including the Bedford Springs. In December 1941, a 35 mile an hour speed limit was imposed nationwide. Gasoline and tires were rationed. Repair parts for vehicles became hard to find.

Despite the many hardships caused by the war, Bedford Springs did play a role in the war effort.

Three Pennsylvania governors and their wives, from left, James A. Beaver, Martin Grove Brumbaugh and Samuel W. Pennypacker.
Courtesy of Omni Bedford Springs Resort.

BEDFORD SPRINGS GOLF COURSE FROM NEW BUILDINGS

BEDFORD SPRINGS COMPANY
Offer for Sale the
Bedford Springs Hotel and Estate of 3600 Acres
Located at BEDFORD, PENNSYLVANIA

HE PROPERTY of the Bedford Springs Company, approximating thirty-six hundred acres, about six hundred acres being cleared and developed and the balance in valuable timber, is located among the foothills of the Alleghany Mountains at an elevation of approximately eleven hundred feet above sea level. Bisecting the estate, and facing directly upon the entire front of the Hotel Buildings, is the Horeshoe Trail, a wide concrete highway, completed in 1926, reaching to Cumberland, Maryland, connecting with National Highway to Washington, Pittsburgh and Shenandoah Valley to the south, and Altoona, Pennsylvania, to the North. This trail crosses the Lincoln Highway at Bedford Village, one and one-half miles from Bedford Springs Hotel, giving the very best of highways west to Pittsburgh, 104 miles, and equally good roads to every point east to the Atlantic Seaboard. At Bedford village the Pennsylvania railroad gives direct rail connection via Altoona, with main line of Pennsylvania Railroad to all points on its system and to Cumberland where the Baltimore and Ohio Railroad is reached. The Huntington and Broadtop Mountain Railway, also with terminus at Bedford, gives additional rail facilities.

Climate The altitude gives, winter and summer, pure, bracing air. In the summer one may always sleep under a blanket, and the days are never uncomfortably warm. In the early Autumn, with the forests taking on their color, no place is more beautiful. Later, with cooler days, the air becomes more bracing, and one would indeed be hopelessly ill who did not benefit with the mountain walks, the bridle paths, and the cheery fire on the hearth.

The Springs Throughout the estate are innumerable flowing springs, the purest water from many, and others highly mineralized and of inestimable value in treatment of Gout, Chronic Rheumatism, Diabetes, Kidney and Bladder troubles, Obesity, and reducing blood pressure. Physicians of note, both in this country and abroad agree that in every particular the waters of Bedford Springs are

The Bancroft years - 123

The CARLSBAD of AMERICA

LOOKING 1

Bedford Springs Estate Comprises 3600 Acr
Springs Hotel and Hotel Farms, a
Famous Bedford Min

the equal of Carlsbad and of the ather noted Spas of Europe. Principal among the springs is one known as the Magnesia Spring, famous for more than two hundred years for its curative qualities. Its waters flow from a cleft in the rock at a temperature of 52° summer and winter, are radio active, and constantly sought after by the leading druggists and physicians throughout the east. The water is carried through a system of pipes to the large bottling plant a few hundred yards distant, where it is bottled as it runs from the spring. With suitable handling and publicity, this water would take lead over any medicinal water known. The Sweet Spring is famous for its purity, and its waters are bottled and shipped extensively, being especially popular as a table water at Palm Beach and Ormond Beach. The Black Spring flows copiously, furnishing abundant supply of the purest of water for hotel uses, under natural pressure and for the ice supply. Several Iron Springs and a sulphur spring are valued members of the curative family. The Limestone spring flows in sufficient volume to furnish ample water supply for a city of one hundred thousand people. Analysis are available for all springs.

BEDFORD SPRINGS HOTE

The Forest A survey, by unquestioned authority, shows approximately ten million feet of merchantable white oak, much of which can be removed without seriously changing the grandeur of the mountain views from the hotel. At the time the survey was made, July, 1927, it was estimated that at prevailing price of labor, this timber could be felled and sawed on the ground at a cost of about $10.00 per M. Every part of the forest is accessible for easy and inexpensive lumbering. The operation would provide fuel for hotel boilers for years, and mine props and ties would produce excellent revenue from small growth.

The Farms Much cleared acreage provides ample staple products for general use, potatoes, corn, hay and all vegetables. There are five dwellings, conveniently located at different points on the estate, and suitable for farmers occupancy.

The barns, stables, ice houses, etc., are amp repairs to place in the best of shape.

The Hotel Bedford Springs Hotel has jus cessful season. Its history ext its register appear the names ander Hamilton, Daniel Webster and man original hotel is still standing, thoroughly columns in rotunda and dining room, larg baths, and balconies overlooking the wond concrete building, the first section of a prop furnished and opened for the summer seas fortable accommodations for more than fo rooms having private baths. At comparati other 100 rooms. One of the finest hotel new, fully equipped with modern machine

---

This property is offered for sale in its entirety to responsible parties financially able to qualify

MR. JOSEPH BANCROFT
Rockford, Wilmington, Delaware

MR. H. E. BEMIS
Vice President, Florida East Coast Hotel Co., (Flagler System)
Royal Poinciana, Palm Beach, Florida

G TOWARD HOTEL

HUNDRED
miles
from
PITTSBURGH

cres of Mountain and Timber Lands, the Bedford
and Eighteen Hole Golf Course, and the
ineral Springs and Baths.

OTEL FACADE AND GROUNDS

mple for the large estate, and require only minor

just completed its one hundred and eleventh suc-
extends back to the early days of America. On
mes of Benjamin Franklin, Henry Clay, Alex-
any of their contemporaries. A portion of the
ly modernized, large airy space, beautiful white
arge rooms with open fireplaces, spacious private
onderful lawns and grounds. A new stone and
roposed large extension was completed, beautifully
eason of 1925. The hotel has ample and com-
four hundred and fifty guests, a majority of the
ratively small cost this could be increased by an-
tel kitchens, of any resort hotel is comparatively
inery, refrigeration and all facilities. An ample

and complete department for the care of the help is provided. The plant is completely equipped with electric lights, power, etc. Current is available from a central generating plant, and the cost for even so large an operation is inconsequental. All refrigerating machinery, the two elevators in the hotel, the large and fully equipped laundry, pumps, etc., are motor driven. Steam for heating purposes and hot water, kitchen and laundry use is generated by two boilers, which are in excellent condition. Fuel is low in price, being practically at the mines.

The public rooms are especially attractive, all finished in white, with green carpets. The lobby is spacious, well furnished, and has two large fireplaces. Winding stair cases, meeting on a balcony overlooking the main lobby, approach the main dining room, a room unequalled for light and air, and the beauty of its white pillars, polished oak floor and lighting effect is most unusual. Smaller dining rooms are provided for needs. The ball rooms, of which there are two, are large, have beautiful floors, and each a stage, and are sufficient to accommodate nearly a thousand people. For conventions and other gatherings they are eminently adapted. Writing rooms, ladies wear shops, formal parlors, hair dressing and beauty shops, barber shop, telegraph office, telephone booths, and all requirements are met.

The enclosed tile swimming pool is the finest in the state. Flowing spring water, properly heated, serves to provide unusually sanitary conditions. A sun parlor, with ample dressing rooms is provided. In the pool building, which is a part of the main hotel building, are the medical baths, the House Physician's office, and all equipment for the treatments made possible at Bedford Springs by the medicinal waters. The department was rebuilt in 1927 and is eminently adapted for the purpose.

The Grounds   The grounds immediately adjoining the hotel buildings are most attractive. Many acres of lawns, over which tower massive trees of many varieties, shrubbery, flower beds and running vines, give a vista from

ify for its purchase and all desired information may be obtained by addressing any of the following:

MR. MARTIN SWEENY
Managing Director, The Berkshire, Madison Avenue at 52nd Street, New York, or care Whitehall, Palm Beach, Florida.

MR. L. R. JOHNSTON
Manager, Florida East Coast Hotel Co., (Flagler System) Hotel Ormond, Ormond Beach, Florida.

the innumerable balconies of the hotel that is unique. Years of care and labor, and the preservation of trees hundreds of years old, have made possible this surrounding.

Golf An eighteen hole golf course, in perfect condition, of more than six thousand yards, is provided. It is topographically one of the most beautiful courses in the state, and years of continued expenditure of large sums have resulted in a course whose merit is quickly apparent to not only the good golfer but to the construction engineer of present-day standards of the best courses. A modern, commodious club house, fully and beautifully equipped and furnished provides for every need of lady or gentleman golfer. The club house, first tee and eighteenth green are only a few yards from the main house.

Tennis Two standard tennis courts were laid down in the spring of 1926, and are of championship construction. Located on rising ground, a few yards from the club house, with excellent view from the club verandas, showers, lockers and all facilities are at hand.

Riding Saddle horses are available, riding being a most attractive feature for patrons.

Motorists A most important part of the business of the hotel, are well provided for. Ample parking space within the hotel grounds. Garage accommodations for over fifty cars, individual locked compartments for each car owner. Facilities are provided for washing, gas and oil.

Owners Residence Located directly adjoining the main building, with a fine view, is the owners residence, a finely constructed building with ample room, baths, heat, fireplaces, a wide veranda, and all facilities for comfortable summer or all year residence.

The Bedford Springs property, with the passing of the owner some years ago, and the extensive and varied interests of those at present controlling it, is offered for sale. It is particularly desired to call attention to the unusual opportunity to acquire a property so well adapted for development along many lines. For a recreation place for any large industrial corporation; for a school; for a sanitarium; a large railroad company, to whom the lumber alone would be a valuable asset for many years to come, in addition to the facilities provided for the care and recreation of their employees; to any city which wishes to co-operate with those looking to the welfare of its people, and would provide a place for its people to recuperate; to any one who wishes to embrace the great opportunity of establishing a health resort that would rival any in Europe, with proper expenditure for publicity and propaganda for the waters. In no other way could one be a benefactor to such a degree or to so many persons who at middle age are not in the best of health, as in the development and use of the waters and the cure at Bedford Springs.

The owners solicit inquiry from any responsible parties who may be interested, and to those financially able to qualify for the purchase of the property in its entirety, will be given all desired information and every facility for inspection.

Any one of the following may be addressed:

MR. JOSEPH BANCROFT,
Wilmington, Delaware.

MR. H. E. BEMIS,
Vice Pres., Florida East Coast Hotel Co., (Flagler System), Royal Poinciana, Palm Beach Florida

MR. MARTIN SWEENY,
Managing Director, The Berkshire, Madison Avenue at 52nd Street, New York, or Care Whitehall, Palm Beach, Florida.

MR. L. R. JOHNSTON,
Manager, Florida East Coast Hotel Co., (Flagler System), Hotel Ormond, Ormond Beach, Florida.

The region's other mineral spring resorts

The Bedford Mineral Springs is the sole survivor of a vanishing breed of once-popular mineral springs resorts in Central Pennsylvania. Spas were once extremely popular, but gradually lost favor when the public began to seek pleasure and entertainment in addition to a cure. Other spas lost their appeal because they were simply difficult to reach in the days when most people traveled by stagecoach.

One such spa, called Warm Springs, was located five miles west of Huntingdon.

What Bedford and Warm Springs have in common is that they were both visited by native Americans long before the white settlers arrived. Huntingdon County historian Albert M. Rung wrote that the Indians once came to Warm Springs from great distances and regarded the springs as having healing powers. "Early Virginia settlers are believed to have learned of the springs from the Indians and were possibly the first white people to make a pilgrimage to the locality."

The Warm Springs were being visited regularly by invalids before 1770, but the first written account of them was made by the Rev. Philip Fithian and recorded in his diary. He arrived at Huntingdon August 21, 1775, where he spent the night. He was determined to pay a visit to the springs, having heard of the ancient resort, and the visit he called a "life long ambition."

The next day he rode a horse to the springs along a path through the woods about four miles, and arrived safety despite apprehensions that there were hostile Indians in the region. The springs are located in Standing Stone Valley.

In his diary, he wrote, "The water rises boiling up with sand and much air in bubbles in a piece of land which is almost level. There is a small descent of a few feet from the highest part of neighboring land to the place of the water rising; and below is a watery flat covered with marsh flowers ... The water rises up in nearly equal quantities in two places about three perches distant. One is used by the invalids for drinking; the other for bathing. They both stand as great nature formed them edged with moss and overhung with boughs....They have also scooped out the bath into a kind of hollow basin about six feet long and four feet wide. The water is quite clear, without any floating scum whatever. The bottom is covered by a white sand and small gravel, which makes the place

The region's other mineral spring resorts - 127

in bare appearance desirable."

The springs at the time of Fithian's visit lacked improvements. He continued, "They must carry all of their provisions and supplies themselves; they live in low cabins built with slabs and boughs, and cook their dinners all at one great common fire; the men for exercise play at quoits, hunt deer, turkeys and pheasants; with their hardships, however, they live in friendship."

Prior to 1800 someone constructed a tavern at the Warm Springs, which provided lodging and meals. It is not known who built the first permanent structure, but in 1807 John Fee owned the Warm Springs Farm and advertised the farm for rent.

On June 27, 1811 Israel Evans placed an ad in the *Huntingdon Gazette* announcing that he has leased the Warm Springs Tavern, and "he has put the old Bath House in a complete state of repair, and intends immediately to erect a new one, for the accommodation of those who may be disposed to attend the Springs..."

Another newspaper advertisement dated March 7, 1816 announced that James McCullach had rented the Warm Springs Tavern.

Sometime in the 1820s (again the exact date is unrecorded) someone erected a two-story frame hotel building on the site and made additional improvements to the spa.

Joseph Forrest, proprietor of the hotel, placed a lengthy notice in the newspaper on February 11, 1844, in which he made a number of comparisons between his spa and the Bedford Mineral Springs. He noted that the hotel is open for the reception of visitors, "where every accommodation can be had by persons in search of health through the use of the waters, or of a retired and pleasant retreat during the hot weather."

He makes it clear that the qualities of these waters were known long before the discovery of the Bedford Springs, which they somewhat resemble. He gives the temperature of the water as 64 degrees, 14 degrees higher than that of any other spring water in the vicinity, as well as citing a medical testimony to the water that was written in 1810.

Historian Rung stated that, from the 1840s through the Civil War, there was a gradual decline in the popular Huntingdon resort, "by reason of Bedford's convenient situation along the greatest traveled highway leading from the East across the Alleghenies." Sporadic attempts were made to revive the popularity of the Warm Springs, but all were unsuccessful.

Then came construction of the Pennsylvania Railroad through Huntingdon, and a new age of prosperity came to Huntingdon County. In 1854 J. Edgar Thomson, chief engineer of the PRR purchased a long strip of land west of Huntingdon for $29,000. There was much speculation as to what Thomson intended to do with this property. But the Civil War came and went, and the land remained idle.

Prior to the war Col. William Dorris of Huntingdon purchased Warm Springs, which was then in operation only sporadically. Shortly after the war concluded, Col. Dorris was contacted by officials of the Pennsylvania Railroad, informing him of their intention to buy his entire tract at Warm Springs, and to have the necessary papers drawn up.

Dorris was on his way to the Courthouse in Huntingdon to fulfill the request, but met an old friend along the way, A. Porter Wilson, an attorney. He told Wilson about his mission, but Wilson answered, "Why, Colonel, you promised to sell the Warm Springs to me if it was ever decided to make disposal of the property."

Dorris could not recall having made such a promise, but thought he might have forgotten about it. So he notified the PRR of his forgotten promise and sold the land to Wilson.

After the purchase was concluded Wilson informed the railroad that he would sell the property to them, but demanded an exorbitant price, which was refused.

Shortly afterwards, the PRR purchased land at Cresson, where the Cresson Springs Resort was later constructed. In its day, Cresson Springs was extremely popular and was regularly patronized by such captains of industry as Andrew Carnegie.

Had Dorris not met Wilson that fateful day, the PRR would have purchased the Warm Springs and may have developed a spa that would have rivaled Bedford Mineral Springs, but fate intervened.

Warm Springs remained in operation for a few years, but 1875 was probably the last year that the hotel was open.

Cresson Springs, once a rival to Bedford Springs, began as a small health institute near the railroad "wye" at Hollidaysburg. It was founded by Dr. Robert Montgomery Smith Jackson, who like Dr. John Anderson of Bedford Springs fame was a man of many interests.

In order to take advantage of what he believed were the healing properties of the mountain environment and springs, he moved to Cambria County in 1846, first residing at Summit. Construction of the Pennsylvania Railroad main line gave birth to the town of Cresson where mineral springs were situated, and he moved there. He incorporated the Allegheny Mountain Health Institute April 29, 1854 and his original Mountain House at Hollidaysburg was dismantled and moved to the grounds of Cresson Springs.

Additions were made to the main Mountain House building, and when completed, it had 89 rooms. The PRR erected a station across from the resort.

Dr. Jackson, while at Cresson, also served as Postmaster and also engaged in the manufacture of fire brick.

In 1861, 32 leased lots around the Mountain House were made available for the construction of cottages.

During the Civil War Dr. Jackson was a surgeon in the 3rd Pennsylvania Regiment, and when the war ended the Pennsylvania Railroad invested heavily in the Mountain House, which was renamed Cresson Springs Resort and owned by the Cresson Springs Company.

The beautiful scenery, cool mountain air, and springs were popular with city dwellers and industrialists, especially from Pittsburgh. One of the cottages, called Braemar, was built by Andrew Carnegie as a summer residence. In his autobiography he spoke of "our cottage at Cresson Springs on top of the Alleghenies where my mother and I spent our summers." In 2009 efforts were being made to restore this cottage.

Some historians believe this particular cottage was built for Benjamin F. Jones, a founder of the Jones & Laughlin Steel Company.

In 1880-81 a new hotel was built that could accommodate 600 guests. The grounds of the Mountain House boasted many walking paths. Spring houses were located along the paths so that patrons could enjoy a refreshing drink of the pure mountain spring water.

Golf tournaments were being held at Cresson a few years before the original Bedford Springs golf course was constructed.

Unlike Bedford Springs, Cresson was in decline not long after the new hotel was built, and in the early 1900s it was used as a sanitarium for patients with tuberculosis. A new sanitarium was constructed by the Commonwealth of Pennsylvania at Cresson in 1912, and in 1916 the hotel was razed.

Two other mineral spring resorts were located near Bedford. One was called Chalybeate Spring, the other White Sulfur Spring.

The ballroom at Chalybeate Spring, as it appears today. Photo by Jon Baughman.

Chalybeate, an iron spring, is located just north of the Pennsylvania Turnpike, north-east of Bedford. In addition to the iron spring, there are two other springs on this property, one sweet and another a limestone spring.

The site was originally called Funk Springs, after George Funk, who acquired the land from the Penn Heirs. In 1786 Funk built a house in which he operated a tavern. Funk's Tavern was gradually expanded into the main building at this resort. The bricks for the additions were made on the property.

As early as 1825, curative powers were ascribed to the waters on this property, especially the iron or chalybeate spring. As was the case with Bedford Springs, valetudinarians began to flock here in search of various cures.

By June, 1867 a new wing had been added to the tavern, and it was being operated as a summer resort by H. M. Chenowith. That year, 44 people registered as guests. After Chenowith took over the hotel, business increased every year and included some very notable guests. Among these were Horace Greeley, 1875; President James G. Garfield, 1878; President Rutherford B. Hayes, Henry Ward Beecher and Robert Ingersoll, 1880; and in 1882, Leo Isenthal, his wife, 12 children and three nurses, stayed at the hotel.

G. H. Dauler of Pittsburgh purchased the resort in 1885; the purchase included 250 acres of land. He made a number of improvements to the property including a large building containing a dining room, dishwashing room, kitchen, and children's dining room, as well as several guest rooms. It was completed in 1887. Then in 1903, a large ballroom was constructed. It was used both as an annex and ballroom. By this time, there were also a billiard room and a card room in the main building, a bath house, an ice house, and an ironing house where laundry was done. The latter had a huge fireplace used for making apple butter. There was also a large barn where hay and grain were stored, and where horses drawing the carriages that met trains bringing guests to the hotel were stabled.

At the turn of the century, the guests included President Benjamin Harrison, accompanied by Jay Gould (1890) and also Mr. and Mrs. William K. Vanderbilt and Little Willie, Mr. and Mrs. Jay Gould, and Mr. Alfred Vanderbilt and Maid.

In "The Kernel of Greatness (1971)" Mr. Dauler recalled "seeing card games running for three and four days, with stakes as high as five and ten thousand dollars. Playboy gamblers would spend a month at the hotel, bringing their own cases of liquor and storing them in the wine cellar. The parlor was used by the elite for entertaining or creating an impression. European violinists or pianists on tour in New York or Philadelphia were often brought here to play recitals in the parlor for a few select friends of the entertaining guests."

In 1898 his son, George H. Dauler, Jr. assumed ownership of Chalybeate Springs. It was reported that "While Bedford Springs was the more fashionable resort, Chalybeate Springs was more the family resort, with many coming year after year and spending entire summers there. In one instance of a family from St. Louis, the "Lady" came on April 1 by train. Her carriage and maids, hand-servants, and governesses arrived by May 1 and remained until November 1. They were regular guests every year from 1889 through 1903."

There was a salve made from the sediment of the Chalybeate Spring, which was quite popular, and at one time the water was barreled and shipped all over the country.

Blackburn's "History of Bedford County" (1906) reports, "Mr. J. Harper Hafer, one of the proprietors of the Bedford House, and whose father at one time owned and conducted the Chalybeate Springs, is the manufacturer of the Celebrated Chalybeate Cure, or Iron Salve, which is compounded by the sediment thrown out by the spring with other healing ingredients, which is now having a large and well deserved sale. Its curative powers as a skin medicine are attested by many leading physicians who have been using it in general practice."

The Daulers closed the hotel for the last time in June, 1913. The hotel, with all its furniture and curtains intact, remained untouched for 35 years, although the Daulers continued to live in one of the buildings. In the summers at least through the 1920s some families continued to stay here, on the basis that they were willing to do their own work.

A contractor purchased the property in 1947 and over the next five years, the buildings were converted into 13 apartments without altering the 19th century architecture. They are still standing and in use today.

White Sulphur Springs is located west of Bedford in a narrow valley called Milligan's Cove. Once a popular resort, it has found new life as the home of the Officers Christian Fellowship, an organization of more than 15,000 members.

During its heyday the resort property consisted of 650 acres in two separate tracts. The older parcel of 58 acres was purchased by Peter Wertz in 1844, and the second by Samuel M. Barclay and William Lyons in 1847.

A log inn or tavern existed on the Wertz property and served as a stopping place for drovers using the Packers' Trail, close to the crest of Wills Mountain. Later, when the Sulphur Spring became popular, the old tavern was remodeled to accommodate visitors coming to "take the waters." Michael Lutz purchased this property in 1857. Following a series of deed transfers, Michael Colvin bought the log inn about 1921. However it remained separate from the main resort complex for many years.

The present White Sulphur Springs Hotel opened in 1887 at the site of the spring by John P. Reed and George M. Lyon, and operated under the name Reed & Lyon. The main hotel building, of two stories, was enlarged with the addition of a third floor in 1894, and could accommodate about 125 guests. Ross and Michael Colvin were the managers.

The popularity of the summer resort was due, in part, by the opening of the Bedford & Bridgeport Railroad connecting Bedford and Cumberland, Md in 1874. After the main hotel building was completed the railroad established a Sulphur Springs station for the convenience of hotel guests, who were brought by carriage to the resort.

The hotel, during its golden years, offered the mineral spring cure, as well as carriage rides, bowling, tennis, teas, dinners, and parties, and most likely, gambling and billiards.

The Colvin Brothers purchased the resort in

White Sulphur Spring pavilion.
Courtesy of Bedford Gazette.

1894 and erected a large frame house near the hotel, which served as their private residence.

World War I and the recession that followed the end of the conflict brought a decline in the resort hotel business, and White Sulphur Springs was no exception. It is said that, going into the 1920s, Michael Colvin, then the sole owner, found it difficult to make a profit. After the Great Depression began, this became almost impossible. It closed in 1941.

In 1946 a Chicago businessman, Paul Cochran purchased the property. He believed that the old hotel still had a future, and was willing to restore the property to its former greatness. According to "The Kernel of Greatness," he and his wife "made extensive changes and additions. They reconstructed the interior, adding heating for the winter months; they excavated a basement, making space for a recreation room, together with utility and storage space. Wells were drilled, one an artesian flow, to provide an adequate domestic water supply. Pools were built, one for swimming, the other for fishing. Hiking and riding trails were cleared and extended. At the hotel itself, wide porches provided rocking chairs and settees for lazy summer visitors. The white sulphur spring was walled in, and its pavilion was rebuilt."

The original two-story hotel at White Sulphur Springs.

million. Under the proposal, Harrison House will be converted into a working museum, a teahouse, a place to house summer staff, and for small group meetings.

Nearby, a modern 54,000 sq. ft. lodge and conference center will be constructed. It will have 50 guest rooms, a meeting room to accommodate 220 people, which will showcase modern technology and will be energy efficient. It will be called Heritage House. The property now has more than 1,000 acres.

The Cochrans had given the old resort a new lease on life. The resort catered to honeymooning couples, served fine meals, catered private parties, and hosted small conventions. It remained open both summer and winter.

The Officers Christian Fellowship was founded during World War II to bind together Christian officers, and to help all ranks, grades and ratings -- all men and women of the armed services -- to come to a knowledge of Jesus Christ. The group's oldest retreat was established at Spring Canyon, Engelwood, Colorado.

In the 1970s OCF was looking for a facility that was closer to Washington, D.C. and found out about White Sulphur Springs. In 1978 it was purchased from Chicago industrialist Paul Cochran to provide military men and women and their families a place where they can ease the strain of military life.

The three-story hotel was renamed Harrison House and could house about 60 people at a time. There were 32 guest rooms, a kitchen, a vintage, 100-year-old bowling alley, a dining room that seated 100 persons, and a meeting room that also seated about 100.

Despite improvements, not all of the guest rooms had private baths, and much of the wiring was out of date.

So in 2008, OCF launched a three-phase campaign to expand the facility at White Sulphur Springs at an estimated cost of $8.5

White Sulphur Springs Hotel after a third floor was added. Both photos, Bedford Gazette.

132 - The Bedford Springs Resort

Bedford Springs during World War II

When Stanley G. Stroup came to Bedford to teach English and history at Bedford High School, the Bedford Mineral Springs was in its glory. Stroup taught here from 1925 through 1927, when he moved to Sewickley, near Pittsburgh.

When he left Bedford, little did he realize that he would return 15 years later under much different circumstances, and that the Bedford Springs Hotel would be the focal point of his new career.

Today, many Bedford residents fondly remember the brilliant Stroup as an attorney, member of the General Assembly (1954 to 1960) and State Senator (1960 to 1971), ably representing Bedford County and the 30th District in all affairs of government. Fewer residents can recall when Stroup, as president of the Keystone Schools threw his full energy in doing his part to crush the Axis powers during World War II -- a role that centered around the Bedford Springs.

Stroup was born at West End, Somerset County, grew up in Altoona, and graduated from Altoona High School. He attended Juniata College, where he was later recognized as a distinguished alumnus. He received advanced degrees from the University of Pennsylvania and University of Pittsburgh.

The annals of broadcasting proclaim that the pioneer radio station in the United States, KDKA in Pittsburgh, went on the air in 1923. One year later, the Keystone Radio Institute was chartered in Pittsburgh under the laws of the Commonwealth of Pennsylvania to train people in the budding new technology -- the second such school in the nation. The institute trained radio operators and engineers for 14 years, at which time it was reorganized as the Keystone Schools. The campus relocated to Pittsburgh's North Side.

In 1939, the year that Stanley G. Stroup became it's president, Keystone began to specialize in a radio airline training program. Its clients included Eastern Airlines, United Airlines, TWA and Pennsylvania Central Airlines.

The outbreak of World War II is generally dated to September 1 1939, with the German invasion of Poland. This invasion caused Britain and France to declare war on Germany, even though the United States did not enter the conflict until the Japanese attack on Pearl Harbor, December 7, 1941.

*Naval Training School graduating class, August 23, 1943.
Photos in this chapter courtesy Bedford Springs Historical Society.*

In 1939, sensing that radio communications would be vital to the war effort, the school's services were offered to the United States government. At this time, the school had 890 civilian students enrolled in a variety of courses.

Training of Army radio operators began at Pittsburgh after the war broke out. In the spring of 1941 the Radio department of Keystone Schools was awarded a contract from the U. S. Army Signal Corps to train 100 men.

Immediately following the attack on Pearl Harbor, the Keystone Schools began to negotiate with the Fourth Naval District to establish a naval training school in radio operating. In February, Stroup and Keystone Schools Secretary Thomas G. Moreland started looking for a facility that could house the school. They had run out of space in Pittsburgh, and Stroup, being familiar with Bedford County, knew where to look.

At that time the Bedford Springs was owned by Pittsburgh interests, thus it was easy to approach the owners about leasing the historic hotel. During the war, the resort business had dried up and the owners were more than interested. They agreed to lease the Bedford Springs property for the duration of the war.

The Colonial Building was hastily prepared to receive the first class, and on May 1, 1942, two hundred Navy men arrived in Bedford and comprised the first training class. Additional classes arrived each month. For the preceding 150 years of its history, the Bedford Mineral Springs was a summer resort, closing each year before cold weather set in. The Naval Training School operated year round. Not all sections of the Hotel were heated, but the Colonial Building and the other structures used by the Navy did have a central heating system. Heat was provided by two steam boilers that were located in the kitchen wing. Steam for heat, as

134 - The Bedford Springs Resort

well as hot water for kitchen, laundry and personal use, was supplied by this boiler plant.

The large dining room was lined with tables and on these were placed the sending and receiving sets on which the men were trained. The convention hall was divided (partitioned off) into four class rooms for theory and typing. The private dining room became the control room.

In the kitchen wing, a large cafeteria was established, capable of serving 500 men. The officers mess was in the old bar. A soda fountain and ice cream bar was also provided for the men. The second floor housed the school offices and the commandant's office, and the third floor, officer's quarters and rooms for visiting Naval officials.

Some other remodeling (called "construction" in the Naval Training Schools newsletters) took place. One photo shows the ground floor porches on the Colonial building and the Evitt building being enclosed using board siding; windows were also installed here.

Each training class took an intensive four-month course in radio transmission. But the stay at Bedford wasn't all work. The men also had an athletic department at Bedford Springs and Bedford High School which included touch football, basketball, baseball, and tennis teams which competed against each other, as well as boxing. There was also swimming in the summer at Lake Caledonia. The athletic department was in charge of Lt. John T. Kelley, Jr.

The recreation director was former Bedford High School football coach John A. Hubicsak who also provided volleyball, calisthenics and instruction in golf. Ping-pong and pool tables were also installed.

Each class, at the completion of their training, was honored with a graduation ceremony in which the Bedford High School Band participated.

Sailors relax at Bedford Springs: Front row, from left, Al Lavin, Thomas Lee, Joseph Lees and Edward McCarthy. Second row, Richard Lounder, Edward Locke, Johnny Rovenz, Charles Males, and Gene Leighton. Back row, Dick Massa, Edward Martin, John Klose, Howard Lamoreaux, John Mullen, Walter Manisto and Arthur Manchester, M.A.

Above, the cafeteria and serving line at the Naval Training School, Bedford Springs.

The snack bar.

For more than two years the school even had its own post office and also a newspaper, called "The Antenna." The final edition of the newspaper was issued on November 21, 1944.

As the war raged on, the Pittsburgh Army Signal Corps training center was unable to handle the demand, and a second Army Signal Corps Institute was opened in Hollidaysburg, PA by the Keystone Schools on September 1, 1942. It began serving as a Naval Training Facility on October 16, 1943 and from that time until it closed, Lt. Cmdr. C. B. Boocock, USNR was commanding officer of both the Bedford Springs and Hollidaysburg Naval Training schools. The school was located at Highland Hall, a former girls' school. It operated until the end of September, 1944.

By the time the Bedford Springs and Hollidaysburg schools closed, more than 7,000 Navy personnel had graduated from the program. The final class of what was fondly called the "Mountain Navy" at Bedford Springs graduated on December 20, 1944. The Bedford Springs became silent. But not for long.

The final edition of "The Antenna" proclaimed, "The Bedford School and the Hollidaysburg School, operated by the Keystone Schools, Inc. under the leadership of Mr. Stanley G. Stroup, have provided over 7,000 radiomen for the Navy, and reports from the navy sources agree that Bedford men have become excellent radiomen."

In a tribute to the men who attended the Bedford Springs school, instructor R. C. Kepplinger wrote, in part, "They all had a story to tell, but each with a different setting. One was a public accountant. He wanted to be a yeoman, but -- he graduated with a 22-22. Another came from a farm in the midwest, and he found the new surroundings strange. He wanted to leave school and go out and fight; said he had a brother lost in action. We convinced him he could avenge his brother in no better way than to do the job picked out for him in as proficient manner as possible. He graduated 23-25 and now adds RM (Radioman) 3/c after his name.

"I could go on and on, telling experience after experience of a stockbroker, a Brooklyn taxi-cab driver, a script writer for CBS, a musician who played with one of the country's best-named bands, or of a welder, a grocery clerk in a grocery store. But these men were not picked at random for my story. They were all in the original Company that started their radio training here at Bedford in May 1942. They didn't pick radio, but they all graduated and went out to do a job, and do it they did. My hat is off to every one of those men, and I am proud to say they were on our side."

As the Navy moved its operation from the Bedford Springs, word was received in Bedford that a group of hotel owners had acquired the stock of the Bedford Springs Company. They were headed by L. Gardner Moore of Washington, D.C., long time manager of the Shoreham Hotel.

Lawrence Gardner Moore was born in 1896, the son of David Moore, a Washington realtor, and Regina McGloughlin Moore. He was a graduate of Georgetown University Law School and worked as a bookkeeper before joining the Air Corps in World War I. He was with the balloon corps scheduled to be the first group to bomb Berlin, but the war end and he returned to Washington.

Moore's long career in the hotel and hospitality industry began in 1919 when he became

Sailors swimming at Lake Caledonia.

assistant manager at the Wardman Park Hotel. Five years later he was named manager and a member of the board of directors. He opened the Shoreham in 1930 and was the general manager there until 1958.

One of Moore's earliest memories was seeing President Teddy Roosevelt ride by on his brown horse, with one man, a sergeant, riding with him. TR, Moore later told an interviewer, would never fail to notice the little boys on Park Street; he would wave, flash his famous toothy smile and shout "Deelighted!"

The little boys, according to Moore's obituary, were invited to play baseball on the White House lawn, and a foul tip off of Moore's bat broke a window in the President's house.

Moore and his partners, upon the departure of the Navy, planned to restore the Bedford Springs to its original use, but they knew this would require extensive, and expensive renovations, and they did not see it opening for the 1945 season. In a letter written by Moore on May 15, 1945, he noted that the hotel had deteriorated under its previous use, and much of the furniture was missing.

It is rumored that a great deal of hotel furnishings was cleared from the buildings when the Navy took over. According to reports, the furniture was simply tossed out the windows, placed in large piles, and burned on the front lawn. This included many antiques that had been in the historic hotel for decades.

Moore was approached by the State Department to lease the hotel to house Japanese diplomats and their families. It is likely that Moore was personally acquainted with a few State Department officials. He met many notable people during his career, among them, Army Major (later General and President) Dwight D. Eisenhower, who had lived in one of Moore's apartments in Washington.

Sailors march in front of the Bedford Springs.

State Department occupancy would begin in the middle of July. Moore's letter indicated that until that time, extensive renovations had to be made. In the meantime, Moore and company began to staff the hotel with their own employees. Oliver Ayres was appointed manager, and Alfred Nadar, manager of the golf course.

The story of the Japanese at Bedford Springs is a fascinating one. In the Spring of 1945 the War in Europe was rapidly drawing to a close, and when the fall of Berlin was imminent the Japanese fled the capital to escape the approaching Allied forces. Some fled to Austria, having been denied entrance to Switzerland.

Many of the Japanese were collected by American units that had retaken Austria from the Nazis. In time, some 130 were held by the American 7th Army at Bad Gastein, an Austrian resort. These included diplomats from ambassador on down, military and technical advisors and their families, and embassy staff members including cooks, chauffeurs, and maids; also Japanese businessmen and reporters. A few of the Japanese had European spouses, which further complicated matters, and a few were Europeans employed by the Japanese.

The prisoners insisted that, as diplomats, they should not be treated as prisoners of war. In the end it was decided they should be treated with some deference, especially in regard to baggage searches and interrogations. The prisoners had value in future exchanges of prisoners with the Japanese; both the Americans and British felt they might be useful for propaganda or psychological warfare purposes. England and the United States agreed that any benefits to be gained would be shared equally. By this time the Japanese held some 150,000 westerners, including civilians and prisoners of war. Only a few exchanges had been made, the last one in December, 1943.

A State Department search for a suitable place to hold the Japanese eventually led them to Bedford Springs. Hotels seemed to offer the simplest and most economical method, based on their experience at the beginning of the war. Bedford was close to Washington, and adequate security was a necessity. Bedford Springs, where the Naval Radio Training School has just been closed, seemed like the best site.

Gardner Moore and his partners said they were willing to lease Bedford Springs to the State Department, if the government would guarantee at least four months occupancy. The owners would charge $3.00 per day for each detainee, and $1.50 per day for each American stationed there. In addition the hotel expected the government to provide the cost of meals and salaries, with a ten percent overhead to the owners. Occupancy by the State Department would begin in the middle of July.

The best account of their stay was written by Arthur E. Barbeau, Professor of History at West Liberty State College at West Liberty WV, and published in the "Western Pennsylvania Historical Magazine," Vol. 64 No. 2, titled, "The Japanese at Bedford." Copies of this article are in the Bedford County Historical Society Library. Barbeau's article was used as a primary reference for this chapter. He also presented the paper in an address to the Historical Society in 1979.

Rumors of the hotel's proposed use were circulating in Bedford. The Bedford Gazette suggested that the coming inhabitants could not be prisoners of war, or the War Department, not the State Department, would have made the arrangements. At this time the Civil Service was advertising for guards, so it had to house prisoners of some kind.

In June a State Department representative took up residence in the Cottage, where Ayers and Nadar were already in residence.

The hotel consisted of six main buildings, the Colonial Building, Evitt, Stone, Swiss Cottage and Anderson buildings (labeled A, B, C, D and E in order, on a map in Dr. Barbeau's article); and behind the Colonial building, was the Barclay, called the Annex. Building A had both hotel rooms and dining rooms, with an attached kitchen and cafeteria wing, and an attached dormitory. There was also an indoor swimming pool attached to Building A; this would be sealed off and unavailable to the Japanese, as were the hotel's other recreational facilities.

Most of the detainees would be housed in the Annex; the remainder would have rooms in Building A. Most of the government employees would be housed in Building C. Hotel employees would stay in the Dormitory.

For security purposes a board fence was constructed to enclose the lawns in front of the Colonial Building, complete with guard boxes.

Even as the necessary work at Bedford Springs was being finished, the arrival of the Japanese was delayed. A lack of transport space put off arrival of most Japanese in the United States until August.

General Oshima was among a group of 33 detainees who arrived by boat at New York July 11, and were taken for customs inspection at Newark Airport before their flight to Washington. On August 8, John R. Hall took custody of General Oshima and the others. These were the first to be interred at Bedford. The convoy carrying them to the hotel consisted of two automobiles and a half-ton truck. Five military policemen served as guards. The convoy arrived at Bedford at 8 p.m. the same evening.

The main group of 147 detainees left Bad Gastein on the morning of July 25, and arrived at Bedford on August 12. They were transported on a B & O Railroad train to Cumberland, MD, then by busses to Bedford, arriving at 7:30 p.m. This group included men, women and children.

From that point through October, other small parties of detainees were taken to Bedford. In all, about 180 Japanese resided at the hotel.

The formal announcement alerting the residents of Bedford of the Japanese coming to Bedford Springs was noted by editor Annie M. Gilchrist in the weekly *Bedford Inquirer* on June 25. She had been telephoned by a State Department official four days before. This confirmed the rumors that had already been circulating.

There was an immediate public outcry in Central Pennsylvania, which is well documented by Prof. Barbeau in his article. Ironically, most of the protests came from outside Bedford County. Let's look at a few examples:

* An article in the *Altoona Mirror* asked, "Since when did we start to play nurse maids to those dirty rats? While our boys are starving to death in their filthy concentration camps."

* One lady complained in a letter, stating that the Japanese should be housed in a prisoner of war camp.

* In a resolution to Senator Frances Myers, American Legion Post 561 of McConnellsburg wrote, "... it was the feeling of the Post that the nip diplomats be accorded the same treatment (as Japan gave to American prisoners) instead of being handled with kid gloves and fed to the Queen's taste."

* The Johnstown *Tribune* published an editorial titled, "Aren't We Being Too Nice?", asking if giving the Japanese complete freedom of the Bedford Springs was justified. Although stating that the prisoners should not be mistreated, the editorial continued, "On the other hand, to house them and dine them as though they were welcome guests come to spend a pleasant vacation seems to us to be piling it on a bit thick."

* Nelson A. Elsasser wrote directly to President Truman complaining that all of the facilities at the hotel were open to the Japanese.

That rumor persisted for weeks. Most of the protests were about the Japanese enjoying the hotel's luxuries, rather than staying there. The State Department tried to outline the facilities that would be used. Joseph Grew wrote to senator Myers that "While it is distasteful for all of us, it is a thing which must be done in the interest of our compatriots who are suffering in the Far East and for their sake we should be prepared to face even more unpleasant things."

Albert Clattenburg told the *Tribune* that even more luxurious facilities had been used to house enemy diplomats at the beginning of the war, and that the main purpose of using Bedford Springs was its close proximity to Washington, D.C.

The State Department asked the FBI to install listening devices in many of the rooms. It was decided to install only 20 "bugs," because of the unimportance of many of the guests. Although J. Edgar Hoover had reservations about it, the FBI reluctantly agreed to carry it out.

As a final measure, the State Department held a meeting at the hotel July 19. John Puerffov, Clattenburg and Robert Bannerman represented the State Department. The guests were carefully selected to include labor leaders, veterans' groups, and members of the news media. This allowed the complainers to "blow off steam." Tours of the areas to be used by the Japanese were conducted. After the meeting, the protests tapered off.

The stay of the Japanese at Bedford was quiet and uneventful, except for a few isolated incidents. One was the death of Tetsuzo Takano, 65, a cook, of a heart attack. Dr. Timmons of Bedford was called, but the man could not be revived. Prof. Barbeau stated that under guard, three of the detainees took the body to Pate's Funeral Home, from where the remains went to Pittsburgh for cremation. The ashes were returned to Bedford and went back to Japan when the internees left.

This was the only death among detainees while at Bedford.

Not all of the internees were Japanese. Imgard Yamamoto was German. She had been separated from her husband and wanted help in locating him. She also wanted to contact her sister who was in England, and feared being forced to go to Japan to live among people she did not know in a land she had never seen. Marguerite Nogami was Hungarian; her husband, Soichi, was a teacher. She had not seen him since April and wanted to divorce him and return to her mother in Germany. She also had a 15-month-old daughter, who received a great deal of attention from all the internees. These are some of the problems the State Department had to deal with in Bedford.

The Bedford Springs internment faced even more trouble after journalist James Young addressed the Bedford Rotary Club. Young had edited a small English - language newspaper in Japan before the war, and was then arrested and held in solitary confinement by the Japanese. When he returned to the United States he authored two anti-Japanese books and was a reporter for the Hearst newspapers. He told the Rotarians that at least twenty of the Bedford detainees were war criminals, which was false. Only one, General Oshima, Japan's Ambassador to Germany before and during the war, was ever put on trial by the Allies, and he was convicted of only one of seven charges (general conspiracy). He served a prison sentence and was released in 1952.

Young also published a nationally syndicated column in which the falsehoods were repeated, as well as new untruths. He had evidence to the contrary from the State Department, and had not visited the hotel personally, although he claimed he had. The State Department wasted no time and effort to calm the outcry that resulted from Young's allegations.

On August 14, the United States announced the unconditional surrender of Japan and World War II came to an end. There were victory celebrations all over the nation, and Bedford was no exception. Hundreds, then thousands of people poured into town to demonstrate their joy.

As Prof. Barbeau wrote, "Though entirely unplanned, there was still a logic in the proceedings. People drove out of town, turned south on Route 220, passed the Bedford Springs Hotel, and then returned to town to repeat the circuit. Cars and trucks were decorated with red, white and blue. Horns tooted; people cheered and shouted. One car sported a loudspeaker which continually played patriotic music. The loudest cheers were reserved for the passage past the old hotel. Perhaps the parade would have gone no farther, except that police would not permit the pedestrians or vehicles to stop. State Policemen, and even firemen, helped control the traffic. They continually waved on the celebrants while others followed in a seemingly endless procession.

"The object of the crowd's attention were the guests at the hotel ... General Oshima, Japanese ambassador to Germany, his colleagues, and members of the embassy staff. They took the news of Japan's surrender unemotionally, even stoically."

By the middle of October, the State Department decided that there was no reason to detain the Japanese in the United States any longer. There were other reasons. The State Department's original four-month contract with the Bedford Springs expired in the middle of November. The weather was getting colder, and many portions of the hotel were not heated. With General Douglas McArthur's concurrence, they would be returned to Japan as soon as shipping was available.

Early in November the State Department

announced that the Japanese would soon leave, and they would get a 12 hour notice before departure. November 16 was the actual date of departure as the internees were placed on busses bound for Cumberland and the B&O Railroad. Two litter cases traveled in an ambulance. They were bound for Seattle and the cars were switched to other railroads several times along the way. The group arrived in Seattle on Nov. 20, and boarded a ship the following morning.

As the busses departed Bedford on Nov. 16, workmen began closing the hotel for the winter. The same day Milton R. Manum, a 60-year-old guard, died of a heart attack while extinguishing a small grass fire.

The *Bedford Gazette* observed on Nov. 21, "Peace settled over the Bedford Springs this week, and the strangest interlude in its long and colorful history as a resort was at an end."

Over the decades some of the Navy radiomen who trained at the Bedford Springs returned to see what the former radio school looked like as a resort.

In July, 2009 Malcolm Kern, 84, and his wife Connie drove to Bedford from Canton, Bradford County to celebrate their 37th wedding anniversary at the resort. Originally from New Jersey, Kern enlisted in the Navy at age 17 with his father's permission.

He stayed at the radio training school at Bedford Springs from January to May 1943, where he learned Morse code and also learned to type. When he left the Springs, he went first to Miami, FL, then to Long Beach, CA, and from there boarded a ship for the Pacific Theater of the war in Samoa and Okinawa.

To Kern, the restored Bedford Springs had an entirely new look.

He remembered being on fire watch duty at the Bedford Springs.

"There were hot air heaters in the ceiling and you couldn't walk on one side or the other. You were dried up by the time you finished your walk.

He also recalled the area on the front lawn of the hotel, where the fire pits are located. He said it was flooded and the sailors could ice skate on it.

Kern concluded, "I'll never understand how we won the war. The majority of us were kids just out of school, like myself."

Classroom and control room, Bedford Springs

142 - The Bedford Springs Resort

The Gardner Moore era

L. Gardner Moore is the man responsible for the modernization of the Bedford Springs Hotel. Under his leadership a methodic restoration of the hotel complex began in 1945, which took years to complete, one step at a time. Moore headed a corporation that was willing to invest money in the hotel complex.

Moore knew that if he wanted to attract the clientele that he served at the Shoreham in Washington, D.C., modernization of the facility was a must. Guests would expect a first class hotel, and he would provide one.

Keep in mind that in many sections of the hotel, guests still faced the "shared bathroom" arrangements of the past. New tiled bathrooms were gradually installed in all rooms. This work was completed by the start of the 1952 season.

The rooms in the Barclay House were remodeled and an outdoor swimming pool was constructed in front of the hotel. Lake Caledonia, now called Red Oaks Lake, was developed for swimming, boating and fishing. The old-fashioned "surrey" was placed back in service to transport guests to numerous outdoor functions, including activities held the lake.

Elegance and personal service became the norm. Under Moore's direction, the lucrative convention trade was targeted, as it had been in the 1920s and 1930s.

G. Bland Hoke, formerly of The Tides in Virginia, had been recruited by Moore to be the new manager of the Bedford Springs. It was Hoke who redecorated the rooms in green and blue French Provincial styles with furniture to match. The French Provincial furniture remained in the Hotel until after the resort closed for good, and a prospective developer sold off the contents at public auction, room by room. Many Bedford County residents still treasure their French Provincial bedroom furniture that was purchased at these sales.

Hoke installed the crystal chandelier in the lobby, which was a Hotel hallmark for many decades.

Hoke was largely responsible for enticing the legendary Glidden Tours of antique automobiles to stop at Bedford on two occasions, 1948 and 1951. The first-hand accounts of the two tours provide a glimpse into the hospitality and elegance offered at Bedford Springs under the direction of Gardner Moore.

On October 10 - 14, 1948, the Glidden Tour Fall Outing stayed at the Bedford Springs on a journey across Pennsylvania, originating in Philadelphia. The following account of the visit was written by George M. Hughes.

"The trip was uneventful for the tourists although in my particular case I was just far enough ahead of the main group to reach Bedford, Penna., in a teeming rain storm. Those

The Gardner Moore era - 143

arriving a little later or those who arrived earlier were able to avoid this drenching rain.

"As I slowly turned into the drive way of the Bedford Springs Hotel both Grace and I heaved a sigh of relief in knowing that we had completed this leg of the trip. With the rain the car started missing seriously although I discovered later it wasn't the storm so much as a faulty magneto that was causing the trouble.

"In approaching the Hotel where a large group of costumed people (replete with handlebar moustaches, high collars and other items of another era) were waiting to greet us, I saw the little red Maxwell of Les Henry and found that he was AACA club host of the day. He introduced the arrivals one by one and it was a pleasure to meet Mr. and Mrs. G. Bland Hoke, our hosts at the hotel. The costumed group brought to our minds a picture of how it must have been forty years prior to this visit, when the 1908 Glidden Tour arrived at Bedford Springs (founded in 1804) coming in from the west. The 1908 Tour was held in July and the motorists spent 11th, 12th, and 13th at the Springs. In 1908 incidentally, there were two women drivers — Mrs. Andrew Cuneo of New York driving a Rainier and Mrs. L. W. Shirley of Jamestown, New York, in an Overland Runabout. Coming from the west, (Pittsburgh) it took the 1908 group approximately eight hours to reach destination, Bedford Springs.

"The record books show that the 1908 group (of grand-daddy cars) was slightly different than the roll call of the 1948 cars. In 1908 there were listed the Pierce, Peerless, Gaeth, Franklin, Marmon, Oakland, Selden, Oldsmobile, Gearless, Gyroscope, Reo, Premier, Thomas, Stevens-Duryea, Haynes, Studebaker, Garford, Packard, Moline, Stodard-Dayton. In the '48 list only Sam Baily's Pierce and Jim Kellog-Clark's Oldsmobile corresponded with the earlier registration.

"By nightfall all the participants had arrived in Bedford Springs, even C. W. Kelsey of Troy, N. Y. in a little three wheeled motorette which he made himself back in 1910 got there. This little two passenger vehicle has just a single driving wheel in the rear and Colonel Augustus Post, who has participated in every Tour from the beginning, characterized it as the car that does everything with three wheels that other do with four wheels. The top speed of this little chugger is 15 miles per hour and it certainly is to the credit of Mr. Kelsey's ingenuity that this car could, thirty-eight years after home manufacture, take a trip such as the Glidden without any hesitation whatsoever. The car apparently never missed a beat and Mr. and Mrs. Kelsey deserve a tremendous amount of credit for their immense courage in attempting a Glidden Tour in the low powered car. Their only protection from the elements was a little wind shield.

"That evening of October 11, 1948, was devoted to an old fashioned ball featuring the square dance and activity such as might have been held forty years earlier. Most of the group (including many Bedford residents) were in costume and dancing to the weird strains of a unique square dance orchestra that hammered again and again on the same tune with more or less casual discord. By 10:30 p. m. most were beginning to seek their

The Colonial Building, with the Colonnade in front, which was added in 1905.
From Blackburn's "History of Bedford County."

144 - The Bedford Springs Resort

beds. It had been a long, hard day.

"Tuesday was a nice day although clouds continually blocked out the sun. Frank Ross, color photographer, was almost in tears (figuratively speaking) at the peculiarities of the sun and clouds. He had been assigned to secure pictures for the Saturday Evening Post and despite his hurried activity in attempting to be in position when the sun was out he found little consolation with the small hand full of gorgeous pictures that he finally achieved. In the early afternoon, after a quiet morning of relaxation, the motorists again cranked up their cars and prepared for a parade through Bedford, Penna., such as was done in 1908. Estimates place the crowd lining the parade route at 5,000 to 6,000 people; they seemed to emerge by magic in mid-afternoon to line the curbs, and many hundreds had come from distant points to see the automobiles. School children of Bedford township arrived by bus, to line up with local grade-schoolers and extend a shrill cheering welcome - one of the most excited and thrilled groups I have ever had the pleasure of seeing. One of the best exhibits of this parade to my mind was an object earlier than the cars themselves-it was an ancient (not antique) band wagon, horse drawn and carrying the band, costumed in the regalia of a long generation ago. This vehicle in the parade presented as much of a spectacle to the Tourists as they themselves did to the townsfolk.

"Evening, after the second great dinner at the hotel, the group gathered in the auditorium — possibly the meeting room forty years ago — and listened to several talks and witnessed some film taken at several earlier antique auto events. This meeting again was presided over by President Jerry Duryea.

"Wednesday morning the dawn was punctuated by the muffled noises of Bill Fleming warming up and taking off for the better than one hundred and forty mile trip to Reading, Penna. Bill and his wife, early birds to say the least, were up and away before the majority even thought of leaving their beds. In the early-bird category can also be listed C. W. Kelsey and Jim Clark. For myself I could just about open one eye to glimpse Bill as he slowly

Scene from 1951 Glidden Tour, at Bedford Springs.
Photo courtesy of Antique Automobile Club of America Library.

chugged down the driveway turned eastward and headed out of sight! Several hours later I was to pass him near the end of the Turnpike but only after the Winton had raced along for an hour or two at speeds of better than 40 mph. After a pleasant breakfast, Grace and I jumped in the Winton and started toward our destination."

The 1951 Glidden Tour, called the Pittsburgh Tour, also visited the Bedford Springs on September 25, where the participants remained two nights. One of the organizers of this event reported, "We were advised by G. Bland Hoke, manager of Bedford Springs Hotel that he was willing and eager to have us visit his hotel in 1951.

"To many the very highlight of the day was our arrival at a small town called Hyndman which is located about half way between Cumberland and Bedford. Here Mr. and Mrs. Earl J. Leap, Tour members and prominent local residents, had prepared an outdoor luncheon at their own expense. A reception committee met us just outside of town and escorted us to the school grounds where lunch was served by members of the student body. We can't recall any other similar occasion where children treated our Antique cars with such great respect. Many noted that not one little hand fondly stroked a brass lamp. That is really something. When finished luncheon Tourists proceeded to Bedford and to the Hotel Bedford Springs as they wished.

"Bedford Springs Hotel presented a truly fine spectacle. Many residents of the town plus all the hotel staff were costumed in clothing reminiscent of the earlier days when the Glidden Tour actually visited Bedford Springs Hotel.

"An official greeter was present—he was John Mansure of Philadelphia fame and gorgeously dressed in an outfit that defies description. Half clown, part something else John gave the warm handshake to each man and a kiss and a taffy to each gal. The welcoming committee went all out and afforded much amusement and fun.

"The afternoon was not scheduled and over 100 cars continued arriving for several hours. Since this was really the first time we could look over each other's cars to any advantage, many an idle moment was spent inspecting the early and the unique of the motor kingdom.

"The evening was taken up with the Gay Nineties Costume Party and Ball. Prizes were awarded for most interesting and authentic costumes. The party lasted into the wee hours. Many went to bed with their minds turned back to the delectable dinner menu. Such items were listed as Roast Prime Ribs of Beef au jus, Robert Hayes; Assorted Fiambres Plate, Robert C. Laurens. It was possible to have Ford 'S" Model Salad with Sherbet Panache Van Sciver. Quite an interesting and amazing menu. Most tucked away these extraordinary menus for future lodging in ye old scrap book.

"Tuesday was a nice clear day—at least it started out that way and lasted to well into the afternoon. This was the day of the parade which was one of the great events in Bedford history. Thousands watched—many coming from long distances.

"It was estimated that more than 10,000 persons crowded the streets of Bedford to view the parade which was a rather slow and difficult one for the old cars.

"After the parade a band concert was given on the front lawn of the hotel from the Old Pavia Band Wagon—a relic of many years ago. This strange old wagon was last used in Bedford when our 1948 Tour visited the hotel.

"A side show of some interest was the hour spent in the hotel swimming pool. This swim was sparked by such luminaries in the swimming field as Eleanor Weiant and Ruth Miller (they are twins and respective wives of Warren Weiant, Newark, Ohio and Frank Miller, Glendale, Ohio) and are former national sprint champions and holders of virtually every women's record of their day, plus Jerry Duryea, a former great water polo champion at the University of Pennsylvania, and New York Athletic Club, plus Colonel Augustus Post, dean of all Glidden Tourists also a swimmer of no mean ability even today.

"A relay race was scheduled and the team of Frank Miller, Sintra Badenhausen, George Hughes and Eleanor Weiant defeated a hasty combination of Leslie Henry, Audrien Henry, Jerry Duryea and Ruth Miller. In the other competitive feature Jerry Duryea won, with ease, the pool plunge for distance. Colonel Post swam a lap and gracefully performed a dive of no mean proportion.

"In discussing Bedford Springs hospitality it should be mentioned that Manager Hoke even went so far as to provide a huge circus tent for the storage of cars and protection from the elements. This tent was under guard at all times. Local automobile dealers provided mechanical services quaintly announced as "Craftsmen skilled in mechanical trades are available for all types of repairs."

"Dinner that night was out of this world. An outside old fashioned New England shore dinner had been planned but due to coolness and dampness it was held in the main dining room. Clams, oysters, shrimp, lobster and other delicacies were available in abundance and anyone not having enough just didn't have energy to go back more than once to the buffet set-up. This was a dinner we will long remember.

"After our feast the group went to the auditorium for a meeting which was under the direction of capable Bill Swigart. Briggs Cunningham of Green Farms, Connecticut was the chief speaker. Briggs had entered three cars in the Tour but only the Simplex was at Bedford, the rest eliminated due to press of business. The Simplex had just come from the shop of "The Know-How Repairers Extraordinaire," owned by Ralph Buckley and Henry Heinsohn, Northfield, New Jersey. It was a gorgeous thing to behold. Briggs gave a delightful and colorful account of his experience at the Le Mans 24 Hour Race of 1951 held at Le Mans, France. Although Briggs did not win, his V-8 Chrysler powered engines with slight Cadillac modifications, gave a fine account of themselves. Accidents and mechanical troubles seemed to be the biggest bugaboo. Imagine running at a speed of something like 150 mph at night in rain. Briggs did.

"Bill Spear of Southport, Connecticut also competed in this race and added his comments.

"After our racing information Bill Swigart called on numerous present including the great steam enthusiast T. Clarence Marshall of Yorklyn, Delaware. Clarence presented us many facts on Stanley Steamer history, some of them little known to many of us. This was a very fine talk. Meeting was adjourned at a reasonably early hour and numerous caught up on sleep lost the previous night."

American illustrator Charles Dana Gibson developed and made famous the Gibson Girl look during a twenty year period spanning the late nineteenth and early twentieth century in the United States. The Gibson Girl was tall, slender yet with ample bosom, hips and bottom in the S-curve torso shape, which was adopted by Hollywood actresses and then became an "ideal" to be copied by young ladies everywhere. There was merchandising of Gibson Girl "saucers, ashtrays, tablecloths, pillow covers, chair covers, souvenir spoons, screens, fans, umbrella stands" all bearing her fictional image.

It was Hotel manager Hoke who adopted the Gibson Girl theme at the Bedford Springs, as part of his "Gay Nineties" look, especially in the bar and cocktail lounge areas.

Also, for the first time in the history of the Springs, the resort began to stay open for the winter, beginning in 1950. The activities included sledding, sleigh rides, ice skating and tobogganing. Photos from this time period show old-fashioned Yule log celebrations in the Hotel with the staff members dressed in Colonial style costumes. Community carol singing also took place in the Hotel lobby.

By 1956 a new sprinkler system had been installed, an emergency generator was placed in an electrical service room under the kitchen, and air conditioning was also added.

Artist James Reynolds (1891 - 1957), who had painted a number of murals at the Shoreham Hotel in Washington, was recruited to decorate portions of the Colonial Building in 1956. He was a friend of Gardner Moore.

Reynolds painted a series of murals depicting the early history of Western Pennsylvania, particularly the French and Indian War period. In the Reynolds Room, which was located next to the indoor swimming pool, Fort Cumberland was depicted. General Forbes was also shown with Col. George Washington.

One observer called Reynolds an "Irish Romantic painter" who "fell under the spell of Bedford Springs and decorated it handsomely with his paintings," including the main dining room and the Bar on the lower level, "and here

The Gardner Moore era

he was particularly successful in recapturing the wild, untamed wilderness of eighteenth-century Bedford."

Many older Bedford County residents can recall their years working at Bedford Springs when it was operated by L. Gardner Moore, which they consider to be the "renaissance years" of the famed hotel.

Darlene (Fix) Long, a Six Mile Run native who worked at the Bedford Springs Resort for 43 years, said her supervisor had high praise for his workers from the local region.

Now living in Cessna, she started working at the Springs as a summer job in 1950, four years before she graduated from Saxton-Liberty High School.

"My family lived near what is now the Six Mile Run Fire Hall. Dad (Russell Fix) was a coal miner, working at the Zeth mine near Langdondale. In the 1950s he did some carpentry work at the Bedford Springs."

"Mother (Edith) worked at the Springs. She kept the dormitory rooms (where employees stayed) clean as well as the Clubhouse (at the golf course). Later she worked in the kitchen, making salads, pancakes, and so on."

She said the Fix family consisted of nine children and money was always short. So her mother told Darlene she could work at the Springs in the summer. "I was only 14; you had to be 16 to get a worker's permit. So our insurance agent Darrell Satterfield drew up some papers so I could get hired." She explained that a student had to be 16 to work in the kitchen around sharp knives and other equipment.

But getting back to Mr. Doyle, he hired many high school area students to work in the summers. He was so pleased with them that they were often called back to work weekends in the fall after classes resumed. If the hotel hosted a convention or large parties, the extra help was in demand.

According to Darlene, Mr. Doyle at the Springs would send a limousine to Saxton-Liberty High School to pick them up early Friday afternoon. "We missed a couple of periods. The principal, Mr. G. Allen Hoover, didn't like it. He was pretty strict but we had permission slips from our parents. When the weekend was over the limousine brought us back home."

She added, "We were dependable. During the 43 years that I worked there, I did not call in sick. The only time I took off was for 11 days when my daughter was ill with spinal meningitis."

She explained that the dormitory building had rooms for employees to stay in. The first floor was for single males, the second floor for married couples, and the third for single girls. "We stayed there all week. We got one day off on which we could go home, and my pay went to my parents."

Dining room and ball room staff: Standing, head waiter Al Doyle; seated from left, Gabe ---; unidentified; George ----; Jerry Schnably, bar tender; 'Zip ---;" Helen ---; and Marian Pettengil, cashier for the ballroom.

Courtesy Bedford Gazette.

She continued, "I didn't mind staying up there. I liked the work. I could always get a ride home with someone from Six Mile Run who worked there. Many families did not have a car in those days.

"I never saw inside the guest rooms; the maids and also the waiters and waitresses who made room service deliveries would have seen them. We were not allowed to go anywhere in the hotel except where we worked. We were not allowed to go anywhere in the hotel in uniform when we were off duty. We could go to the snack bar in our street clothes. If caught, we had to do extra work.

"Mr. Doyle taught us right. There was no compromise in cleanliness. When he had roll call, he looked closely at our appearance. Our white shoes had to be polished. Our uniforms had to be pressed and the collars had to be starched. Many of the girls did not want to stay up late to press their uniforms, so my mother, who stayed in the dormitory also, would do it for them for 25¢. A quarter was a lot of money in those days. But she made me do my own," Darlene recalled.

When she stayed in the employee dormitory, room and board was deducted from her salary at the rate of $25.00 for two weeks.

Mr. Doyle also taught them if they saw anything on the floor of the dining room, they were to pick it up. His favorite saying was, "If the shoe fits, wear it."

After graduation, she married Robert Long of Six Mile Run (Mosquito Hollow), a 1952 S-L graduate, now deceased. Bob and Darlene are the parents of three children.

She remembers that many of the hotel employees went to Florida to work in the winters. The Bedford Springs was a seasonal enterprise, open only from April to October. Due to family obligations she did not have an opportunity to work in Florida. After her marriage, she no longer had to stay in the dormitory.

She waited on a number of famous people while a waitress at the Springs. Perhaps the best known was President Dwight D. Eisenhower, who came there in 1962 to attend a fundraising banquet for William Scranton, candidate for Governor of Pennsylvania. Scranton, by the way, won the election.

Darlene recalled, "I was waiting on the head table where the President was seated. They brought him in through the kitchen for security reasons, and he was escorted by Mr. Moore, who was then the owner of the Bedford Springs, and also by a policeman."

She continued, "I have a framed photo of Mr. Eisenhower, which was taken in the kitchen. He autographed a Bedford Springs doily for me, and also provided autographs for my three children. I still have his autograph. He also kissed me on the cheek."

Another notable person she waited on was the Duke of Bedford -- the Fort, the town of Bedford, and the County were named in honor of his ancestor. She was 21 years old at the time (1958), and her photo was taken with the Duke in the Bancroft Room. She still has that photo, which also shows State Senator and

From left, Judge and Mrs. Snyder; the Duke of Bedford and wife; and State Senator Stanley G. Stroup. The waitress is Darlene Long.
Courtesy Darlene Long.

Mrs. Stanley Stroup and Judge and Mrs. Snyder.

The Duke's visit coincided with the Bicentennial of the construction of Fort Bedford, during which time an all-summer-long celebration was held in Bedford.

She remembers when evangelist Rex Humbard was a guest at the Springs, but she and the other employees were not fond of Humbard's wife, whom they called "uppity." Darlene said she wore a lot of jewelry and flaunted her wealth. Some of the employees felt this was odd since all of the Humbards' money had been donated to them for evangelism.

She served the Beach Boys and The Platters, and she has autographs of these also.

She remembers when the popular band "Alabama" stayed at the Springs. They wanted to eat there, but refused to wear the required dinner jackets, even though Mr. Doyle, the Maitre d' brought jackets to them. "So they did not get to eat at the Springs," Darlene added.

Other famous persons she remembers being at the Springs included evangelist Billy Graham, then - Governor of California Ronald Reagan (later to become President Reagan); and Prescott Bush, President George W. Bush's grandfather. "Clair Chaney of Six Mile Run, now living in Texas, served Mr. Bush," she added. Prescott Bush was a well known businessman and a United States Senator.

For the Fix children, it was a family affair. "All eight of my brothers and sisters worked there at one time or another. Two of my brothers worked in the kitchen. Gene Fix was an executive chef, and he stayed in one of the log houses on the Springs property which was called the Chefs' House. In 1968, he became ill at work, went home, and suffered a massive heart attack and died. He was 37 years old."

"My brother Sherman Fix, the oldest brother, was a cook at the Springs from 1937 to 1940. He is still working, helping out at the Carriage House Restaurant at Bedford. My nephew, Wesley Fix was a chef at the Springs. He is the owner of the Carriage House."

Chef Wesley Fix worked at the Bedford Springs between 1971 and 1981. His mother, Ruth Ann, was a waitress at the Springs.

"I was born in Kearney and grew up in Six

Rex Humbard and daughter in the gift shop. Courtesy Bedford Gazette.

Mile Run," Sherman Fix explained. "I started working at Bedford Springs as a cook in 1937. In 1940 I went to Howard Johnson's Restaurant on the newly-opened Pennsylvania Turnpike at Bedford, and worked there as a cook for 45 years."

As the Springs was only a seasonal resort, Sherman went to Howard Johnson's so he could work year round.

Wesley Fix worked at Bedford Springs, "off and on for ten years," starting in the stock room, where all of the goods from vendors were received. He worked as an executive chef at the Springs in 1980 and 1981.

"In those days, you didn't go to school to become a chef. You got paired up with a chef and learned from him. That way I worked with four or five chefs, sometimes changing every six months," Wesley said. "Each had a specialty, whether pastry, desserts, salads, main courses, and so on. I could learn to prepare many different foods."

Among the chefs he worked for at the Springs were Tom Spence and John Hicks.

He also went to Florida to work in the winter when the Springs was closed. "At that time the chefs went to Clearwater, FL in the winter, then came back in late April. After 1981 I bypassed the Springs and worked in New England. I was an executive chef at Kennebunkport, ME." Among the notable people he served there at The Colony Hotel, perhaps the most notable was the first President Bush, who was then the director of the CIA. Other guests included Senators Edmund Muskie and "Tip" O'Neill. "From there I worked at Cape Cod's Chatham Hotel, Long Island, and Connecticut."

Fix studied under Executive Chef David Bouley, an acclaimed 4-star chef who *The New York Times* has called perhaps the best chef in the United States. Bouley grew up in Rhode Island and studied in France. He owns Bouley Restaurant at 120 West Broadway, New York.

But during his career, Fix traveled from place to place and never owned a home. So he and his wife decided to move their family back to Bedford. He borrowed $10,000 from his father to start his own restaurant, The Carriage House. Since that time, his "Whiskey Rebellion steak" has been a popular menu item.

He said the Carriage House is known for a variety of comfort foods and for good steaks (the same choice steaks that are served at larger hotels). "I know meats, I also worked as a butcher," Fix said.

Fix and his aunt Darlene both remember the destructive fire in June, 1970 in the Bedford Springs kitchen, which caused between $75,000 and $125,000 damage to the building. The kitchen and the employees cafeteria on the floor below suffered heavy damage. In the kitchen, all of the ranges and other equipment had to be replaced. Fix pointed out that the ranges and other equipment were very old and out of date. "It was a huge, open kitchen," he said. "Today they have three or four kitchens." Until the kitchen could be reopened, meats were cooked at the nearby Bedford Elks Club and transported to the Hotel in employees' cars. Some food was prepared at the Springs Clubhouse.

Fix also remembers a few weekends when all of the 275 guest rooms at the Springs were filled, and the overflow of guests went to the Fort Bedford Inn in downtown Bedford.

The Springs menu, Fix said, was based on what is called the American Plan, which features eight main menu items, which were changed daily. On the menu were one beef item, one pork, one lamb, one poultry, one fish, and so on. One day the specialty item might be chicken, the next day duck.

For some guests, he said the meals were included in the price of a room.

Now fast forward in time to 2007, when the newly restored and renovated Bedford Springs Resort was getting ready to open. The Springs kitchens were not yet ready for use, but the Springs owners were bringing in 40 to 50 people at a time from Baltimore, Washington, Philadelphia, Pittsburgh and other cities to tour the new facility. They needed a place to prepare meals.

Fix explained, "For two months, mid-April through June, the Springs chefs used my kitchen at The Carriage House to prepare the food, and took it to the Elks where the guests were served. They also held employee seminars in my kitchen."

During that time, Fix said he got to know Konrad Meier, executive chef at the Springs, very well.

Darlene Long continued, in addition to the large kitchen, the kitchen area also included a stock room, linen room, glass pantry where glasses were washed and stored; a salad preparation area, and a dessert room where desserts were prepared. Pastry chefs made desserts also. The Springs had a bakery, too.

"Parfaits were the specialty dessert at the Springs, especially for banquets and conventions. They were made with vanilla ice cream. One was made with creme de menthe; chocolate parfaits were made with chocolate syrup; sometimes they were made with strawberries. All were topped with whipped creme and a green cherry," Darlene explained. "Hundreds of these were prepared in advance and frozen."

The Gardner Moore era - 151

She said, "We (the waitresses) had to carry 25 parfaits at a time to the dining room."

She said that each dining room at the Springs had a different menu. If a party was held, they would order in advance.

In addition to the main dining room, the Hotel also had the Garfield Room, the Bancroft Room, the Garden Room and the Anderson Room. "Many days I worked 14 to 16 hours, with a couple hours break in the afternoon, when I went home to check on the children. Then I returned to serve dinner."

She said the Springs had sauce plates which were inscribed with "Che Sara Sara," the Bedford County motto. Onto these were placed the plates of appetizers and soup. We had to walk to the kitchen and back with every course we served at a meal. The plates were covered, but sometimes the vegetables got cold."

For special parties, she said the Springs used gold service china.

She also delivered room service, but usually after 11 a.m. because those guests got up late. Tables were carried up to the rooms along with the items ordered.

'Mr. Doyle, the Maitre d' liked flowers on the tables and would pick flowers and bring them in. Many waitresses were asked to pick flowers along the roads or bring them from home. If a convention was held, they ordered their own flowers."

"Some of the guests invited us for drinks, usually Bloody Mary's, on the porch. We were allowed to do this after continental breakfast was served," she added.

The standard tip for waitresses, included with the bill, was 25¢ for breakfast, 50¢ for lunch, and $1.00 for dinner. "We worked in pairs and it was split with your partner. If they wanted to give you extra, they left it at the front desk."

"The tips were very good. A waitress could make money if they worked hard -- the more tables you turned over, the more people you served and the more tips you received." She remembers an elderly gentleman, a millionaire who stayed alone, giving her a $100 tip.

Perhaps the most embarrassing moment for Darlene was the time she accidentally set fire to a man's suit jacket.

'We were serving a 25th Anniversary Party. For dessert they had ordered cherries jubilee, and each plate of dessert was lit before being served. So that the flames would be visible, the lights were turned down," Darlene recalls.

When the lights were dimmed it was difficult to see, and Darlene had accidentally tipped one dessert so that the liquor ran down on the floor. "When I lit it the flames went down across the floor and right up his suit coat. I actually caught the man on fire!"

The hotel staff reacted promptly and rolled him on the floor to put out the flames. Apparently the man was not injured, but Darlene was embarrassed. "I thought about not coming in to work the next day, but Mr. Doyle reassured me that everything was alright."

There were many long hours for the waitresses and others who worked the dining rooms. The day began with regular breakfast, which was followed by continental breakfast. Then the tables had to be torn down and set for lunch. If meeting rooms were in use, those people came up for lunch plus the regular lunch crowd. Lunch was also served in the Clubhouse to golfers.

If a convention or private party was being held at the Springs, Darlene recalled that the main banquet room was set up with tables, a head table and a podium for speakers to use. The meal was served, then the staff had to wait until both the meal and the meeting were over. Then they had to tear everything down and set it up as a dining room.

Between Friday and Sunday, between 400 and 500 people ate dinner in the dining rooms each day, she said.

The last few years that Darlene worked at the Springs, business had dropped off. The hotel was losing money.

In 1980 owner Gardner Moore and his son-in-law, E. Harris Knight, sold the hotel to a group headed by West Virginia architect J. Holden Kieffer. The new owners invested money in the Springs golf course and it looked like things were going to get better.

Both Darlene Long and her brother Sherman vividly remember what happened next. On June 21, 1983 there was a flash flood along Shober's Run, which was compounded by the partial breach of a dam located between Caledonia and Sweetroot Road. Between 2 and 4 a.m., a freak storm dumped between 6.5 and 8 inches of rain on the region between Friends Cove and Manns Choice; the Springs property was right in the middle of this storm.

Pavement along old Route 220 was ripped up and deposited in the parking lot of the Bedford Springs. Cars in the parking area were carried downstream. Many of the golf course improvements were destroyed. The water rose so high that it covered the black and white tile floor in the hotel lobby.

The Springs property suffered an estimated $2 million loss, including damage to the Clubhouse, which was knocked off its foundation. By 1984, the Clubhouse had been restored to its foundation and the hotel and golf course were back in operation.

Noted Darlene, I stayed until the very end. By that time the hotel had closed. After the dining room closed the Clubhouse remained open to serve golfers at the golf course. She was then pressed into service to provide food and drinks to the golfers. "I drove a golf cart out to the 9th hole with iced tea, hot dogs and candy bars."

Today the dormitories where Darlene stayed are gone. They were taken down to make room for the new Spa and guest suites. The Clubhouse, too, has been demolished.

Up on the hill, the grand Barclay House had its upper stories removed; two stories remain, and have been completely remodeled for guests.

Darlene remembers when the entire Barclay House was reserved for conventions. "The people would attend the convention, and then play golf. I cooked breakfast for them," she said.

Hazel Marie (Hastings) Taylor of Six Mile Run remembers working at the Springs in the summer after she graduated from high school (1954). "I worked in the glass pantry," she said. "I stayed in the dormitory at that time."

Her job was washing dirty glasses, shining them, and then placing them in the pantry. There was always someone to inspect them to make sure they were done right. "It is unbelievable the amount of glasses that had to be washed. When we got done, we could go up to our rooms and visit with other employees."

Hazel Marie never had a problem getting a ride to or from Bedford, because quite a few Six Mile Run residents were employed at the Springs.

Dick Spargo of Saxton, as a young man, worked at the Springs as a doorman. Dick said he could never get used to holding out his hand for tips. "I always thought that you got paid to do your job, and that's all you got."

One incident that he remembers took place when he worked late into the evening. That night the crickets and tree frogs were especially loud. A young couple from out of the area stopped and asked him where they could buy one of those electric crickets.

"They're not electric. They are real crickets," he replied to their amazement. Apparently, in the city, they never heard real live crickets before.

Max Adolphson of Dudley worked for several years at the Bedford Springs in the kitchen. Said Max, "I worked with members of the Fix family. I especially remember executive chef Gene Fix. He was a fine man."

Max has in his possession a number of mementos from the glory days at the Bedford Springs.

Linda Kurtz of Bedford worked as a waitress in the 1960s. In 2007 she recalled waiting on President Eisenhower during his 1962 visit. "I was so nervous I couldn't stand it. I had to use two hands to hold the cup of tea I was carrying."

She continued, the President made her feel comfortable. "He reached up and took the cup and saucer from me, and said, 'Why are you so nervous?' I said, 'Because you're you!'"

In those days, she said the Springs was known for its elegance. "It was all real flowers, not artificial flowers."

In 2002 students of teacher Beth Engle of Everett Area High School spent four months producing a professional quality video about the Bedford Springs' glorious past. The students were able to uncover some little-known tidbits, which are discussed in the 33-minute production.

Among the notable people mentioned in the video are Pat Boone and Bobby Riggs. It is confirmed that Boone sang in the mid-sixties in a tent theater where Equity actors from New York

City staged plays, and that Riggs was the tennis pro at the Resort in 1983. In the 1980s, according to the video, tennis was so popular that a grandstand was erected around the courts for viewers.

Former cocktail waitress Hazel Malone recalls a clambake where seafood unheard of in Bedford was served, and conventioneers gambled so much they'd lose their homes.

One time hotel bellhop David Thompson, and later Bedford County Commissioner, remembers an elderly elevator operator joining him on the porch during a slow period, telling Thompson about a big Packard car pulling up one day, and a spiffy gentleman getting out and asking directions to Cumberland. The gentleman tossed a $20 gold piece to the respondent, telling him, "Now you can say you met John Dillinger."

Former bellhop Joe Koontz recalls earning $100 in tips per shift, and Charles O'Shea remembers when 500 college girls checked in, and when he walked evangelist Rex Humbard's dog.

In a paper written for the Bedford County Historical Society, former employee Edythe Timmerman called the Bedford Springs "the Grand Old Dame of Bedford!" Her paper was written prior to the massive restoration project that brought the Springs back to life. She said, "I know people who never knew her in her prime or never worked for her cannot understand how the rest of us feel. They cannot know how much we would like to see her come back to life again. She was like home to us and we truly love her.

"Many of the workers relied on her for their livelihood and others made money there to help obtain a college education. She employed many generations in the same family."

She continued, "My father worked there as a waiter when they set up tents on the front lawn for meetings and served meals there. My daughter and my son both worked there, my daughter in the drug store and my son parked cars. I personally worked there for almost 20 years. I worked under managers Ayers, Hoke, Shoemaker, Moore, and Knight. We had excellent assistant managers such as Miller Baumgardner, Paul Faber, Bill Kelley, and Paul Howell. There was also Al Doyle who maintained the dining room and kept it up to its high standards. In the accounting office was Mr. Dudash and Edna Sill. Joe Koontz was Bell Captain and Don Jones was reservation manager.

"Even though the hotel was closed in the winter we opened up for snow emergencies. We had a skeleton crew but we managed to house many people stranded in snow storms.

"We were like one big happy family. We all worked very hard. It was nothing to have 500 people checking in and 500 people checking out all in the same day. If we were needed somewhere other than our regular job we would fill in wherever needed and were happy to do so.

"We also had fun. We had picnics and wiener roasts at Egolf Park, and other parties at the barn at Lake Caledonia including masquerade parties at Halloween.

"My job was mainly switchboard operator. We moved from a one position board in the Barclay building to a two position board at the front desk in the main lobby, and from there to the present front desk in what was once the drug store and soda fountain.

"I for one would like nothing better that to see the beautiful crystal chandelier (which we washed by hand one crystal at a time before it was installed) light up again. I would love to see the dining room so tastefully set and its mouth watering food open for people to enjoy again. I would love to hear the orchestra play in the ballroom and see the "surrey with the fringe on top" taking people for rides."

L. Gardner Moore, who had guided the operation of the Bedford Springs Hotel since 1945, officially became president of the Bedford Springs Corp. in 1957. That same year, he and his wife, Florence McGregor Moore, moved to Bedford from Washington, D.C.

The following year he officially retired from the Shoreham Hotel. Florence Moore passed away February 17, 1958 at age 57. They had been married since 1921. In her obituary she was listed as vice-president and treasurer of the Bedford Springs Corp.

Many still remember the kitchen fire of June 2, 1970 that damaged the kitchen area of the Bedford Springs Hotel and sent two firemen to

The outdoor pool was constructed in front of the indoor pool building.
Courtesy Omni Bedford Springs Resort.

the hospital. Fortunately, only a small number of guests were at the hotel when the blaze broke out -- fewer than 50 from Union Carbide and a small number of other guests.

News reports stated that the fire first showed up as a red glow under the range in the kitchen at 5:30 p.m. Chef Pedro Rivera and Bobby Monnett were working nearby and turned a fire extinguisher on the spot, while handyman Robert Davis of Defiance worked with a fire extinguisher from below, in a room housing electric panels and an emergency generator.

Other electric panels were turned off by hotel manager and son-in-law of Gardner Moore, E. Harris Knight but the men were driven out by smoke.

More than 100 volunteer firemen responded from five volunteer fire companies and fought the blaze for over four hours. Two firemen -- Lee Sallada of Bedford and Ross Williams of Schellsburg -- suffered smoke inhalation and were admitted to the intensive care unit of Memorial Hospital of Bedford County. Also admitted were Joseph Miller and Gary Smith, both Bedford firemen and Springs employee Oliver Keel.

Later that evening Joe Straub, Bill Sallada and Joe Smith were admitted for smoke inhalation and Joe Hershberger for blistered feet.

Everett fireman Herb Gump fell through a hole in the kitchen floor, but escaped serious injury, as did Bedford fireman Carl Wilson when he fell partially through the floor.

The outdoor swimming pool was pumped dry by the fire companies, after which a pond and Shober's Run were utilized to get water to fight the blaze. Bedford called for additional men at 7:30 p.m., and Everett issued a similar call at 9:25 p.m.

The fire appeared to be concentrated in the kitchen floor and in wall partitions. Bedford Fireman Gary Nouse said that initially, there was very little smoke but in ten minutes it was all smoke. The dense smoke persisted in pouring out roof vents and eventually clouded the front of the hotel.

The blaze was brought under control shortly after 11:00 p.m. Oddly, a sprinkler system in the kitchen failed to activate, possibly due to a lack of sufficient heat.

The Gardner Moore era - 155

During the blaze hotel employees carried food to waiting vans supplied by Queen City Produce Co. and the Bedford Dairy Dell, to be moved to the Bedford Elks Club.

A gaping hole was found in the kitchen floor, which sagged a foot and a half. The high side of the floor rested on a stone wall foundation. The kitchen, the main electric switchboard below, and the employees' cafeteria below suffered heavy damage. Some 100 employees living in the dormitory, which connected to the employees' cafeteria, were temporarily evacuated.

On Tuesday evening and Wednesday morning, guests were given supper and breakfast at the golf clubhouse nearby.

A portion of the kitchen and the dining room in the Colonial building were soon back in service. Meat was cooked at the Elks Club and driven back to the Springs in employees' cars. A quick return to normal was expected because the first of some 400 Pennsylvania National Insurance claims agents were expected to arrive on Thursday for a convention. The kitchen floor was shored up and a temporary railing was placed around the hole in the floor.

Gardner Moore said he felt it was electrical in nature and probably related to the switchboard that stood away from the walls, and ran to the ceiling below the kitchen.

Damage was estimated at between $75,000 and $125,000.

By the spring of 1971, the year that Bedford County residents celebrated the county's bicentennial year, extensive renovations had been completed to the kitchen wing. All new ranges and other equipment had been installed. A new floor of concrete and steel had been constructed. Also included were a new bake shop, new staff dining room, and a completely refurbished employee cafeteria.

A news article from 1971 pointed out that "Over two thirds of the hotel's over 250 guest rooms have been repainted.

"The famed hotel, Bedford's host to travelers since 1804, expects to see more than 25,000 guests this season.

"With conventions booked well into June, Manager E. Harris Knight predicts it should be a very good year.

"The first convention opening here today is Danforth Associates of Washington, D.C., a professional group interested in international affairs.

"A broad spectrum of state and regional groups is expected throughout the remainder of the year. Over 280 persons will be employed by the Springs this summer."

A description of the Bedford Springs Resort of the 1970s is found in a radio script originally aired on WQED-FM, Pittsburgh, part of the Public Broadcasting System, dating from 1977 or 1978 and later published in book form. A copy of the script is found in the Bedford County Historical Society's Bedford Springs collection, but unfortunately the author is not known.

The unidentified broadcaster titled his piece, "The Ghost of President Buchanan, and a Town." His broadcast is reprinted here, in parts:

"Spa life has never been quite so important in America as it has in Europe, although possibly this is an overstatement, because therapeutic waters certainly did play a refulgent role in the social history of the United States during the nineteenth and early twentieth centuries. Wherever there was a spring whose waters would seem to have curative or ameliorative properties, a hotel was sure to be built, or even a series of lodging places. Perhaps the most famous American spa of the nineteenth century was Saratoga Springs, in northern New York state -- a glittering resort of sin and fashion celebrated in song and story.

"Pennsylvania never had anything in the way of spas so fabulous as Saratoga, but there were several in the western part of the state. The Cambridge Springs Riverside Hotel of 1886, in Crawford County, was a quiet, well-run establishment noted for its waters, but it recently has closed. Long one of the most popular health spas was that of Frankfort Mineral Springs, in Beaver County, with a large hotel that burned in 1906. Still extant and flourishing is the Bedford Springs near Bedford, which was established shortly after 1800, when Dr. John Anderson of the town located a lodging house at a magnesia mineral spring. By mid-century additional quarters had been built with a frontage of almost six hundred feet.

156 - The Bedford Springs Resort

"Many people prominent in the social, political and business life of the Eastern Seaboard have been summer guests here, but its most famous visitor was James Buchanan (1791 - 1868), Pennsylvania's only President (1857 - 1861). During that strange, uneasy, lurid period just before the Civil War, Bedford Springs was Buchanan's Summer White House. In those days there was no Camp David.

"I consider it my favorite American spa of all possible spas -- and it seems to me that the long echoing verandas and solemn Greek Revival halls of the hotel are haunted by the ghost of President Buchanan. In fact, so sure am I of his haunting presence that I have even entertained the idea of some kind of reincarnation. Once, a year or two ago, when I was sitting on one of the verandas with the high summer sun shining through my expansive white hair and whiskers, a passing summer lady, struck by my mid-nineteenth century appearance, asked me who I was. "The ghost of President Buchanan," I replied solemnly.

"From the town squares one approaches the Bedford Springs Hotel via Route 220, after having passed through the calm residential streets of Victorian and Edwardian Bedford. One skirts a golf course that surrounds another old, high-veranda-ed hotel now belonging to the Elks....The road enters a narrow gap between two mountains through which flows a small creek. One passes a stone mill of 1797 and, on the other side of the road, a log house of 1798 -- both of them in excellent condition. Here, in the green shade cast by the looming mountains, it is not too difficult to imagine what the Bedford countryside must have been like two hundred years ago.

"The gap widens again into the beginning of a tree-studded lawn, with the creek murmuring along at the other side of the road. As the valley slowly unfolds and expands, suddenly the hotel unfurls on the right like a long snake of brick and timber. Long lines of verandas terminate, at the hotel entrance, in a large Classical portico, part of the Greek Revival main building that President Buchanan would have known so well.

"The chief dimension of these nineteenth century resort hotels was almost invariably horizontal; height was eschewed for obvious reasons until elevators began to be introduced toward the end of the century. It is interesting that horizontal construction has come back into fashion with the advent of the motel. But in the old days, if more rooms were needed, another wing was attached to existing ranges of three-and-four-story structures, whose varying styles attest to the dates of their construction. At Bedford Springs verandas abound, especially on some of the later wooden buildings; the Victorians loved to take the air sedately. I myself prefer a room with a porch. Being elderly and sedentary, I like to sit in the dappled summer light, reading and writing or just contemplating reflectively the past. For those guests who prefer vertical living there is a high-rise tower of the 1920s, attached to the up-valley end of the hotel.

"For the younger and more active guests there are all the amenities of the modern resort hotel, save winter sports, because Bedford Springs is open only from May to November (The season has since been lengthened). Up the valley is a great golf course, one of the chief attractions of the hotel. One may ride, like the Victorians in a surrey or on horse-back, walk, hike, or "jog." There are several tennis courts and places for shuffleboard. On the long green lawns in front of the hotel, I have seen ladies and gentlemen playing croquet or practicing archery. Or were these the shades of long ago visitors? At night, if you want to dance, you may do so at the week-end. If you like to eat and drink, the meals are abundant and good, and they go with the price of your room.

"If you want to take the therapeutic waters, they are still there, but they are not so fashionable as they once were. With the development of modern medicine in the last few decades, there has been less and less emphasis on hydrotherapy of the nineteenth century type. One of the chief springs is located in a small Classical pavilion on the other side of the valley from the main entrance building of the hotel, and it may be reached by an elevated bridge from the Greek Revival veranda.

"The architecture of the hotel, in all its variety, is a constant pleasure. The interior of the Greek Revival main building was remodeled in

The Gardner Moore era - 157

the 1890s with a handsome "grand" staircase and a huge fireplace that always has a blazing fire on cool days or evenings...

"Bedford Springs is old, and yet always new. Here you may have both the past and the present, while you enjoy all the comforts of modernity. As I have said, it is my own favorite spa, and my commendation of it is a labor of love."

During the L. Gardner Moore years the Bedford Springs Hotel hosted dozens of famous people, including Ralph Nader, Ambassador Andrew Young, Lee Iacocca, Billy Casper, Joe Paterno and countless congressmen, judges and governors.

In 1975, another (future) president visited the Bedford Springs. Ronald Reagan stayed one night at the hotel and made a speech before the Maryland Chamber of Commerce.

In his address, as reported in the *Bedford Gazette,* he blamed the country's economic problems on the growing power of government and called for a return of power to the states.

Reagan said, "The belief that government, especially the federal government, has the answer to our ills, and that the proper method of dealing with social problems is to transfer power from the private to the public sector..." has led to inflation, rising unemployment, and "the absorption of revenue at all levels of government."

Government at all levels, according to Reagan, will absorb 37 percent of the gross national product and 44 percent of our total personal income by the end of this fiscal year next June.

"Federal authority ... has created more problems in welfare, education, housing, food stamps, Medicaid, community and regional development, and revenue sharing, to name a few," Reagan said. "The sums involved and the potential savings to the taxpayer are large."

The speech set the stage for Reagan's candidacy for President of the United States a few years later.

In the 1970s it was no secret that the Bedford Springs was for sale. Gardner Moore, who was 78 years old when Reagan paid his visit to Bedford, had already handed over management of the hotel to his son-in-law, E. Harris Knight. In the late 1970s occupancy rates had been dropping, and the number of conventions being booked was also in decline.

In the 1970s a Huntington, West Virginia couple who would later become the owners of the Bedford Springs were forced off the Pennsylvania Turnpike during the snow storm, and almost by accident "discovered" the old hotel. Oralee Kieffer and then - husband J. Holden Kieffer thought it was magnificent and returned several times.

In a July 2007 interview she recalled, "We came back, we had a good time. It had a European comfortable feel."

Now the owner and operator of Oralee's Golden Eagle Inn at 131 E. Pitt Street, Bedford, she remembers those visits well. "What sold me on the place was one of those visits when the Washington Board of Realtors were meeting there. They were having a banquet and a beautiful young woman in a white gown slid down the banister. How could you not like a place like that where people felt comfortable to do something like that?"

The Bedford Springs Lobby. From a postcard.

At that time the Moore and Knight families had the historic hotel on the market. In 1979 Harris Knight reached a deal with Holland & Lyons Associates, a Washington, D.C. real estate firm. The option to purchase the Springs was for $4 million -- a bargain -- and the buyer pledged to invest $5.5 million in the property, which would include an indoor tennis building which would double as a banquet hall to seat 3,500 people.

Weeks later, Holland & Lyons suffered a financial setback and was unable to exercise the option. The hotel remained on the market.

In 1980 architect J. Holden Kieffer put together a group of three investors to purchase the Bedford Springs. The others were Bedford Springs golf pro Frank Trovato and William B. Pace, manager of Lakeview Resort in Morgantown, WV. They got the entire property for $3.6 million, financed through the Bedford County Industrial Development Authority.

Years of deferred maintenance and a gradual decline in guests had been hard on the hotel. The new owners began to make improvements. One of the first projects was the installation of a new watering system and shale cart paths around the golf course.

Oralee Kieffer recalls, "I had a wonderful time and I learned a lot. It was my introduction to the hospitality industry."

She also vividly remembers the disastrous flood that followed a freak downpour that took place in the early morning hours of June 21, 1983. The rainfall from the cloudburst was estimated at 6.5 to 8 inches, mostly between 2 and 4 a.m. Affected were the Shober's Run watershed, as well as the nearby valley of Friend's Cove and Mann's Choice.

Shober's Run turned into a raging torrent, knocking out all of the golf course bridges. One pedestrian bridge was rammed into the Club House, knocking it off its foundation. Asphalt paving on the curve in old Route 220 was lifted up and dumped into the hotel lawn. Golf carts were strewn along the road.

On that fateful night, Southern Alleghenies Planning and Development Commission was holding its annual conference at the Springs, which included planners and county officials from a six county region. Many of the guests who are still active in government remember that conference, and where their vehicles were found the next day. The raging, angry flood waters flipped the parked cars around the parking lot. Some were carried away and found at the upper end of the Bedford Elks golf course.

The water rose high enough to flow over the black and white tile floor of the main lobby and the enclosed promenade along the front of the Evitt and Stone Buildings.

"The first thing Bill Pace did," Oralee Kieffer remembered, "was set up a bar. I wouldn't have thought of it at that hour, but he thought the guests might need a drink when they started coming downstairs about 4:30 a.m." The guests were not waked during the flood. The managers thought that lives might be lost if the guests tried to save their vehicles. Nearly 100 cars were damaged.

Despite the damage, the hotel did not close, and the dining room was open that night. A Washington realtors group did postpone their convention for a few days; they were scheduled to arrive that evening.

Kieffer and Pace estimated the damage and lost revenue at $2 million.

Oralee continued, "It's really hard to bounce back from that. It was a huge expense, and we never could have done it without the staff and friends who gave their time." She remembers getting fish out of the indoor pool and the Bedford fire company pumping it and hosing down the place. Almost everyone who worked there found ways to walk in and help clean up, as did neighbors from Sweet Root Road; local teenagers scrubbed mud from the tennis courts; women golfers cleaned the clubs, clothing and shoes in the club house.

Ironically Bedford -- and the Springs -- did not qualify for Federal disaster assistance because not enough homes, roads or infrastructure was lost.

The year after the flood -- after the club house had been returned to its foundation -- the nearby golf cart barn burned and destroyed the golf carts.

A couple of weeks after the flood the golf course had been put back in shape. Three weeks after the flood, the Ladies Professional

The Gardner Moore era - 159

Golf Association held a pro-am tournament at the Springs. The tournaments continued for three summers but did not attract enough interest.

The Kieffer group did participate an ambitions venture to bring first class entertainment to the Bedford area. The seven year summer program was billed as the Bedford Springs Festival for the Performing Arts. A large yellow and white striped tent that could seat 1,000 was pitched in a meadow a half a mile below the hotel in the direction of Bedford. The meadow is on the hotel grounds. That summer the festival drew about 12,000 attendees.

In the first season, 1982, dozens of young people formed a symphony orchestra for the event. By the second season, the orchestra had grown to include professional musicians from orchestras and faculties from more than 20 states and Canada.

The first season featured Natasha Snitkovsky, a Baku, Russia born pianist, then living in the United States. A Steinway concert grand piano was trucked to the Springs specifically for her performance, on loan from the Steinway and Sons factory at Long Island City, NY.

The symphony orchestra was under the direction of Jacques Brourman, of Rumanian heritage, acting director of the New Orleans Philharmonic and music director of the Charlotte Symphony.

Brourman returned to Bedford for the second season, which ran from July to August 21, 1983. The schedule included symphony concerts, chamber music, solo recitals, poetry readings, lectures and a film series, plus, an elegant benefit ball held at the Bedford Springs, "reminiscent of social events of the pre-Civil War era when, for a time, the Springs served as an informal summer White House."

A steering committee of several hundred people from several states successfully solicited funds from more than 300 corporations, foundations and individual patrons to finance the Festival. They also set up a half dozen local committees from Washington, DC to Pittsburgh to promote the activities, and to "let many more people in on the secret of the most delightful cultural season in this region," stated Festival President Marcia Johnson, wife of noted Washington attorney Arnold C. Johnson.

The Bedford Springs Festival continued for seven seasons before it ran out of steam and money.

Not long after the Festival ended its last season, an even more ambitious plan was in the works to bring a symphony to Bedford -- the Pittsburgh Symphony Orchestra. In 1989 the Pittsburgh Symphony had been looking at several locations that could serve as the group's summer home. Bedford was one of these. In February, 1990 the Symphony announced that they had selected State College.

Bedford County's Board of Commissioners had spent $1,000 in secret for a study that concluded that the County could raise $3 million over a seven year period to support the summer home project. When the report became public, there was an outcry among county residents.

In May 1991, the Symphony took a renewed interest in Bedford and revealed that the orchestra would look at three potential sites for a summer home: Shawnee State Park, the Bedford Springs (which was then closed), and the Samuel Bussard, Jr. property located about 12 miles south of the Springs. At a public meeting, local residents voiced their opposition to two sites, but agreed that the Bedford Springs was a good location.

Unfortunately the Springs property was already embroiled in controversy. By 1985 the Kieffer group was having financial problems. Stated simply, the Bedford Springs Hotel was losing money. They were unable to secure financing to make the needed improvements, even with the promise of income tax credits for historic reconstruction. The hotel was for sale.

A buyer emerged in the form of Washington real estate developer F. Bruce Corneal and Altoona business owner Asher Sky. Sky Brothers, a wholesale food distributor, had just been sold to Sara Lee Corp. (now U.S. Foodservice, Inc.). Sky agreeing to take a 50% interest in Bedford Springs, with Corneal getting the other half. A deal was inked December 31, 1985, awaiting financing.

Throughout 1986 the Kieffer group remained in control of the property, as no bank would lend the money for the purchase and restoration of the historic hotel.

The 1987 season began with the Keiffers still operating the hotel. On July 30, 1987, Union National Bank of Pittsburgh approved a $7.5 million loan. Oralee Kieffer recalls staying on at the Springs, "working at everything from the front desk to bookkeeping. I guess the only job I didn't have was waitressing."

She then went to Key West, FL for three years to manage a guest house, but returned to Bedford where she purchased an historic property at 131 East Pitt Street. The three story green brick building was remodeled into a lodging and dining facility that is called Oralee's Golden Eagle Inn.

The Corneal - Sky partnership would not last long. Each partner wanted to control the project and had different ideas as to what should be done; they ended up in court in August 1987. The dispute and litigation dragged on for the remainder of the year, and for most of 1988. In January, 1989 a Federal bankruptcy judge gave control of the Bedford Springs to Sky.

Due to the Corneal - Sky dispute, all reconstruction work was halted on June 16, 1988. The golf course and hotel dining rooms were opened for the season, but the hotel itself did not open at all in 1988. The last year the hotel operated, until the 2007 reopening, was 1990.

Over the next two years Sky was unable to find a buyer or a lender to finance restoration of the hotel. At one point Sky was unable to make payments on the original $7.5 million loan, which had never been fully disbursed. In June 1991 Integra, the new owner of Union National Bank, said it would put the property up for Sheriff's sale for debt of $6.398 million.

This was, in brief, the situation at the Bedford Springs when the Pittsburgh Symphony decided to look at the Springs as a summer home, and negotiations began with Bedford County Commissioners and economic development leaders as partners. Initially, the Symphony said $10 million had to be raised locally, and a developer would put up the $50 to $60 million needed to restore the hotel.

Among the citizens of the county, opposition to the project was growing. People wondered why the Symphony, with its generous endowments, could not put up the money. When the Symphony asked the county to provide $20.5 million in tax increment bonds, political support evaporated and it started to look like a lost cause. By September 1992, the Symphony project was dead.

Even as the Symphony project was struggling to attract the needed financing, a group of county residents had been working behind the scenes to get the Bedford Springs Hotel designated as a National Historic Landmark. Bedford architectural engineer William Defibaugh, journalist Sally Frear, and members of the county Historical Society worked diligently with Gerald Kuncio, historic preservation specialist with the Pennsylvania Historic and Museum Commission to provide the documentation

The dining room staff is shown preparing a huge buffet in 1949.
Courtesy Bedford Gazette.

needed for the designation.

Kuncio said the architecture of the buildings, while significant, was secondary in importance to the cultural and historical importance. He pointed to its association with President James Buchanan, who used the resort as his summer White House, and because it is an important example of 19th century resort/spa life.

"This is a tremendous place. I'm really impressed with what good condition it's in after being basically vacant" for three years, Kuncio said.

On April 25, 1991, the Secretary of the Interior's National Park System Advisory Board, meeting in Olympic National Park in Washington state, recommended that the Springs and 25 other historic sites be designated as National Historic Landmarks.

Ben Levy, administrator of the National Historic Landmarks Survey, noted that it was one of 40 sites reviewed, of which 26 were chosen. Levy said nearly 2,000 sites had been so designated, in comparison to more than 60,000 properties that were listed on the National Register of Historic Places.

The hotel, still the property of Union National Bank, "could become the recipient of restoration funding which would not be available to other properties. Additionally, tax credits would be available on rehabilitation costs," it was reported.

Still, those benefits did not come automatically. The only thing presented was a plaque noting the landmark designation. Nor did the designation guarantee that the historic hotel buildings would be preserved.

With the Pittsburgh Symphony out of the picture, the Bedford County Commissioners took the lead. The county spent $10,000 on a feasibility study that concluded that the Springs could be revitalized under federal redevelopment regulations with little risk to the county. The study was the work of Michael Shaul of Harrisburg. In all, Shaul received $100,000 for the study and his unsuccessful efforts to find a developer that had the financial resources to do the project. AIHP (now Allegheny Ridge Corporation) contributed $44,000 of the cost.

In 1994 Gov. Robert Casey delivered on a promise to provide a $5 million state grant for the project, and Congressman Bud Shuster added $6.1 million in federal highway funds. The county had made a deal in December 1993 with Integra Bank to sell the Bedford Springs property for a bargain basement price of $1.625 million, but only if a developer was found who had the money. The Bedford County Redevelopment Authority would hold the title.

No deal was made until mid-1995 when the prospective developer, Marcus Fields, agreed to put up $1.5 million and another $2.5 million came from the Dauphin County General Authority. In exchange for the money, the Dauphin Authority would own and (hopefully) operate the Springs golf course. In fact, the course was maintained and remained open until June, 1996.

The $1.5 million from Fields enabled the Bedford County Authority to buy the hotel property. Fields promised to raise another $4 million to get the project rolling.

For the next three years not much happened with the project. Fields was searching for either financing, a partner, or both. Fields and both

The Fix family: From left, Sherman Fix, Darlene Long, Chef Wesley Fix and Ruth Ann Fix. All worked at the Bedford Springs.
Photo by Jon Baughman.

162 - The Bedford Springs Resort

authorities were constantly at odds with each other.

Finally in 1998 the project was handed over to a new developer, Shober's Run Development Corp., with Mark Langdale, a Houston, Texas developer holding a majority interest, and Marcus Fields retaining a minority interest. Later, Fields and his partner, William DeForrest were sued by Shober's Run for $1 million for misleading them on the cost of the project by $10 million. By December, 1998 the total cost to renovate the Bedford Springs had climbed to $70 million.

The golf course renovations began in May, 1999 and once the course opened, it was heavily used. Otherwise, not much was happening.

By 2001 Shobers Run went public with a new proposal. Restoration was out, new construction was in. Shober's Run had stated officially the previous March that they could not find the $70 million to pay for historic restoration. The fears of the county Historical Society -- expressed back in 1991 when the National Historic Landmark designation was approved -- had come true. The historic portions of the hotel would be demolished. Only "some" portions would be saved.

In March, 2001 the "New Vision" was unveiled to the Redevelopment Authority.

The "some" that would be restored boiled down to the brick Colonial Building and the attached indoor pool building. Everything else would be demolished. It was reasoned that everybody still wanted a hotel project, and it was better to save some of the Springs buildings than none.

The presentation made to the Authority described the new facility as a hotel, spa and conference center with 230 guest rooms, to be located on the hillside where the Barclay Building was located. This is the same location where Pittsburgh architect Eric Fisher Wood had designed a new hotel complex for the Bancrofts, of which only the Barclay portion was completed. The projected cost of the project was $60 million. The new complex would face down the valley, toward the golf course. A new golf club house was also planned.

Shober's Run Corp. and Stormont Hospitality Group of Atlanta, the hotel management group still interested in the Springs, had employed architects RTKL, to prepare the concept drawings. Dick Stormont had personally examined the hillside and saw it as the perfect location for the new complex.

The county historical society was not happy with the project, especially the plans to demolish most of the historic structures. At an authority meeting held July 10, 2001, Sally Frear of the historical society was accepted as an advisor to the authority. Specifically, the historical society wanted to work on restoration of the lobby of the Colonial Building and the two-room suite of President James Buchanan, also in the Colonial Building. In addition, the society wanted the Stone Building preserved.

Frear told the authority that the Stone Building is structurally sound, and is a fine example of the Springs early history with its tapered walls of stone, hand hewn beams and its original hearth from the hotel. She said the historical society had formed a committee to accumulate information to use to try and save the oldest structure -- the Stone Building, if the whole hotel cannot be saved. Committee members had been exploring the building, crawling into the attic to find beams and chimney flues no longer visible in the lower floors.

Authority member Tom Cunningham said he wanted the authority to back the historical society's effort to catalog what artifacts remain at the Springs, "so they don't disappear. The last five or six owners have ravaged it. They've flat out stolen things."

Cunningham also noted that former developer Marcus Fields had sold a lot of the furniture, antiques, ledger and record books and other contents of the hotel at auction. Some of the antique furniture and many of the ledger books had been purchased by Bedford architectural engineer William Defibaugh and were being preserved by him for future use at a restored Bedford Springs.

Bedford County Commissioner David Thompson told the authority that the Pennsylvania Historic and Museum Commission had indicated that tearing down portions of the historic hotel most likely would cost the Springs its National Historic Landmark designation.

The Gardner Moore era - 163

James Petrarca, Redevelopment Authority chairman, explained his group's position by saying, "We've finally admitted that there is no way to do a complete restoration. More than half the hotel needs to be replaced."

The decaying part has rotting wood and rooms about half the size of those in today's Marriotts or Sheratons. Petrarca explained that many walls are covered with mold, and parts of the roof are caving in.

The tax breaks for the project, the Authority said, would hopefully come from a new program under which the hotel property would be designated a Keystone Opportunity Expansion Zone. The Authority had filed an application before the February 28, 2001 deadline. Bedford Township, Bedford County and the Bedford Area School District all had to give their blessing. They did. By mid-year, the Bedford Springs property had received the designation and the tax incentives that went with it over a ten year period.

State Senator Robert C. Jubelirer of Altoona was the driving force behind the KOEZ designation and also some $26 million in state funding that was eventually approved.

Senator Jubelirer devoted 17 years of his political career on the Bedford Springs project, which in a 2007 interview he described in one word -- "Frustration." Early in the process, he said, there "were actually more setbacks than anything. We never gave up and I know those in Bedford didn't either."

Following the unveiling of the plans for a new hotel in 2001, the former State Senator recalls that there was a big hurdle, and that was approval by the Pennsylvania Historic and Museum Commission because the hotel had National Historic Landmark designation. The PHMC was not comfortable with demolition of the older portions of the hotel in favor of new construction and would not give the needed approvals.

Che Sara Sara plate from the 1950s; table water bottle from the 1920s.
Photo by Jon Baughman.

By the year 2005 a compromise had been reached between the developer, Mark Langdale, and the PHMC under which most of the historic property would be preserved and restored; a smaller portion would be demolished and replaced with entirely new facilities.

Jubelirer said, "It almost made you sick to your stomach sometimes as one developer fell," and what started out as a $3 million rehab grew to a $40 to $50 million project.

"Three governors helped fund the project," Jubelirer recalled. "It was virtually the last hours of Mark Schweiker's tenure that he emailed we had $16 million that made the difference (in the success of the project). Gov. Bob Casey was first with the $5 million to start and Gov. Ed Rendell has helped ($3.9 million). We begged and borrowed to convince these administrations this was a good project, and that we had the match."

He continued, "Finding that match was a substantial struggle." Langdale came to the project in 1998 through a chance encounter with Marcus Fields, who had spent three years looking for money. Langdale spent until 2005 finding private funding and securing approval of the project, particularly through the PHMC.

Between 2001 and 2005, as investors and public officials worked feverishly behind the scenes, there wasn't much news about the project. The parties had agreed to remain silent until a project was in place.

William L. Defibaugh

Walk through the halls of the restored and renovated Bedford Springs Resort, and you will see the handiwork of William L. Defibaugh, P.E. everywhere, but you may not realize the scope of his involvement.

The historic photos, framed and displayed on the walls, the antique chairs on display in several of the dining rooms, the framed flyers and posters, the cast iron kettles and cooking utensils, the hand-embroidered samplers hanging on the walls -- even the hotel guest books came from Bill's collection.

"A previous owner of the Bedford Springs sold the furnishings and even the hotel guest registers at public auction. I didn't want these treasures to leave Bedford County, so I bid on them. I kept them in the basement of my home until the restoration of the Springs could become a reality," he pointed out.

Bill grew up in Michigan, but his family made many visits to Bedford when he was growing up. "As I grew up, I came to love the Bedford Springs, and the stories about my family's connection to it. I started buying things at auctions and I had others go to auctions for me while I was living and working in Detroit. If I had to go to Pittsburgh on business, I always made a side trip to Bedford," Bill said. As a professional engineer and architect, business trips took him to many regions of the country. But if he had business in Pennsylvania, Bedford was also on the itinerary.

Defibaugh's parents worked at the Springs, both as pin setters in the bowling alley before leaving for Michigan, and they had many stories to tell.

Eventually he and his wife came to realize that Bedford was their true home, and they moved from Detroit, even though he knew full well that he would make a lot less money here. But as the years passed, he knew that he had made the right decision. After moving to Bedford he was able to attend the auctions personally and was able to add greatly to his Bedford Springs collections.

The vast array of items, from books and maps, to ledgers, store account books and diaries, bottles, photographs, newspapers and antiques, are all housed in a spacious room in the basement of his home, except for the items already taken to the Springs (which are numerous). The Springs staff still stops by the house to pick up additional items, as required. "These items needed to be at the Springs," he added. The photo collection alone included more than 460 historic photos of the Bedford Springs Hotel.

Defibaugh is a founder of the Bedford Springs Historical Society. He has also been active in the Bedford County Historical Society and served as president for several years. That group (formerly called Pioneer Historical Society) has an extensive Bedford Springs collection; much of that material originated with Bill Defibaugh.

The Bedford Springs Historical Society serves as the repository of the Bedford Springs - related material owned by Defibaugh. The management of the resort has provide secure space at the Resort in which the collection is being housed, organized, and indexed.

The hotel guest registers are the gems of this collection. The ledgers have been returned to the Hotel. Bedford Springs Resort hosted many great Americans, from presidents to senators, military men to the captains of industry, Defibaugh said. Nine presidents have visited, and President Buchanan, the only president from Pennsylvania, spent decades relaxing there.

"I have the ledgers with signatures of people like Henry Clay and Daniel Webster. Both Clay and Webster were declared to be among the top five most important senators in American history. Aaron Burr, Henry Ford and Henry Clay Frick were also guests. They could come here and live a wonderful lifestyle."

Much of his information is contained in a 100 page soft-cover book that Bill has self-published. *The First Days of Bedford Springs* by William L. Defibaugh, P.E. is on sale at selected locations in and around Bedford, as well as the Bedford Springs Resort gift shop. One of the outstanding things about this book, other than the fine detail paid to the early history of the Resort, are the architectural drawings and hand-sketched maps that show the very first buildings constructed at the Resort, followed by additional buildings as they were constructed, enlarged or removed. This traces the Resort from its early beginnings up to the 1880s and 1890s. It is a must - read for anyone interested in the early history of this grand resort.

Bill Defibaugh at the Springs.
Photo by Jon Baughman.

Today, the completely restored indoor pool at the Omni Bedford Springs Resort bears testimony to the quality and expert craftsmanship that went into the Bedford Springs restoration.
Courtesy Bedford Gazette.

Bedford Springs reborn

In the summer of 2005 there were plenty of rumors circulating, but few facts, about the Bedford Springs project. The rumors were really flying when word leaked out in early August that Mark Langdale had purchased the Bedford Springs golf course from the Dauphin County Authority.

An announcement wasn't long in coming. A groundbreaking ceremony was planned for September 1 in front of the still - deteriorating hotel.

About a hundred public officials, citizens and members of the press turned out on that historic Thursday to hear Mark Langdale make the announcement. "On September 1, 2007, the Bedford Springs will be 202 years old and new. It's rare for people to come and experience a hotel that's been around for 200 years," but, he added, "We have a project."

With a massive project estimated to cost $80 million, Langdale said the hotel would be back in business in less than two years. The official groundbreaking ceremony included Langdale, State Senate President Pro Tem Robert C. Jubelirer, and 9th District Congressman Bill Shuster.

The state pledged $24.9 million for the project from the Redevelopment Assistance Capital Program -- money that had been allocated under three governors. The federal government invested $2.2 million for new water and sewer lines, and $7.7 million in highway funds to relocate Route 220 behind the hotel complex. The road relocation crossed through 22 acres of land owned and donated by the resort. Some 600,000 cubic yards of rock were dynamited out of the ridge for the new road.

Jubelirer was overjoyed, explaining, "Curiosity was rising because activity was picking up, but not much was being said. We agreed some time ago that there would not be any more public events until the goal line was crossed and we were assured of a win."

In 2003 Langdale began working with Benchmark Hospitality International, a Houston, TX based hotel operator, which would manage the Springs. Beginning that year, Benchmark participated in the planning process that would serve as a blueprint for the project.

Other partners with Langdale were the Ferchill Group, a Cleveland, OH real estate development company, and Chevron TCI Inc., an investor in tax credit rehabilitation projects. They joined forces as owners of the Bedford Springs under the name, Bedford Resort Partners, Ltd..

Langdale, who was appointed Ambassador to Costa Rica by President George W. Bush and who served in that capacity until April, 2008, outlined what the restored Bedford Springs would offer: 216 guest rooms, a spa, restored golf course, conference rooms and fine dining. He said the Springs would target business and conference groups, in addition to recreational travelers.

Managing partner Keith Evans was placed in charge of the massive construction project. Evans, a Dallas, TX developer, was first shown the property by business partner Langdale early in the project. "When I turned the corner, I couldn't help but fall in love. The history, the setting, the architecture, all just sitting there, waiting to come alive....like a Grand Lady waiting patiently for someone to do something."

Some feared that most sections of the old hotel were just beyond repair. Deterioration of the buildings actually began before the property changed hands in the 1980s. Previous developers had ripped up floors in the Colonial Building which were never replaced. For years the Springs was listed as one of Pennsylvania's most endangered historic properties.

In the end, the PHMC, the National Park Service and Bedford Resort Partners settled on a plan that allowed demolition of some portions of the hotel, new construction, and restoration. The NPS oversees the granting of historic preservation tax credits. The golf clubhouse and the old Dormitory building would be demolished. At the Barclay building on the hill, the top three floors would be removed; the remaining two floors would be renovated for office space, an employee cafeteria, maintenance and shipping and receiving. In place of the Dormitory, the owners would erect a new wing that would provide spacious guest suites and the Springs Eternal Spa.

Slated for restoration and renovation would be the indoor pool, Colonial Building, and the four structures that had guest rooms: Evitt House, Stone Inn, Swiss Cottage and Anderson House -- an expensive undertaking.

As the project moved forward, Adrian Scott Fine of the National Trust for Historic Preservation told reporters that it is always easier to start from scratch rather than restore. "A restoration means doing a lot of investigative work plus bringing the building up to current standards of safety and building codes. It's a pretty daunting task."

Rikki Boparai, Bedford Springs first general manager under the new partnership, and employed by Benchmark, said, "Restoration costs much more money than to demolish and then rebuild. But the beauty of a restoration is that you are preserving history." He pointed to the challenge of retaining the historic qualities of a building, while incorporating such modern essentials as electricity, high speed internet connections, cable TV, telephone, heating, ventilation and air conditioning, more spacious hotel rooms and even private baths in buildings where shared bathrooms were once the norm, or when outside toilets were in use.

In the Anderson House, Boparai said, "There were community bathrooms or none at all. They were outside. Today people expect bathrooms to be luxurious."

In the older portions of the hotel the contractors and architects were able to make the

State Senator Robert C. Jubelirer, in tan suit, talks with a reporter during the Grand Opening of the Resort. Courtesy Bedford Gazette.

rooms larger, and add the required bathrooms, by reducing the total number of guest rooms to 216. In the Anderson, Evitt and Swiss Cottage, the contractors took three old rooms to make two new ones. In the Stone Inn, two old rooms became one new guest room. The new bathrooms were designed like a "little spa." The interior color schemes were based on an Historic color palate.

Beneath the Swiss Cottage the remains of what was possibly a frontier fort was found. In the stone wall were gun ports for defense, which were still visible under the building.

One of the architects working on the project, David Rau of architectural firm 3 North of Richmond, VA, added, "Obviously you want to preserve the past, but you need to sort of re-envision it and transform it for a new generation. It doesn't do any good to just turn it into a museum."

An example of the painstaking restoration work undertaken at Bedford Springs is the fact that over 70 percent of the original windows were refinished. Many, if not most of the original windows were made from hand-blown glass. In the 19th Century, window glass was produced by blowing large cylinders, which were cut open and flattened, and then cut into panes. This process limited the size of the panes resulting in windows divided by transoms into rectangular panels.

The panes were marked by varying thicknesses, ripples, bubbles and other imperfections. Noted Boparai, "In the olden days people would pay any money to get perfect windows. Now they pay more for the imperfections."

Some window panes are engraved with former guests' initials. Former Resort employees noted that 19th Century brides often used their diamond rings to etch their names and dates onto the windows. These kinds of details help make the Springs "a national treasure," David Rau explained.

As in the past the porch ceilings were painted blue. The explanation given for this is because birds will not build nests in what looks like the sky.

The massive restoration and reconstruction would last two years and employ hundreds of construction workers and craftsmen, many from Bedford and surrounding counties. These men and women took a great deal of pride in their work as they wanted to see the Springs returned to its former glory. Dozens of contractors participated in the project.

Keith Evans observed, "I can't come to Bedford without someone telling me how excited they are. The chance to work on and invest in something like this -- it comes along only once in one's career."

Jeff Farina, chief development officer for Benchmark, explained, "This is a facility unlike any other because there's a complete ground-up restoration. You have this historic hotel that's going to be completely modern in every respect."

The actual reconstruction contractor, Reynolds Construction, supervised the numerous contractors that performed the work, as well as the craftspersons employed by them. James Paschke, senior project manager, explained, "We started working on pre-construction activities in 1998. Then we had selective demolition in 2005 and built the foundations for the spa. Our work on the historic portion of the property began in March of 2006," and from there, took about 15 months from gutting to finish.

"The restoration, one of the most comprehensive of its kind ever attempted in the nation, dealt with both structural and architectural challenges. The work included many important construction tasks from the removal of asbestos to the structural reinforcement of the buildings. There were many details attended to, as well. For example, glass resembling that of the hotel's glory days was used to replace broken windows. Old mortar, brick and stone was cleaned and original wood was removed, refurbished and replaced." -- *Bedford Gazette,* July 12, 2007.

"The most challenging thing about the restoration of the Bedford Springs Resort has been dealing with unforeseen conditions. But it has also been a very rewarding experience for all of us. It took a great deal of vision to see the grandeur of the place, considering the conditions when we began. That vision of the managing partners was what sustained us," Paschke added.

As construction moved into high gear, Bedford County's retailers were warned that they needed to get ready for the grand opening of the Bedford Springs Resort. At meetings sponsored by the Bedford County Chamber of Commerce, Todd Gillespie of Benchmark explained that the new Springs would offer an offbeat blend of old-fashioned elegance and modern-day convenience.

"We'll have an advantage over the Greenbrier and the Homestead," Gillespie said, referring to other historic resorts that competed against Bedford Mineral Springs in the past and would continue to do so in the future. "They've been open 225 years, but they don't have modern amenities like flat screen TV's."

According to Gillespie the new resort would be open year round, and the average guest would have a household income of over $75,000 a year. Benchmark predicted that about 125,000 guests would stay at the Springs the first season -- an average of 342 guests a day.

Alice Estrada, Main Street Manager for Gettysburg, told the Bedford group that the challenge would be to entice guests to stay at the resort and shop downtown.

Sharon Turkovich, Bedford Main Street Manager, added that before the Springs closed in 1990, guests flooded downtown and spent money. "Everybody in town would anxiously await opening day in May," she said. The challenge is for each business to be prepared to deal with that target market.

Early in the year 2007 Bedford Resort Partners, Ltd. announced that the Springs would reopen for Memorial Day -- at least, that was the target date. By this time, the total cost of the massive project had reached nearly $120 million and the state's investment in the Springs restoration was nearly $30 million.

In mid-April Keith Evans announced that about 40 people had been hired, mostly for the golf course maintenance crew. Sales teams and senior managers would be next, followed by general hiring in the middle of May.

Boparai said, in an interview published April 25, that the general contractor was pushing furiously to open on Memorial Day weekend. "Everyone is working hard and very long hours to get the job done. Most of the furniture for the historical guest rooms is in, and we will be installing our kitchen equipment this week. Work on the spa is going well and the landscapers are making progress on the front of the building."

As the Memorial Day holiday approached it became clear that the deadline would not be met. It was agreed to push back the grand opening to ensure that everything was ready. The new target would be July 12.

Excitement began building even before summer arrived. A steady stream of local residents and curiosity seekers drove out old Route 220 every day to see the miracle that was taking shape. A neglected, crumbling hotel that was still listed in some tourism guide books as having "since declined into disrepair and decay" had come back to life.

"We look forward to celebrating the completion of

The Crystal Room.
Courtesy Bedford Gazette.

Bedford Springs Resort," said Keith Evans. "This remarkable, historic property is the culmination of years of planning, persistence in our commitment to the restoration and assistance from the State of Pennsylvania and civic leadership. All of this and more assisted us in getting us to this exciting day."

He explained that some of Bedford Springs Resort's oldest living guests and former employees will be in attendance to celebrate the resort's re-opening and help welcome first-time guests to the newly restored historic destination. Also on hand for the ceremony will be representatives of Bedford Resort Partners Ltd., owners and developers of Bedford Springs Resort; Benchmark Hospitality International, and community officials.

Evans continued, "The Greenbrier in West Virginia and The Homestead in Virginia are listed as two of the 1,000 places to see before you die, and Bedford Springs Resort will be 1001!"

Finally the big day arrived. In Bedford, there was much excitement in the air, even though the July 12 festivities were by invitation only. The management promised that, once the formalities were over, tours of the restored resort would be given to the public.

The opening ceremonies began at 10 a.m., and Bedford Springs Old Course, its classic design now restored to its former glory, officially re-opened at 12 noon.

After setting idle for 20+ years, and many years of neglect, the Bedford Springs Resort officially opened amid much pomp and celebration. The project to renovate and restore the historic Springs cost $120 million and took two years to complete.

Managing partner Keith Evans told the crowd of employees and guests, "This is a happy day. There is no other project like this. To be part of such a special piece of history -- it's truly, truly a privilege."

Former State Senator Robert C. Jubelirer, who played a major role in obtaining funding for the project, called it "A dream come true."

Special guests at the opening were Nellie Burger Over, who was a waitress at the Springs from 1937-38, and Max and Mary Francis Elbin, who met at the Springs in 1938. They were the hotel's first guests and arrived in horse drawn carriages, and to the strains of the Bedford Springs March, composed in 1878 by Adam Geibel.

Due to the famed mineral springs on the property, the original Bedford Springs was a spa, but over the decades grew into a full-service resort, complete with its legendary golf course.

The new owners returned to the Resort's beginning as a spa. Evans explained, "It's all about the history. And it's all about the water." Mineral water, that is.

The new owners demolished the old dormitory building, where employees once stayed, and in its place developed the new 30,000 sq. ft. Springs Eternal Spa, featuring 14 treatment

The outdoor pool. Courtesy Bedford Gazette.

rooms. But it is no ordinary spa. Richmond, VA architect David Rau, who worked on the project, said the spa is the cornerstone of the resort. "Today there are spas on every corner" across the country, "but they have tap water. This spa is fed by natural mineral springs, just like in the resort's early years." So are the restored indoor pool, constructed in 1905, and the new outdoor pool.

Completely restored are the original hotel sections, the Evitt House, Stone Inn, Swiss Cottage and the Anderson House. All rooms feature a 32-inch LCD flat screen TV, i-Pod docking station, alarm clocks and high-speed wireless internet. The hotel has a total of 216 rooms, including suites.

The main building, the Colonial, no longer contains guest rooms. Dining options include the Crystal Room, the Frontier Tavern, 1796 Room, Che Sara Sara Cafe, and the Turtle Shell. The kitchen has been completely modernized.

The Crystal Dining Room, the Resort's largest, seats 142 persons in two distinct dining areas. It features wood floors, rich area carpets, and linen covered tables with Victorian round back chairs.

The Frontier Tavern takes its name from the old Defibaugh Tavern, also called The Willows, that once served chicken dinners to Bedford Springs guests arriving aboard the Talley-Ho stage. Located on the ground floor of the Stone Inn, it provides a relaxed dining area and also serves as the main bar and lounge. There are a number of historic artifacts on display, such as an old bear trap, tools, wood-fired kitchen stove, antique china and crockery. Also located here is a dining room known as the 1796 Room. Inside, antique chairs, quilts, and coverlets -- all vintage and locally made, are on display. Located inside this room is the original fireplace on which the very first meals for Bedford Springs guests were prepared.

The Che Sara Sara Cafe (based on the motto on the crest of the original Duke of Bedford) is a specialty shop for tea, coffee, ice cream and confections, soups, sandwiches, sodas, beer and wines.

The Turtle Shell is located at the outdoor pool.

The 20,000 sq. ft. conference center offers the most current meeting technology. The conference facilities include the ballroom; junior ballroom; Reagan meeting room which seats up to 120 persons; 16 soundproof, climate controlled meeting rooms and 10 breakout rooms. The largest room is 5,550 sq. ft. and the smallest, 768 sq. ft.

The Springs Eternal Spa features spas fed by the famed mineral springs. An eighth spring uncovered during the excavation for the new spa and christened the Eternal Spring, was pressed into service to supply water for the spa.

In earlier times, this spring was located in the old boiler room.

Spa services include body treatments, massage, hydrotherapy, facial treatments, manicures and pedicures, couples' treatments, and more. Guests can relax while sampling the historic Bedford Baths using products inspired by local herbs and botanicals.

Five guest suites are located in the spa building. The Donald Ross Suite, named for the famed golf course designer, contains 2 bedrooms, 2-1/2 baths and a grand terrace that can hold 75 people.

The Clay and Calhoun Suite is actually two connecting suites overlooking the golf course.

The James K. Polk Suite features sweeping vistas of the golf course and the Cumberland Valley.

The Junior Suite has a small private balcony.

Half Way House is located near the 10th green of the golf course and serves snacks, sandwiches, and drinks.

The rooms off of the Lobby display hundreds of framed vintage photos and other documents portraying the history of the Bedford Springs, many of which were donated by Bill Defibaugh. Among these is a contract for the construction of the Stone Inn. In the spa, a large glass display case is filled with bottles of all shapes, sizes and colors that were once used in the sale of bottled Bedford Springs mineral water.

The painstaking attention given to historically accurate details throughout the resort's landmark structures have been praised by architectural and historical experts. Bedford Springs Resort was among the most threatened landmarks on the National Register of Historic

Keith Evans, managing partner, welcomes the first guests to the new Bedford Springs Resort. From left are Nellie Burger Over, a waitress at the Springs in 1937-38; and Max and Mary Frances Elbin, who met at the Springs in 1938.   Courtesy Bedford Gazette.

Places prior to the $120 million investment infused into this national treasure.

Nellie Burger graduated in 1937 from Altoona High School in Altoona, Pennsylvania and remembers how hard jobs were to find during the Depression-era years. Her aunt was the head hostess at Bedford Springs Hotel and she found Nellie a waitress job in the Crystal Dining Room.

Mr. Burger, Nellie's dad, hesitated as his daughter was only 17 and had never left home. But her aunt reassured him that Nellie would be well supervised because all the others waitresses were school teachers on summer break.

"I really loved it at the hotel and enjoyed working in the main dining room, the Crystal Room," Mrs. Over said. "Bill Welch was the hotel gardener then and kept the most beautiful flower beds. He always had fresh flowers in the dining room and the annex."

"Every night," Nellie remembers, "A five-piece band played dinner music at the hotel. My sister, Viola, also worked at the hotel for two years and met her husband there. He played in the band."

Nellie met her husband, Edgar Over, a Bedford native, while she worked at the hotel. "He was a postal clerk at the Bedford Post Office and a volunteer fireman. His mother owned the tourist home on East Pitt Street called Lincoln Lodge," she explained.

"I have lots of fond memories of the hotel and am so happy it has been restored and re-opened," she said during the grand opening.

Bedford Springs reborn - 173

1796 Room: Fine Dining

174 - The Bedford Springs Resort

Max Elbin was 18 years old in 1938 and a recent graduate of Allegany High School in Cumberland, Maryland, when he participated in a golf tournament at Bedford Springs. The same day, the woman who would later become his bride, Mary Frances Kelly, was 17 and a senior at Ursuline Academy, also in Cumberland, and along with several girlfriends, attended Camp Sunshine, not far from the resort.

Carrene Elbin Ressa, the couple's daughter, further unfolded the story about how her father, Carl Maxwell Elbin, Sr. (Max), went on to achieve a career in golf that would honor him with induction into the PGA Golf Hall of Fame in 2005, and how her parents met the day he played in the Bedford Springs golf tournament.

"My father was dating one of mother's friends at the camp and she wanted to see my father play golf that day. My mother went along with her friend for something to do. When the tournament was over, my parents were introduced. Shortly after meeting dad at the tournament, my mother's friend announced that she had found another boyfriend. Dad was available! Mother and dad began dating and were married in 1943," said Ressa.

"The Bedford Springs golf tournament was also the reason that my parents left western Maryland for Silver Spring, and finally, settled in Bethesda," Ressa went on to say. "Dad not only met my mother at the tournament, but also Lew Worsham, one of the golfers who played in the tournament and the head golf professional at Burning Tree Golf Club in Bethesda. Worsham needed an assistant and hired dad for the job."

Max Elbin took over as head golf professional at Burning Tree when Worsham left to pursue his dream of playing on the professional golf tour. In fact, Worsham won the 1947 U.S. Open Championship, defeating Sam Snead in an 18-hole playoff, as well as the Tam O'Shanter World Championship in 1953, golf's first $100,000 tournament.

Elbin remained at Burning Tree for 50 years, retiring in 1996.

During his golf career, he served as secretary and president of the Mid-Atlantic Professional Golfers Association (PGA) and president of the PGA of America from 1966-68. In his capacity as head professional, he taught or talked golf with U.S. presidents, kings, diplomats, senators, congressmen and notable entertainers.

"I think it is safe to say that none of this would have happened if it were not for the Bedford Springs golf tournament," said Ressa.

The promised open house was scheduled for Monday, July 16 after the official opening. Visitors were instructed to park at the Bedford Fairgrounds and five buses were used, 55 passengers per bus, plus 29 on a smaller, sixth bus, to shuttle the visitors to Bedford Springs with the first tour to begin at 4:00 p.m. The turnout for the tours was beyond belief. Cars started showing up at the Fairgrounds at 1:30 p.m. causing the Fair board to open the restrooms there.

It is estimated that 2,500 people toured the Springs that evening. This figure doesn't count the number of people who got caught in a traffic jam on Pitt Street trying to get to the Fairgrounds. Many never made it. The Fairground lots were filled to capacity by 6:45 p.m., and some cars were parked in the back fields.

During the open house, Keith Evans observed, "I have no idea how many people are here, but its amazing. I also continue to be surprised by the wonderful stories from people about their experiences at the Springs from the past."

Rikki Boparai added, "It was our pleasure to provide this open house. It's their property (Bedford County residents) and I think they wanted it to be transformed like this."

Even before the ribbon was cut on July 12, many golfers were checking out the golf course. "I first saw this place in 1988 and it was a wreck," golf course architect Ron Forse of Forse Design, Hopwood, PA said of the hotel and surrounding property. Forse explained that the Bedford Springs Old Course is a hybrid of three eras of golf and three designers, Oldham, Tillinghast and Ross. He said his firm "put its heart and soul into this" project, which cost $8 million.

An official opening tee-off was also held July 12. Taking a whack at the ball with a vintage wooden 1924 driver was Michael Fay of

Hartford, CT, executive director of the Donald Ross Society. Fay stood out in his authentic 1920s golf attire, which consisted of "plus fours" and a flat tartan cap. Fay said he was proud to take part in initiating the Bedford Springs course.

"The course and the hotel are an ambitious undertaking."

Fay continued, "I've played 145 Ross courses and I'd give this one an 'A' just looking at it."

A new barn for golf carts was completed on the opposite side of Sweet Root Road and the old clubhouse was demolished. The course is being operated from a desk next to a new gazebo near the location of the old clubhouse, and from a pro shop in the spa wing of the hotel.

Bedford Springs hosted its first wedding reception on August 25, with 250 people attending. Within a few weeks, 16 more weddings had been booked. In mid-September sixteen judges held a golf tournament at the resort, and more tournaments were planned.

By October, 21 holiday parties had been booked, and a special event was planned for Thanksgiving. Pennsylvania's newest resort was off to a great start.

As the 2008 travel season approached, general manager Rikki Boparai and Courtney Lowe, who had joined the Springs staff, arriving from Equinox Resort in Manchester, Vermont, said the goal for 2008 was 60 percent occupancy year round, and 80 percent in the summer and fall. But businesses everywhere were hurt that year by ever - increasing gasoline prices which approached $4.00 a gallon that summer, followed by a recession that was caused, in part, by the sudden decline in real estate prices and a mortgage crisis.

In 2008, the Old Course at Bedford Springs had 11,500 total rounds of golf played.

In November the Springs received the Phoenix Award from the Society of American Travel Writers. The award recognizes conservation, preservation, beautification and anti-pollution campaigns by travel destinations worldwide.

The golf course has won many awards and was named "one of the best golf courses in America" for the 2009-2010 season by Zagat, the world's leading provider of consumer survey - based information. Golf Week Magazine has named Bedford Springs Old Course as the number one playable classic course in Pennsylvania.

In December it was announced that Omni Hotels and Resorts would be taking over the management of Bedford Springs from Benchmark. Both Benchmark and Omni are based in Texas. In a press release explaining the change, it was stated that "Ownership recently made the determination that it needed to bring in a new financial partner, which in this case, came with its own management group attached."

On January 1, 2009 the resort's name was officially changed to Omni Bedford Springs Resort. Omni is a privately held company, headed by billionaire Robert Rowling who founded TRT Holdings, the holding company for Omni Hotels.

In announcing the change, Benchmark said the company "is extremely proud of the tremendous performance of its executive team at Bedford Springs Resort throughout every phase of the project, and is equally pleased to have successfully accomplished the initial mission, helping lay a strong foundation for the future growth of this premier destination resort."

Under Omni, Scott Stuckey was appointed general manager. A graduate of the University of Wisconsin - Stout in 1988 with a degree in hotel and restaurant management, Stuckey was employed by Marriott Hotels before joining Omni in 2005. He served as general manager at the Omni Jacksonville Hotel, but came to Bedford by choice. He said, in a January 22 interview with the *Bedford Gazette,* that he grew up in a small town in Wisconsin and thoroughly enjoyed his childhood there. The Bedford area, he explained, gives him a wonderful place to raise his three children. "It was important to me that I could be somewhere to get my kids through school -- so from my standpoint this is a long-term commitment."

While at Jacksonville Stuckey was involved with the local community and said he would continue that tradition in Bedford by building and strengthening ties between the community and the Bedford Springs Resort.

Despite a down economy Stuckey said he

planned to increase business at the resort in 2009. Through the summer of 2009 he did just that, with the hotel completely booked on most weekends.

In January he took advantage of the Inauguration of President Obama with an inauguration package offering special rates for Washington, D.C. area residents who wanted to escape the huge crowds that descended on the city. From January 9 through 25, the inauguration package filled several hundred rooms during a seasonally slow period.

In the fall Stuckey introduced the Penn State Football packages to offer fans an alternative to staying in State College or Altoona. The packages included overnight accommodations, golf, and spa, as well as transportation to and from the game.

According to Stuckey, the Omni brand name will increase both occupancy and revenue at Bedford Springs. "We see great opportunities here to leverage the Omni brand. We have some wonderful historic hotels and this blends in very well. Bedford Springs will be a great addition to our portfolio."

Omni Hotels and Resorts partnership with Bedford Resort Partners, Ltd. is part of what the company describes as its ongoing strategic expansion, through ownership and long term management agreements across North America.

On May 6, Omni president Michael Deitmeyer was the guest speaker at the Bedford County Development Association's annual meeting. He provided an overview of both Omni and the company's vision for the Omni Bedford Springs Resort.

Having served as president since 2004, Deitmeyer explained that he was part of a group that bought eight Omni Hotels in 1996. Deitmeyer said his firm, TRT, was in real estate and Omni was then operating mostly with franchises of differing qualities.

The group phased out the franchises and reinvented Omni. "Our goal and vision was to bring long-term value to the real estate."

He told the Association that, rather than focus on five diamond luxury rating -- "There is a lot of expense to maintain five diamonds among luxury hotels -- we wanted to balance the rating against sustainability," Omni selected a luxury level below the "ultra" level of the Four Seasons or the Ritz, but above the Weston or Hilton hotels.

The closest Omni hotels to Bedford are the William Penn in Pittsburgh and the Shoreham in Washington, D. C. He said that, for a smaller chain, "We do rely on word of mouth" and referrals. For example, the Shoreham or the William Penn might refer guests to Bedford Springs for a different type of experience and to lengthen their stay with Omni.

Deitmeyer said Omni won the J. D. Powers Award three times for customer satisfaction which he attributed to leadership and focusing on personal service. "I always read the comment cards from the past months when I go to one of our hotels, and many of those center on the connection guests make with the staff. We have 13,000 employees and by the end of the day, they need to feel valued. We have a lower turnover than the industry average," he continued.

"We want people to go to town and to the local attractions." He contrasted that with The Greenbrier, which is now going through bankruptcy. Deitmeyer said he felt The Greenbrier had become too much of its own community. "If you want to go off their property for dinner, they refer you to someplace 20 miles away."

For the Springs, Deitmeyer said he is shooting for 70,000 hotel guests in 2009, despite the economy, and added that he saw no reason why that couldn't reach 100,000 in the future. The 70,000 works out to about 190 people each day. The hotel has 216 guest rooms and suites.

He explained that putting the Omni name in front of Bedford Springs Resort "adds to the quality level ... its part of our investment" and helps potential guests find the resort and understand its quality level.

As for the coming years, Deitmeyer predicted a bright future for the Omni Bedford Springs, and for the hotel industry in general. For 2011, he said the industry expects five percent growth; and 2012-13 should be "off the charts because there aren't a lot of new hotels coming on line."

As this book went to press, the National Trust for Historic Preservation presented a

Preservation Honor Award to Bedford Resort Partners, Ltd. for restoration of the Omni Bedford Springs Resort. Along with Bedford Resort Partners, the co-recipients of the Bedford Springs restoration award were The Ferchill Group, Corgan Associates, Sandvick Architects, Inc.; 3North; Reynolds Construction Management, Inc.; Forse Design and Frontier Construction Company.

The Bedford Springs restoration was one of 23 award winners so honored at the 2009 National Preservation Conference held in Nashville, TN.

"After two decades of tireless, monumental efforts to save it, the Bedford Springs Hotel is once again one of America's finest historic destinations, a perfect blend of past and present," said Richard Moe, president of the National Trust for Historic Preservation.

"In addition to the obvious benefits to travelers, the rehabilitation of Bedford Springs has spurred job creation, additional tax revenues and public works projects. This project is a 'win-win' for the community and for discerning travelers," he said.

Bedford Springs Old Course

The Bedford Springs Old Course is one of the best known features of the Omni Bedford Springs Resort. The history of the course is rich and significant. Three of America's famed golf course architects had a hand in its creation and evolution. The course started with Spencer Oldham and continued with A. W. Tillinghast and Donald Ross.

The course started out in the 1890s with 18 holes designed by Oldham, who was from Baltimore. Seventeen years later Tillinghast reduced the course to nine holes. In 1923 Donald Ross created what is known as the course's "enduring character."

As part of the $120 million Bedford Springs restoration project, the Old Course was restored by Forse Designs of Hopwood, PA. The Bedford Springs Old Course marks the 37th Donald Ross course the firm has restored. The company is run by Ron Forse and Jim Nagle. "A good course is one that tests the golfer's wit as well as his ball-striking ability," Forse said.

Land Studies, Inc., an environmental consulting firm, resolved stream erosion problems along Shober's Run and restored the stream's natural flow patterns. Native plants were retuned to the site and important wetlands were created.

Frontier Golf collaborated on the course restoration. The Old Course restoration work cost $9 million.

The 1923 design was selected for the restoration. The course retains features that were designed by all three pioneers: Oldham, Tillinghast and Ross.

Hole No. 1's tee box sits near the Hotel. This hole is called Springs. The ball is hit 230 yards over Shober's Run and four bunkers cut into the hillside. The green is located at the top of a hill.

Hole No. 2, called Spencer Oldham, dates back to 1895. It is a 205 yard par 3.

No. 3, Steeplechase, earned its name from Oldham's left side bunkers. It is representative of the geometric era of golf course architecture and features an S-curve bunker and donut bunker.

No. 4, Volcano, is the first of six Donald Ross holes still intact here. The golfer must make a steep uphill shot to the green. The long, narrow putting surface drops off on every side.

No. 5, Oaks, weaves through dense tree lines. You have to make a good shot between two giant trees, an oak and a sycamore.

No. 6, Ross's Cathedral, is a par 4, 361 yards. Thick stands of oak, maple and hickory line a classic green.

No. 7, named Shober's Run, is a par 4, 395 yard hole. It demands a strategy: how to deal with the stream.

No. 8, Overbrook, takes the ball over the stream; the green is guarded by Donald Ross bunkers.

No. 9, Meadow, has the putting green divided into three plateaus to present a subtle triangle.

No. 10, Gully, starts 55 feet above a ravine and heads toward a sloping green cut into a hillside.

No. 11, Lang Dale, par 4, 468 yards -- the tee shot must clear a brook and a hillside to hit the fairway.

No. 12, Sweetroot: on this par 4, 409 yard hole the green is backed by a chest deep bunker.

No. 13, Long, is a par 5, 613 yard hole, with a dogleg.

No. 14, Tiny Tim, is Tillinghast's classic hole.

No. 15, Bunker Hill, a par 4, 347 yards along a rising hillside to a dogleg left, resembles its 1895 layout.

No.16, Hole O'Cross resembles a Maltese cross. It is a par 5, 593 yard monster.

No. 17, Ronnie, is completely rebuilt to Tillinghast specifications; a par 3, 169 yards.

No. 18, Home, has an S-curve fairway bordered by three large bunkers on the left. Par 4, 367 yards.

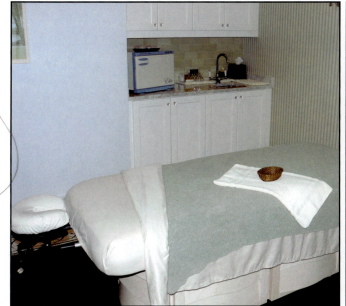

Above, inside the Springs Eternal Spa.

At right, and below: the new Spa wing; the Barclay House is on the hill.

Photos, pages 179 - 184 by Jon Baughman.

Bedford Springs reborn - 179

Above, the Colonnade Ballroom. Below, the Constitution Room.

Reagan Room (Ballroom), in the Evitt Building

The Buchanan Room, now used as a conference room on the second floor of the Colonial Building, was once a suite of rooms occupied by President James Buchanan.

This comfortable reading room is located just off the Hotel's main lobby.

Bedford Springs reborn - 181

182 - *The Bedford Springs Resort*

*Opposite page:
The Grand Stairway is one of the most striking features of the Hotel.*

*Top photo:
The Main Lobby looking toward the Grand Stairway.*

At right: Numerous antiques are on display in the Frontier Tavern. These are from the collection of William L. Defibaugh.

Above, the First Ladies Lounge.

Below, this historic American flag has been restored and is on display behind the main desk.

About the author

Jon D. Baughman has been editor and publisher of the weekly newspaper, *Broad Top Bulletin*, at Saxton, Pennsylvania since 1973.

Baughman is a graduate of The Pennsylvania State University with a degree in Journalism. He also completed additional study at Juniata College and earned a Pennsylvania teaching certificate in Social Studies.

His column, A Moment In History, appears regularly in the *Bedford County Shoppers Guide*.

He is the author of four other books on the history of the region, and co-author of seven books on local history, written with Ron Morgan. He has also been honored as Bedford County Historian of the Year.

He and his wife, the former Judy Black, reside in Dudley, PA. They are the parents of two grown sons, both Penn State graduates.

The historic Nawgle (Anderson's) Mill and the Miller's house still greet visitors as they approach the Bedford Springs property. Photos by Jon Baughman.

Four separate but inter-connected historic buildings provide luxurious rooms for guests at the Bedford Springs Resort. They are, from left, Evitt House, Stone Inn, Swiss Cottage and Anderson House. Below is a twilight view of the same four buildings, taken on a cold winter evening in 2009, with lights all aglow. Photos by Jon Baughman.

Above, the Indoor Pool wing and Colonial Building.

At right, the hallway at the Indoor Pool is lined with framed vintage photos and historic documents.

Bedford Springs reborn - 187

For many years Bedford Springs mineral water was bottled by the Bedford Springs Company and sold to customers far and wide. These vintage bottles are on display in glass cases at the entrance to the Springs Eternal Spa.

At left, these antique chairs were once used at the Bedford Springs and are now displayed in the 1796 Room.

Photos by Jon Baughman.

Looking behind the Colonial Building, looking toward the Barclay House, the Spa wing, and the Golf Course. The sweet spring is located on this hillside.

At right, the Cottage traditionally has been the general manager's residence. Today it provides space for offices.

Photos by Jon Baughman.

Bedford Springs reborn - 189

An Omni Bedford Springs Christmas

190 - The Bedford Springs Resort

Above, an antique sleigh and a nutcracker collection were on display in the main entrance during Christmas, 2009.

At left, Jon Baughman, author of "The Bedford Springs Resort: Its History and Rebirth" signs a copy of the first edition for Oralee Kieffer of Bedford, who was a part owner of the Bedford Springs from 1981 to 1987.